THE LETTERS OF
WILLIAM JAMES

WILLIAM JAMES

FROM A PHOTOGRAPH TAKEN ABOUT 1895

THE LETTERS OF WILLIAM JAMES

EDITED BY HIS SON
HENRY JAMES

IN TWO VOLUMES
VOLUME II

THE ATLANTIC MONTHLY PRESS
BOSTON

CONTENTS

*of Mental Healers — Excessive Climbing in the
Adirondacks.*

*Two Years of Illness in Europe — Retirement from
Active Duty at Harvard — The First and Second
Series of the Gifford Lectures.*

CONTENTS

The Last Period (III) — Hibbert Lectures in Oxford — The Hodgson Report.

LETTERS:—

CONTENTS

LIST OF ILLUSTRATIONS

THE LETTERS OF
WILLIAM JAMES

THE LETTERS OF WILLIAM JAMES

XI

1893–1899

Turning to Philosophy — A Student's Impressions — Popular Lecturing — Chautauqua

WHEN James returned from Europe, he was fifty-two years old. If he had been another man, he might have settled down to the intensive cultivation of the field in which he had already achieved renown and influence. He would then have spent the rest of his life in working out special problems in psychology, in deducing a few theories, in making particular applications of his conclusions, in administering a growing laboratory, in surrounding himself with assistants and disciples — in weeding and gathering where he had tilled. But the fact was that the publication of his two books on psychology operated for him as a welcome release from the subject.

He had no illusion of finality about what he had written.[1] But he would have said that whatever original contribution he was capable of making to psychology had already been made; that he must pass on and leave addition and revision to others. He gradually disencumbered himself

---

[1] "It seems to me that psychology is like physics before Galileo's time — not a single elementary law yet caught a glimpse of. A great chance for some future psychologue to make a greater name than Newton's; but who then will read the books of this generation? Not many, I trow. Meanwhile they must be written." To James Sully, July 8, 1890.

of responsibility for teaching the subject in the College. The laboratory had already been placed under Professor Münsterberg's charge. For one year, during which Münsterberg returned to Germany, James was compelled to direct its conduct; but he let it be known that he would resign his professorship rather than concern himself with it indefinitely.

Readers of this book will have seen that the centre of his interest had always been religious and philosophical. To be sure, the currents by which science was being carried forward during the sixties and seventies had supported him in his distrust of conclusions based largely on introspection and *a priori* reasoning. As early as 1865 he had said, apropos of Agassiz, "No one sees farther into a generalization than his own knowledge of details extends." In the spirit of that remark he had spent years on brain-physiology, on the theory of the emotions, on the feeling of effort in mental processes, in studying the measurements and exact experiments by means of which the science of the mind was being brought into quickening relation with the physical and biological sciences. But all the while he had been driven on by a curiosity that embraced ulterior problems. In half of the field of his consciousness questions had been stirring which now held his attention completely. Does consciousness really exist? Could a radically empirical conception of the universe be formulated? What is knowledge? What truth? Where is freedom? and where is there room for faith? Metaphysical problems haunted his mind; discussions that ran in strictly psychological channels bored him. He called psychology "a nasty little subject," according to Professor Palmer, and added, "all one cares to know lies outside." He would not consider spending time on a revised edition of his textbook (the "Briefer Course") except for a bribe that was too great ever to be urged upon him. As time went on, he became more and more irritated at being addressed or referred to as a "psychologist." In June, 1903, when he became aware that Harvard was intending to confer an honorary degree on him, he went about for days before Commencement in a half-serious state of dread lest, at the fatal moment, he should hear President Eliot's voice naming him "Psychologist, psychical researcher, willer-to-believe, religious experiencer." He could not say whether the impossible last epithets would be less to his taste than "psychologist."

Only along the borderland between normal and pathological mental states, and particularly in the region of "religious experience," did he continue to collect psychological data and to explore them.

The new subjects which he offered at Harvard during the nineties are indicative of the directions in which his mind was moving. In the first winter after his return he gave a course on Cosmology, which he had never taught before and which he described in the department announcement as "a study of the fundamental conceptions of natural science with especial reference to the theories of evolution and materialism," and for the first time announced that his graduate "seminar" would be wholly devoted to questions in mental pathology "embracing a review of the principal forms of abnormal or exceptional mental life." In 1895 the second half of his psychological seminar was announced as "a discussion of certain theoretic problems, as Consciousness, Knowledge, Self, the relations of Mind and Body." In 1896 he offered a course on the philosophy of Kant for the first time. In 1898 the announcement of his "elective" on Metaphysics explained that the class would consider "the unity or pluralism of the world ground, and its knowability or unknowability; realism and idealism, freedom, teleology and theism." [1]

But there is another aspect of the nineties which must be touched upon. After getting back "to harness" in 1893 James took up, not only his full college duties, but an amount of outside lecturing such as he had never done before. In so doing he overburdened himself and postponed the attainment of his true purpose; but the temptation to accept the requests which now poured in on him was made irresistible by practical considerations. He not only repeated some of his Harvard courses at Radcliffe College, and gave instruction in the Harvard Summer School in addition to the regular work of the term; but delivered lectures at teachers' meetings and before other special audiences in places as far from Cambridge as Colorado and California. A number of the papers that are included in "The Will to Believe and Other Essays in Popular Philosophy" (1897) and "Talks to Teachers and Students on Some of Life's Ideals" (1897) were thus prepared as lectures. Some of them were read many times before they were published. When he stopped for a rest in 1899, he was exhausted to the verge of a formidable break-down.

Even a glance at this period tempts one to wonder whether this record would not have been richer if it had been different. Might-have-beens can never be measured or verified; and yet sometimes it cannot be doubted that possi-

---

[1] President Eliot, in a memorandum already referred to (vol. 1, p. 32, note), calls attention to these courses and remarks: "These frequent changes were highly characteristic of James's whole career as a teacher. He changed topics, text-books and methods frequently, thus utilizing his own wide range of reading and interest and his own progress in philosophy, and experimenting from year to year on the mutual contacts and relations with his students." James continued to be titular Professor of Psychology until 1897, just as he had been nominally Assistant Professor of Physiology for several years during which the original and important part of his teaching was psychological. His title never indicated exactly what he was teaching.

bilities never realized were actual possibilities once. By 1893 James was inwardly eager, as has already been said, to devote all his thought and working time to metaphysical and religious questions. More than that — he had already conceived the important terms of his own *Welt-anschauung*. "The Will to Believe" was written by 1896. In the preface to the "Talks to Teachers" he said of the essay called "A Certain Blindness in Human Beings," "it connects itself with a definite view of the World and our Moral relations to the same. . . . I mean the pluralistic or individualistic philosophy." This was no more than a statement of a general philosophic attitude which had for some years been familiar to his students and to readers of his occasional papers. The lecture on "Philosophical Conceptions and Practical Results," delivered at the University of California in 1898, forecast "Pragmatism" and the "Meaning of Truth." If his time and energy had not been otherwise consumed, the nineties might well have witnessed the appearance of papers which were not written until the next decade. If he had been able to apply an undistracted attention to what his spirit was all the while straining toward, the disastrous breakdown of 1899–1902 might not have happened. But instead, these best years of his maturity were largely sacrificed to the practical business of supporting his family. His salary as a Harvard professor was insufficient to his needs. On his salary alone he could not educate his four children as he wanted to, and make provision for his old age and their future and his wife's, except by denying himself movement and social and professional contacts and by withdrawing into isolation that would have been utterly paralyzing and depressing to his genius. He possessed private means, to be sure; but, considering his family, these amounted to no more than a partial insurance against accident and a moderate supplement to his salary. His books had not yet begun to yield him a substantial increase of income. It is true that he made certain lecture engagements serve as the occasion for casting philosophical conceptions in more or less popular form, and that he frequently paid the expenses of refreshing travels by means of these lectures. But after he had economized in every direction,— as for instance, by giving up horse and hired man at Chocorua,— the bald fact remained that for six years he spent most of the time that he could spare from regular college duties, and about all his vacations, in carrying the fruits of the previous fifteen years of psychological work into the popular market. His public reputation was increased thereby. Teachers, audiences, and the "general reader" had reason to be thankful. But science and philosophy paid for the gain. His case was no worse than that of plenty of other men of productive genius who were enmeshed in an inadequately supported academic system. It would have been much more distressing under the conditions that prevail today. So James took the limitations of the situation as a matter of course and made no complaint. But when he died, the systematic statement of his philosophy had not been "rounded out" and he knew that he was leaving it "too much like an arch built only on one side."

James's appearance at this period is well shown by the frontispiece of this volume. Almost anyone who was at Harvard in the nineties can recall him as he went back and forth in Kirkland Street between the College and his Irving Street house, and can in memory see again that erect figure walking with a step that was somehow firm and light without being particularly rapid, two or three thick volumes and a note-book under one arm, and on his face a look of abstraction that used suddenly to give way to an expression of delighted and friendly curiosity. Sometimes it was an acquaintance who caught his eye and received a cordial word; sometimes it was an occurrence in the street that arrested him; sometimes the terrier dog, who had been roving along unwatched and forgotten, embroiled himself in an adventure or a fight and brought James out of his thoughts. One day he would have worn the Norfolk jacket that he usually worked in at home to his lecture-room; the next, he would have forgotten to change the black coat that he had put on for a formal occasion. At twenty minutes before nine in the morning he could usually be seen going to the College Chapel for the fifteen-minute service with which the College day began. If he was returning home for lunch, he was likely to be hurrying; for he had probably let himself be detained after a lecture to discuss some question with a few of his class. He was apt then to have some student with him whom he was bringing home to lunch and to finish the discussion at the family table, or merely for the purpose of establishing more personal relations than were possible in the class-room. At the end of the afternoon, or in the early evening, he would frequently be bicycling or walking again. He would then have been working until his head was tired, and would have laid his spectacles down on his desk and have started out again to get a breath of air and perhaps to drop in on a Cambridge neighbor.

In his own house it seemed as if he was always at work; all the more, perhaps, because it was obvious that he possessed no instinct for arranging his day and protecting himself from interruptions. He managed reasonably well to keep his mornings clear; or rather he allowed his wife to stand guard over them with fair success. But soon after

he had taken an essential after-lunch nap, he was pretty
sure to be "caught" by callers and visitors. From six
o'clock on, he usually had one or two of the children sitting,
more or less subdued, in the library, while he himself read
or dashed off letters, or (if his eyes were tired) dictated
them to Mrs. James. He always had letters and post-cards
to write. At any odd time — with his overcoat on and
during a last moment before hurrying off to an appointment or a train — he would sit down at his desk and do one
more note or card — always in the beautiful and flowing
hand that hardly changed between his eighteenth and his
sixty-eighth years. He seemed to feel no need of solitude
except when he was reading technical literature or writing
philosophy. If other members of the household were talking and laughing in the room that adjoined his study, he
used to keep the door open and occasionally pop in for a
word, or to talk for a quarter of an hour. It was with the
greatest difficulty that Mrs. James finally persuaded him
to let the door be closed up. He never struck an equilibrium between wishing to see his students and neighbors
freely and often, and wishing not to be interrupted by even
the most agreeable reminder of the existence of anyone or
anything outside the matter in which he was absorbed.

It was customary for each member of the Harvard Faculty
to announce in the college catalogue at what hour of
the day he could be consulted by students. Year after
year James assigned the hour of his evening meal for such
calls. Sometimes he left the table to deal with the caller
in private; sometimes a student, who had pretty certainly
eaten already and was visibly abashed at finding himself
walking in on a second dinner, would be brought into the
dining-room and made to talk about other things than his
business.

He allowed his conscience to be constantly burdened with a sense of obligation to all sorts of people. The list of neighbors, students, strangers visiting Cambridge, to whom he and Mrs. James felt responsible for civilities, was never closed, and the cordiality which animated his intentions kept him reminded of every one on it.

And yet, whenever his wife wisely prepared for a suitable time and made engagements for some sort of hospitality otherwise than by hap-hazard, it was perversely likely to be the case, when the appointed hour arrived, that James was "going on his nerves" and in no mood for "being entertaining." The most comradely of men, nothing galled him like *having to be* sociable. The "hollow mockery of our social conventions" would then be described in furious and lurid speech. Luckily the guests were not yet there to hear him. But they did not always get away without catching a glimpse of his state of mind. On one such occasion,— an evening reception for his graduate class had been arranged,— Mrs. James encountered a young man in the hall whose expression was so perturbed that she asked him what had happened to him. "I've come in again," he replied, "to get my hat. I was trying to find my way to the dining-room when Mr. James swooped at me and said, 'Here, Smith, you want to get out of this *Hell*, don't you? I'll show you how. There!' And before I could answer, he'd popped me out through a back-door. But, really, I do not want to go!"

The dinners of a club to which allusions will occur in this volume, (in letters to Henry L. Higginson, T. S. Perry, and John C. Gray) were occasions apart from all others; for James could go to them at the last moment, without any sense of responsibility and knowing that he would find congenial company and old friends. So he continued to go to these dinners, even after he had stopped accepting all invitations to dine. The Club (for it never had any name) had been started in 1870. James had been one of the original group who agreed to dine together once a month during the winter. Among the other early members had been his brother Henry, W. D. Howells, O. W. Holmes, Jr., John Fiske, John C. Gray, Henry Adams, T. S. Perry, John C. Ropes, A. G. Sedgwick, and F. Parkman. The more faithful diners, who constituted the nucleus of the Club during the later years, included Henry L. Higginson, Sturgis Bigelow, John C. Ropes, John T. Morse, Charles Grinnell, James Ford Rhodes, Moorfield Storey, James W. Crafts, and H. P. Walcott.

Every little while James's sleep would "go to pieces," and he would go off to Newport, the Adirondacks, or elsewhere, for a few days. This happened both summer and winter. It was not the effect of the place or climate in which he was living, but simply that his dangerously high average of nervous tension had been momentarily raised to the snapping point. Writing was almost certain to bring on this result. When he had an essay or a lecture to prepare, he could not do it by bits. In order to begin such a task, he tried to seize upon a free day — more often a Sunday than any other. Then he would shut himself into his library, or disappear into a room at the top of the house, and remain hidden all day. If things went well, twenty or thirty sheets of much-corrected manuscript (about twenty-five hundred words in his free hand) might result from such a day. As many more would have gone into the waste-basket. Two or three successive days of such writing "took it out of him" visibly.

Short holidays, or intervals in college lecturing, were

often employed for writing in this way, the longer vacations of the latter nineties being filled, as has been said, with traveling and lecture engagements. In the intervals there would be a few days, or sometimes two or three whole weeks, at Chocorua. Or, one evening, all the windows of the deserted Irving Street house would suddenly be wide open to the night air, and passers on the sidewalk could see James sitting in his shirt-sleeves within the circle of the bright light that stood on his library table. He was writing letters, making notes, and skirmishing through the piles of journals and pamphlets that had accumulated during an absence.

The impression which he made on a student who sat under him in several classes shortly before the date at which this volume begins have been set down in a form in which they can be given here.

"I have a vivid recollection" (writes Dr. Dickinson S. Miller) "of James's lectures, classes, conferences, seminars, laboratory interests, and the side that students saw of him generally. Fellow-manliness seemed to me a good name for his quality. The one thing apparently impossible to him was to speak *ex cathedra* from heights of scientific erudition and attainment. There were not a few 'if's' and 'maybe's' in his remarks. Moreover he seldom followed for long an orderly system of argument or unfolding of a theory, but was always apt to puncture such systematic pretensions when in the midst of them with some entirely unaffected doubt or question that put the matter upon a basis of common sense at once. He had drawn from his laboratory experience in chemistry and his study of medicine a keen sense that the imposing formulas of science that impress laymen are not so 'exact' as they sound. He was

not, in my time at least, much of a believer in lecturing in
the sense of continuous exposition.

"I can well remember the first meeting of the course in
psychology in 1890, in a ground-floor room of the old Lawrence Scientific School.   He took a considerable part of the
hour by reading extracts from Henry Sidgwick's Lecture
against Lecturing, proceeding to explain that we should use
as a textbook his own 'Principles of Psychology,' appearing
for the first time that very week from the press, and should
spend the hours in conference, in which we should discuss
and ask questions, on both sides.   So during the year's
course we read the two volumes through, with some amount
of running commentary and controversy.   There were four
or five men of previous psychological training in a class of
(I think) between twenty and thirty, two of whom were
disposed to take up cudgels for the British associational
psychology and were particularly troubled by the repeated
doctrine of the 'Principles' that a state of consciousness
had no parts or elements, but was one indivisible fact.   He
bore questions that really were criticisms with inexhaustible
patience and what I may call (the subject invites the word
often) *human* attention; invited written questions as well,
and would often return them with a reply penciled on the
back when he thought the discussion too special in interest
to be pursued before the class.   Moreover, he bore with us
with never a sign of impatience if we lingered after class,
and even walked up Kirkland Street with him on his way
home.   Yet he was really not argumentative, not inclined
to dialectic or pertinacious debate of any sort.   It must
always have required an effort of self-control to put up with
it.   He almost never, even in private conversation, contended
for his own opinion.   He had a way of often falling back on
the language of perception, insight, sensibility, vision of

possibilities. I recall how on one occasion after class, as I parted with him at the gate of the Memorial Hall triangle, his last words were something like these: 'Well, Miller, that theory's not a warm reality to me yet — still a cold conception'; and the charm of the comradely smile with which he said it! The disinclination to formal logical system and the more prolonged purely intellectual analyses was felt by some men as a lack in his classroom work, though they recognized that these analyses were present in the 'Psychology.' On the other hand, the very tendency to *feel* ideas lent a kind of emotional or æsthetic color which deepened the interest.

"In the course of the year he asked the men each to write some word of suggestion, if he were so inclined, for improvement in the method with which the course was conducted; and, if I remember rightly, there were not a few respectful suggestions that too much time was allowed to the few wrangling disputants. In a pretty full and varied experience of lecture-rooms at home and abroad I cannot recall another where the class was asked to criticize the methods of the lecturer.

"Another class of twelve or fourteen, in the same year, on Descartes, Spinoza, and Leibnitz, met in one of the 'tower rooms' of Sever Hall, sitting around a table. Here we had to do mostly with pure metaphysics. And more striking still was the prominence of humanity and sensibility in his way of taking philosophic problems. I can see him now, sitting at the head of that heavy table of light-colored oak near the bow-window that formed the end of the room. My brother, a visitor at Cambridge, dropping in for an hour and seeing him with his vigorous air, bronzed and sanguine complexion, and brown tweeds, said, 'He looks more like a sportsman than a professor.' I think that the sporting men in college always felt a certain affinity to themselves on one side in the freshness and manhood that distinguished him in mind, appearance, and diction. It was, by the way, in this latter course that I first heard some of the philosophic phrases now identified with him. There was a great deal about the monist and pluralist views of the universe. The world of the monist was described as a 'block-universe' and the monist himself as 'wallowing in a sense of unbridled unity,' or something of the sort. He always wanted the men to write one or two 'theses' in the course of the year and to get to work early on them. He made a great deal of bibliography. He would say, 'I am no man for editions and references, no exact bibliographer.' But none the less he would put upon the blackboard full lists of books, English, French, German, and Italian, on our subject. His own reading was immense and systematic. No one has ever done justice to it, partly because he spoke with unaffected modesty of that side of his equipment.

"Of course this knowledge came to the foreground in his 'seminar.' In my second year I was with him in one of these for both terms, the first half-year studying the psychology of pleasure and pain, and the second, mental pathology. Here each of us undertook a special topic, the reading for which was suggested by him. The students were an interesting group, including Professor Santayana, then an instructor, Dr. Herbert Nichols, Messrs. Mezes (now President of the City College, New York), Pierce (late Professor at Smith College), Angell (Professor of Psychology at Chicago, and now President of the Carnegie Corporation), Bakewell (Professor at Yale), and Alfred Hodder (who became instructor at Bryn Mawr College, then abandoned academic life for literature and politics). In this seminar I was deeply impressed by his judicious and often judicial quality. His range of intellectual experience, his profound cultivation in literature, in science and in art (has there been in our generation a more cultivated man?), his absolutely unfettered and untrammeled mind, ready to do sympathetic justice to the most unaccredited, audacious, or despised hypotheses, yet always keeping his own sense of proportion and the balance of evidence — merely to know these qualities, as we sat about that council-board, was to receive, so far as we were capable of absorbing it, in a heightened sense of the good old adjective, 'liberal' education. Of all the services he did us in this seminar perhaps the greatest was his running commentary on the students' reports on such authors as Lombroso and Nordau, and all theories of degeneracy and morbid human types. His thought was that there is no sharp line to be drawn between 'healthy' and 'unhealthy' minds, that all have something of both. Once when we were returning from two insane asylums which he had arranged for the class to visit, and at one of which we had seen a dangerous, almost naked maniac, I remember his saying, 'President Eliot might not like to admit that there is no sharp line between himself and the men we have just seen, but it is true.' He would emphasize that people who had great nervous burdens to carry, hereditary perhaps, could order their lives fruitfully and perhaps derive some gain from their 'degenerate' sensitiveness, whatever it might be. The doctrine is set forth with regard to religion in an early chapter of his 'Varieties of Religious Experience,' but for us it was applied to life at large.

"In private conversation he had a mastery of words, a voice, a vigor, a freedom, a dignity, and therefore what one might call an authority, in which he stood quite alone. Yet brilliant man as he was, he never quite outgrew a perceptible shyness or diffidence in the lecture-room, which showed

sometimes in a heightened color. Going to lecture in one
of the last courses he ever gave at Harvard, he said to a colleague whom he met on the way, 'I have lectured so and so
many years, and yet here am I on the way to my class in
trepidation!'

"Professor Royce's style of exposition was continuous,
even, unfailing, composed. Professor James was more
conversational, varied, broken, at times struggling for
expression — in spite of what has been mentioned as his
mastery of words. This was natural, for the one was
deeply and comfortably installed in a theory (to be sure a
great theory), and the other was peering out in quest of
something greater which he did not distinctly see. James's
method gave us in the classroom more of his own exploration and *aperçu*. We felt his mind at work.

"Royce in lecturing sat immovable. James would rise
with a peculiar suddenness and make bold and rapid strokes
for a diagram on the black-board — I can remember his
abstracted air as he wrestled with some idea, standing by
his chair with one foot upon it, elbow on knee, hand to chin.
A friend has described a scene at a little class that, in a still
earlier year, met in James's own study. In the effort to
illustrate he brought out a black-board. He stood it on a
chair and in various other positions, but could not at once
write upon it, hold it steady, and keep it in the class's
vision. Entirely bent on what he was doing, his efforts
resulted at last in his standing it on the floor while he lay
down at full length, holding it with one hand, drawing
with the other, and continuing the flow of his commentary.
I can myself remember how, after one of his lectures on
Pragmatism in the Horace Mann Auditorium in New York,
being assailed with questions by people who came up to the
edge of the platform, he ended by sitting on that edge him-

self, all in his frock-coat as he was, his feet hanging down, with his usual complete absorption in the subject, and the look of human and mellow consideration which distinguished him at such moments, meeting the thoughts of the inquirers, whose attention also was entirely riveted. If this suggests a lack of dignity, it misleads, for dignity never forsook him, such was the inherent strength of tone and bearing. In one respect these particular lectures (afterwards published as his book on Pragmatism) stand alone in my recollection. An audience may easily be large the first time, but if there is a change it usually falls away more or less on the subsequent occasions. These lectures were announced for one of the larger lecture-halls. This was so crowded before the lecture began, some not being able to gain admittance, that the audience had to be asked to move to the large 'auditorium' I have mentioned. But in it also the numbers grew, till on the last day it presented much the same appearance as the other hall on the first."

To Dickinson S. Miller.

CAMBRIDGE, *Nov.* 19, 1893.

MY DEAR MILLER,— I have found the work of recommencing teaching unexpectedly formidable after our year of gentlemanly irresponsibility. I seem to have forgotten everything, especially psychology, and the subjects themselves have become so paltry and insignificant-seeming that each lecture has appeared a ghastly farce. Of late things are getting more real; but the experience brings startlingly near to one the wild desert of old-age which lies ahead, and makes me feel like impressing on all chicken-professors like you the paramount urgency of providing for the time when you 'll be old fogies, by laying by from your very first year of service a fund on which you may be enabled to "retire" before you 're sixty and incapable of any cognitive operation that was n't ground into you twenty years before, or of any emotion save bewilderment and jealousy of the thinkers of the rising generation.

I am glad to hear that you have more writings on the stocks. I read your paper on "Truth and Error" with bewilderment and jealousy. Either it is Dr. Johnson *redivivus* striking the earth with his stick and saying, "Matter exists and there 's an end on 't," or it is a new David Hume, reincarnated in your form, and so subtle in his simplicity that a decaying mind like mine fails to seize any of the deeper import of his words. The trouble is, I can't tell which it is. But with the help of God I will go at it again this winter, when I settle down to my final bout with Royce's theory, which must result in my either *actively* becoming a propagator thereof, or actively its enemy and destroyer. It is high time that this more decisive attitude were generated in me, and it ought to take place this winter.

I hardly see more of my colleagues this winter than I did last year. Each of us lies in his burrow, and we meet on the street. Münsterberg is going really *splendidly* and the Laboratory is a bower of delight. But I do not work there. Royce is in powerful condition. . . . Yours ever,

W. J.

Although, in the next letter, James poked fun at reformed spelling, he was really in sympathy with the movement to which his correspondent was giving an outspoken support — as Mr. Holt of course understood. "Is n't it abominable" — Professor Palmer has quoted James as exclaiming — "that everybody is expected to spell the same way!" He lent his name to Mr. Carnegie's simplified spelling program, and used to wax honestly indignant when people opposed spelling reform with purely conservative arguments. He cared little about etymology, and saw clearly enough that mere accident and fashion have helped to determine orthography. But in his own writing he never put himself to great pains to reëducate his reflexes. He let his hand write *through* as often as *thro'* or *thru*, and only occasionally bethought him to write 'filosofy' and 'telefone.' When he published, the text of his books showed very few reforms.

To Henry Holt.

CAMBRIDGE, *March* 27 [1894].
Autographically written, and spelt spontaneously.

DEAR HOLT,— The Introduction to filosofy is what I ment — I dont no the other book.

I will try Nordau's Entartung this summer — as a rule however it duzn't profit me to read Jeremiads against evil — the example of a little good has more effect.

A propo of kitchen ranges, I wish you wood remoov your recommendation from that Boynton Furnace Company's affair. We have struggld with it for five years — lost 2 cooks in consequens — burnt countless tons of extra coal, never had anything decently baikt, and now, having got rid of it for 15 dollars, are having a happy kitchen for the 1st time in our experience — all through your unprinsipld recommendation! You ought to hear my wife sware when she hears your name!

I will try about a translator for Nordau — though the only man I can think of needs munny more than fame, and cood n't do the job for pure love of the publisher or author, or on an unsertainty.

Yours affectionately,
WILLIAM JAMES.

To Henry James.

PRINCETON, *Dec.* 29, 1894.

DEAR H.,— I have been here for three days at my co-psychologist Baldwin's house, presiding over a meeting of the American Association of Psychologists, which has proved a very solid and successful affair.[1]   Strange to say, we are getting to be veterans, and the brunt of the discussions was borne by former students of mine.   It is a very healthy movement.   Alice is with me, the weather is frosty clear and cold, touching zero this A.M. and the country robed in snow.   Princeton is a beautiful place. . . .

To Henry James.

CAMBRIDGE, *Apr.* 26, 1895.

. . . I have been reading Balfour's "Foundations of Belief" with immense gusto.   It almost makes me a Liberal-Unionist!   If I mistake not, it will have a profound effect eventually, and it is a pleasure to see old England coming to the fore every time with some big stroke.   There is more real philosophy in such a book than in fifty German ones of which the eminence consists in heaping up subtleties and technicalities about the subject.   The English genius makes the vitals plain by scuffing the technicalities away.   B. is a great man. . . .

To Mrs. Henry Whitman.

SPRINGFIELD CENTRE, N.Y., *June* 16, 1895.

MY DEAR FRIEND,— About the 22nd!   I will come if you command it; but reflect on my situation ere you do so. Just reviving from the addled and corrupted condition in which the Cambridge year has left me; just at the portals

At this meeting he delivered a presidential address "On the Knowing of Things Together," a part of which is reprinted in *The Meaning of Truth*, p. 43, under the title, "The Tigers in India."   *Vide*, also, *Collected Essays and Reviews*.

of that Adirondack wilderness for the breath of which I have sighed for years, unable to escape the cares of domesticity and get there; just about to get a little health into me, a little simplification and solidification and purification and sanification — things which will never come again if this one chance be lost; just filled to satiety with all the simpering conventions and vacuous excitements of so-called civilization; hungering for their opposite, the smell of the spruce, the feel of the moss, the sound of the cataract, the bath in its waters, the divine outlook from the cliff or hill-top over the unbroken forest — oh, Madam, Madam! do you know what medicinal things you ask me to give up?　Alas!

I aspire downwards, and really *am* nothing, *not becoming* a savage as I would be, and failing to be the civilizee that I really ought to be content with being!　But I wish that *you* also aspired to the wilderness.　There are some nooks and summits in that Adirondack region where one can really "recline on one's divine composure," and, as long as one stays up there, seem for a while to enjoy one's birth-right of freedom and relief from every fever and falsity.　Stretched out on such a shelf,— with thee beside me singing in the wilderness,— what babblings might go on, what judgment-day discourse!

Command me to give it up and return, if you will, by telegram addressed "Adirondack Lodge, North Elba, N.Y." In any case I shall return before the end of the month, and later shall be hanging about Cambridge some time in July, giving lectures (for my sins) in the Summer School.　I am staying now with a cousin on Otsego Lake, a dear old country-place that has been in their family for a century, and is rich and ample and reposeful.　The Kipling visit went off splendidly — he's a regular little brick of a man; but it's strange that with so much sympathy with the insides of every living thing, brute or human, drunk or sober, he should have so little sympathy with those of a Yankee — who also is, in the last analysis, one of God's creatures. I have stopped at Williamstown, at Albany, at Amsterdam, at Utica, at Syracuse, and finally here, each time to visit human beings with whom I had business of some sort or other. The best was Benj. Paul Blood at Amsterdam, a son of the soil, but a man with extraordinary power over the English tongue, of whom I will tell you more some day. I will by the way enclose some clippings from his latest "effort." "Yes, Paul is quite a *correspondent!*" as a citizen remarked to me from whom I inquired the way to his dwelling. Don't you think "correspondent" rather a good generic term for "man of letters," from the point of view of the country-town newspaper reader? . . .

Now, dear, noble, incredibly perfect Madam, you won't take ill my reluctance about going to Beverly, even to your abode, so soon. I am a badly mixed critter, and I experience a certain organic need for simplification and solitude that is quite imperious, and so vital as actually to be respectable even by others. So be indulgent to your ever faithful and worshipful,

W. J.

To G. H. Howison.

CAMBRIDGE, *July* 17, 1895.

MY DEAR HOWISON,— How you *have* misunderstood the application of my word "trivial" as being discriminatively applied to your pluralistic idealism! Quite the reverse — if there be a philosophy that I believe in, it's that. The word came out of one who is unfit to be a philosopher because at bottom he hates philosophy, especially at the beginning of a vacation, with the fragrance of the spruces and sweet ferns all soaking him through with the conviction that it is better to *be* than to define your being. I am a victim of neurasthenia and of the sense of hollowness and unreality that goes with it. And philosophic literature *will* often seem to me the hollowest thing. My word trivial was a general reflection exhaling from this mood, vile indeed in a supposed professor. Where it will end with me, I do not know. I wish I could give it all up. But perhaps it is a grand climacteric and will pass away. At present I am philosophizing as little as possible, in order to do it the better next year, if I can do it at all. And I envy you your stalwart and steadfast enthusiasm and faith. Always devotedly yours,

WM. JAMES.

To Theodore Flournoy.

GLENWOOD SPRINGS,
COLORADO, *Aug.* 13, 1895.

MY DEAR FLOURNOY,— Ever since last January an envelope addressed to you has been lying before my eyes on my library table. I mention this to assure you that you have not been absent from my thoughts; but I will waste no time or paper in making excuses. As the sage Emerson says, when you visit a man do not degrade the occasion with apologies for not having visited him before. Visit him now! Make him feel that the highest truth has come to see him in you its lowliest organ. I don't know about the highest truth transpiring through this letter, but I feel as if there were plenty of affection and personal gossip to express themselves. To begin with, your photograph and Mrs. Flournoy's were splendid. What we need now is the photographs of those fair *demoiselles!* I may say that one reason of my long silence has been the hope that when I wrote I should have my wife's photograph to send you. But alas! it has not been taken yet. She is well, very well, and is now in our little New Hampshire country-place with the children, living very quietly and happily. We have had a rather large *train de maison* hitherto, and this summer we are shrunken to our bare essentials — a very pleasant change.

I, you see, am farther away from home than I have ever been before on this side of the Atlantic, namely, in the state of Colorado, and just now in the heart of the Rocky Mountains. I have been giving a course of six lectures on psychology "for teachers" at a so-called "summer-school" in Colorado Springs. I had to remain for three nights and three days in the train to get there, and it has made me understand the vastness of my dear native land better than I ever did before. . . . The trouble with all this new civilization is that it is based, not on saving, but on borrowing; and when hard times come, as they did come three years ago, everyone goes bankrupt. But the vision of the future, the dreams of the possible, keep everyone enthusiastic, and so the work goes on. Such conditions have never existed before on so enormous a scale. But I must not write you a treatise on national economy!— I got through the year very well in regard to health, and gave in the course of it, what I had never done before, a number of lectures to teachers in Boston and New York. I also repeated my course in Cosmology in the new woman's College which has lately been established in connection with our University. The consequence is that I laid by more than a thousand dollars, an absolutely new and proportionately pleasant experience for me. To make up for it, I have n't had an idea or written anything to speak of except the "presidential address" which I sent you, and which really contained nothing new. . . .

And now is not that enough gossip about ourselves? I wish I could, by telephone, at this moment, hear just where and how you all are, and what you are all doing. In the mountains somewhere, of course, and I trust all well; but it is perhaps fifteen or twenty years too soon for transatlantic telephone. My surroundings here, so much like those of Switzerland, bring you before me in a lively manner. I enclose a picture of one of the streets at Colorado Springs for Madame Flournoy, and another one of a "cowboy" for that one of the *demoiselles* who is most *romanesque*. Alice, Blanche — but I have actually gone and been and forgotten the name of the magnificent third one, whose resplendent face I so well remember notwithstanding. *Dulcissima mundi nomina*, all of them; and I do hope that they are being educated in a thoroughly emancipated way, just like true American girls, with no laws except those imposed by their own sense of fitness. I am sure it produces the best results! How did the teaching go last year? I mean your own teaching. Have you started any new lines? And how is Chantre? and how Ritter? And how Monsieur Gowd? Please give my best regards to all round, especially to Ritter. Have you a copy left of your "Métaphysique et Psychologie"? In some inscrutable way my copy has disappeared, and the book is reported *épuisé*.

With warmest possible regards to both of you, and to all five of the descendants, believe me ever faithfully yours,

W. JAMES.

To his Daughter.

EL PASO, COLO., *Aug.* 8, 1895.

SWEETEST OF LIVING Pegs,— Your letter made glad my heart the day before yesterday, and I marveled to see what an improvement had come over your handwriting in the

short space of six weeks. "Orphly" and "ofly" are good
ways to spell "awfully," too. I went up a high mountain
yesterday and saw all the kingdoms of the world spread
out before me, on the illimitable prairie which looked like
a map. The sky glowed and made the earth look like a
stained-glass window. The mountains are bright red. All
the flowers and plants are different from those at home.
There is an immense mastiff in my house here. I think
that even you would like him, he is so tender and gentle
and mild, although fully as big as a calf. His ears and face
are black, his eyes are yellow, his paws are magnificent,
his tail keeps wagging *all* the time, and he makes on me the
impression of an angel hid in a cloud. He longs to do good.

I must now go and hear two other men lecture. Many
kisses, also to Tweedy, from your ever loving,

DAD.

On December 17, 1895, President Cleveland's Venezuela
message startled the world and created a situation with
which the next three letters are concerned. The boundary
dispute between Venezuela and British Guiana had been
dragging along for years. The public had no reason to
suppose that it was becoming acute, or that the United
States was particularly interested in it, and had, in fact,
not been giving the matter so much as a thought. All at
once the President sent a message to Congress in which he
announced that it was incumbent upon the United States
to "take measures to determine . . . the true" boundary
line, and then to "resist by every means in its power as a
willful aggression upon its rights and interests" any appro-
priation by Great Britain of territory not thus determined
to be hers. In addition he sent to Congress, and thus
published, the diplomatic despatches which had already

passed between Mr. Olney and Lord Salisbury. In these Mr. Olney had informed the representative of the Empire which was sovereign in British Guiana "that distance and three thousand miles of intervening ocean make any permanent political union between a European and an American state unnatural and inexpedient," and that "today the United States is practically sovereign on this continent, and its fiat is law upon the subjects to which it confines its interposition." Lord Salisbury had squarely declined to concede that the United States could, of its own initiative, assume to settle the boundary dispute. It was difficult to see how either Great Britain or the United States could with dignity alter the position which its minister had assumed.

James was a warm admirer of the President, but this seemingly wanton provocation of a friendly nation horrified him. He considered that no blunder in statesmanship could be more dangerous than a premature appeal to a people's fighting pride, and that no perils inherent in the Venezuela boundary dispute were as grave as was the danger that popular explosions on one or both sides of the Atlantic would make it impossible for the two governments to proceed moderately. He was appalled at the outburst of Anglophobia and war-talk which followed the message. The war-cloud hung in the heavens for several weeks. Then, suddenly, a breeze from a strange quarter relieved the atmosphere. The Jameson raid occurred in Africa, and the Kaiser sent his famous message to President Kruger.[1] The

[1] In a brief letter to the *Harvard Crimson* (Jan. 9, 1896), James urged the right and duty of individuals to stand up for their opinions publicly during such crises, even though in opposition to the administration. Mr. Rhodes, in his *History of the United States, 1877–1896*, makes the following observation: "Cleveland, in his chapter on the 'Venezuelan Boundary Controversy,' rates the un-Americans who lauded 'the extreme forbearance and kindness of England.' . . . The reference . . . need trouble no one who allows himself to be guided by two of Cleveland's trusted servants and friends. Thomas F. Bayard, Secretary of State during the

English press turned its fire upon the Kaiser. The world's attention was diverted from Venezuela, and the boundary dispute was quietly and amicably disposed of.

To E. L. Godkin.

CAMBRIDGE, *Christmas Eve* [1895].

DARLING OLD GODKIN,— The only Christmas present I can send you is a word of thanks and a *bravo bravissimo* for your glorious fight against the powers of darkness. I swear it brings back the days of '61 again, when the worst enemies of our country were in our own borders. But now that defervescence has set in, and the long, long campaign of discussion and education is about to begin, you will have to bear the leading part in it, and I beseech you to be as non-expletive and patiently explanatory as you can, for thus will you be the more effective. Father, forgive them for they know not what they do! The insincere propaganda of jingoism as a mere weapon of attack on the President was diabolic. But in the rally of the country to the President's message lay that instinct of obedience to leaders which is the prime condition of all effective greatness in a nation. And after all, when one thinks that the only England most Americans are taught to conceive of is the bugaboo coward-England, ready to invade the Globe wherever there is no danger, the rally does not necessarily show savagery, but only ignorance. We are all ready to be savage in *some* cause. The difference between a good man and a bad one is the choice of the cause.

Two things are, however, *désormais* certain: Three days

first administration, and actual ambassador to Great Britain, wrote in a private letter on May 25, 1895, 'There is no question now open between the United States and Great Britain that needs any but frank, amicable and just treatment.' Edward J. Phelps, his first minister to England, in a public address on March 30, 1896, condemned emphatically the President's Venezuela policy." See Rhodes, *History,* vol. VIII, p. 454; also p. 443 *et seq.*

of fighting mob-hysteria at Washington can at any time undo peace habits of a hundred years; and the only permanent safeguard against irrational explosions of the fighting instinct is absence of armament and opportunity. Since this country has absolutely nothing to fear, or any other country anything to gain from its invasion, it seems to me that the party of civilization ought immediately, at any cost of discredit, to begin to agitate against any increase of either army, navy, or coast defense. That is the one form of protection against the internal enemy on which we can most rely. We live and learn: the labor of civilizing ourselves is for the next thirty years going to be complicated with this other abominable new issue of which the seed was sown last week. *You* saw the new kind of danger, as you always do, before anyone else; but it grew gigantic much more suddenly than even you conceived to be possible. Olney's Jefferson Brick style makes of our Foreign Office a laughing-stock, of course. But why, oh why, could n't he and Cleveland and Congress between them have left out the infernal war-threat and simply asked for $100,000 for a judicial commission to enable us to see exactly to what effect we ought, in justice, to exert our influence. That commission, if its decision were adverse, would have put England "in a hole," awakened allies for us in all countries, been a solemn step forward in the line of national righteousness, covered us with dignity, and all the rest. But no — *omnia ademit una dies infesta tibi tot præmia vitæ!* — Still, the campaign of education may raise us out of it all yet. Distrust of each other must not be suffered to go too far, for that way lies destruction.

Dear old Godkin — I don't know whether you will have read more than the first page — I did n't expect to write more than one and a half, but the steam will work off. I have n't slept right for a week.

I have just given my Harry, now a freshman, your "Comments and Reflections," and have been renewing my youth in some of its admirable pages. But why the dickens did you leave out some of the most delectable of the old sentences in the cottager and boarder essay?[1]

Don't curse God and die, dear old fellow. Live and be patient and fight for us a long time yet in this new war. Best regards to Mrs. Godkin and to Lawrence, and a merry Christmas. Yours ever affectionately,

WM. JAMES.

To F. W. H. Myers.

CAMBRIDGE, *Jan.* 1, 1896.

MY DEAR MYERS,— Here is a happy New Year to you with my presidential address for a gift.[2] *Valeat quantum.* The end could have been expanded, but probably this is enough to set the S. P. R. against a lofty *Kultur-historisch* background; and where we have to do so much champing of the jaws on minute details of cases, that seems to me a good point in a president's address.

In the first half, it has just come over me that what I say of one line of fact being "strengthened in the flank" by another is an "uprush" from my subliminal memory of words of Gurney's — but that does no harm. . . .

Well, our countries will soon be soaked in each other's gore. You will be disemboweling me, and Hodgson cleaving Lodge's skull. It will be a war of extermination when it comes, for neither side can tell when it is beaten, and the last man will bury the penultimate one, and then die himself. The French will then occupy England and the Span-

---

[1] "The Evolution of the Summer Resort."

[2] "Address of the President before the Society for Psychical Research." *Proc. of the (Eng.) Soc. for Psych. Res.* 1896, vol. XII, pp. 2–10; also in *Science*, 1896, N. S., vol. IV, pp. 881–888.

iards America. Both will unite against the Germans, and no one can foretell the end.

But seriously, all true patriots here have had a hell of a time. It has been a most instructive thing for the dispassionate student of history to see how near the surface in all of us the old fighting instinct lies, and how slight an appeal will wake it up. Once *really* waked, there is no retreat. So the whole wisdom of governors should be to avoid the direct appeals. This your European governments know; but we in our bottomless innocence and ignorance over here know nothing, and Cleveland in my opinion, by his explicit allusion to war, has committed the biggest political crime I have ever seen here. The secession of the southern states had more excuse. There was absolutely no need of it. A commission solemnly appointed to pronounce justice in the Venezuela case would, if its decision were adverse to your country, have doubtless aroused the Liberal party in England to espouse the policy of arbitrating, and would have covered us with dignity, if no threat of war had been uttered. But as it is, who can see the way out?

Every one goes about now saying war is not to be. But with these volcanic forces who can tell? I suppose that the offices of Germany or Italy might in any case, however, save us from what would be the worst disaster to civilization that our time could bring forth.

The astounding thing is the latent Anglophobia now revealed. It is most of it directly traceable to the diabolic machinations of the party of protection for the past twenty years. They have lived by every sort of infamous sophistication, and hatred of England has been one of their most conspicuous notes. . . .

I hope *you 'll* read my address — unless indeed Gladstone will consent!!

Ever thine — I hate to think of "embruing" my hands in (or with?) your blood.

W. J.

[S. P. R.] *Proceedings XXIX* just in — hurrah for your 200-odd pages!

I have been ultra non-committal as to our evidence,— thinking it to be good presidential policy,— but I may have overdone the impartiality business.

To F. W. H. Myers.

CAMBRIDGE, *Feb.* 5, 1896.

DEAR MYERS,— *Voici* the proof! Pray *send me a revise* — Cattell wants to print it simultaneously *in extenso* in "Science," which I judge to be a very good piece of luck for it. When will the next "Proceedings" be likely to appear?

I hope your rich tones were those that rolled off its periods, and that you did n't flinch, but rather raised your voice, when your own genius was mentioned. I read it both in New York and Boston to full houses, but heard no comments on the spot. . . .

As for Venezuela, Ach! of that be silent! as Carlyle would have said. It is a sickening business, but some good may come out of it yet. Don't feel too badly about the Anglophobia here. It does n't mean so much. Remember by what words the country was roused: "Supine submission to wrong and injustice and the consequent loss of national self-respect and honor." [1] If any other country's ruler had expressed himself with equal moral ponderosity would n't the population have gone twice as fighting-mad as ours? Of course it would; the wolf would have been aroused; and when the wolf once gets going, we know that there is no

---

[1] From the last paragraph of Cleveland's Venezuela message.

crime of which it does n't sincerely begin to believe its oppressor, the lamb down-stream, to be guilty.   The great proof that civilization *does* move, however, is the magnificent conduct of the British press.   Yours everlastingly,

W. J.

To Henry Holt, Esq.

CAMBRIDGE, *Jan.* 19, 1896.

MY DEAR HOLT,— At the risk of displeasing you, I think I won't have my photograph taken, even at no cost to myself.   I abhor this hawking about of everybody's phiz which is growing on every hand, and don't see why having written a book should expose one to it.   I am sorry that you should have succumbed to the supposed trade necessity. In any case, I will stand on my rights as a free man.   You may kill me, but you shan't publish my photograph.   Put a blank "thumbnail" in its place.   Very very sorry to displease a man whom I love so much.   Always lovingly yours,

WM. JAMES.

To his Class at Radcliffe College which had sent a potted azalea to him at Easter.

CAMBRIDGE, *Apr.* 6, 1896.

DEAR YOUNG LADIES,— I am deeply touched by your remembrance.   It is the first time anyone ever treated me so kindly, so you may well believe that the impression on the heart of the lonely sufferer will be even more durable than the impression on your minds of all the teachings of Philosophy 2A.   I now perceive one immense omission in my Psychology,— the deepest principle of Human Nature is the *craving to be appreciated*, and I left it out altogether from the book, because I had never had it gratified till now.

I fear you have let loose a demon in me, and that all my actions will now be for the sake of such rewards. However, I will try to be faithful to this one unique and beautiful azalea tree, the pride of my life and delight of my existence. Winter and summer will I tend and water it — even with my tears. Mrs. James shall never go near it or touch it. If it dies, I will die too; and if I die, it shall be planted on my grave.

Don't take all this too jocosely, but believe in the extreme pleasure you have caused me, and in the affectionate feelings with which I am and shall always be faithfully your friend,

WM. JAMES.

To Henry James.
[CAMBRIDGE] Apr. 17, 1896.

DEAR H.,— Too busy to live almost, lectures and laboratory, dentists and dinner-parties, so that I am much played out, but get off today for eight days' vacation *via* New Haven, where I deliver an "address" tonight, to the Yale Philosophy Club. I shall make it the title of a small volume of collected things called "The Will to Believe, and Other Essays in Popular Philosophy," and then I think write no more addresses, of which the form takes it out of one unduly. If I do anything more, it will be a book on general Philosophy. I have been having a bad conscience about not writing to you, when your letter of the 7th came yesterday expressing a bad conscience of your own. You certainly do your duty best. I am glad to think of you in the country and hope it will succeed with you and make you thrive. I look forward with much excitement to the fruit of all this work. . . . Just a word of good-will and good wish. I think I shall go to the Hot Springs of Virginia for next week. The spring has burst upon us, hot and droughtily, after a glorious burly winter-playing March. Yours ever,

W. J.

The next letter begins by acknowledging one which had alluded to the death of a Cambridge gentleman who had been run over in the street, almost under William James's eyes. Henry James had closed his allusion by exclaiming, "What melancholy, what terrible duties *vous incombent* when your neighbours are destroyed. And telling that poor man's wife! — Life *is* heroic — however we 'fix' it! Even as I write these words the St. Louis horror bursts in upon me in the evening paper. Inconceivable — I can't try; and I *won't*. Strange how practically all one's sense of news from the U. S. here is huge Horrors and Catastrophes. It's a terrible country *not* to live in." He would have exclaimed even more if he had witnessed the mescal experiment, that is briefly mentioned in the letter that follows. He might then have gone on to remark that the "fixing" of life seemed, in William's neighborhood, to be quite gratuitously heroic. William James and his wife and the youngest child were alone in the Chocorua cottage for a few days, picnicking by themselves without any servant. They had no horse; at that season of the year hours often went by without any one passing the house; there was no telephone, no neighbor within a mile, no good doctor within eighteen miles. It was quite characteristic of James that he should think such conditions ideal for testing an unknown drug on himself. There would be no interruptions. He had no fear. He was impatient to satisfy his curiosity about the promised hallucinations of color. But the effects of one dose were, for a while, much more alarming than his letter would give one to understand.

To Henry James.

CHOCORUA, *June* 11, 1896.

Your long letter of Whitsuntide week in London came yesterday evening, and was read by me aloud to Alice and Harry as we sat at tea in the window to get the last rays of the Sunday's [sun]. You have too much feeling of duty about corresponding with us, and, I imagine, with everyone. I think you have behaved most handsomely of late — and always, and though your letters are the great *fête* of our lives, I won't be "on your mind" for worlds. Your general feeling of unfulfilled obligations is one that runs in the family — I at least am often afflicted by it — but it is "morbid." The horrors of *not* living in America, as you so well put it, are not shared by those who do live here. All that the telegraph imparts are the shocks; the "happy homes," good husbands and fathers, fine weather, honest business men, neat new houses, punctual meetings of engagements, etc., of which the country mainly consists, are never cabled over. Of course, the Saint Louis disaster is dreadful, but it will very likely end by "improving" the city. The really bad thing here is the silly wave that has gone over the public mind — protection humbug, silver, jingoism, etc. It is a case of "mob-psychology." Any country is liable to it if circumstances conspire, and our circumstances have conspired. It is very hard to get them out of the rut. It *may* take another financial crash to get them out — which, of course, will be an expensive method. It is no more foolish and considerably less damnable than the Russo-phobia of England, which would seem to have been responsible for the Armenian massacres. That to me is the biggest indictment "of our boasted civilization"!! It *requires* England, I say nothing of the other powers, to maintain the Turks at that business. We have let our little place, our tenant arrives the day after tomorrow, and Alice and I and Tweedie have been here a week enjoying it and cleaning house and place. She has worked like a beaver. I had two days spoiled by a psychological experiment with *mescal*, an intoxicant used by some of our Southwestern Indians in their religious ceremonies, a sort of cactus bud, of which the U. S. Government had distributed a supply to certain medical men, including Weir Mitchell, who sent me some to try. He had himself been "in fairyland." It gives the most glorious visions of color — every object thought of appears in a jeweled splendor unknown to the natural world. It disturbs the stomach somewhat, but that, according to W. M., was a cheap price, etc. I took one bud three days ago, was violently sick for 24 hours, and had no other symptom whatever except that and the *Katzenjammer* the following day. I will take the visions on trust!

We have had three days of delicious rain — it all soaks into the sandy soil here and leaves no mud whatever. The little place is the most curious mixture of sadness with delight. The sadness of *things* — things every one of which was done either by our hands or by our planning, old furniture renovated, there is n't an object in the house that is n't associated with past life, old summers, dead people, people who will never come again, etc., and the way it catches you round the heart when you first come and open the house from its long winter sleep is most extraordinary.

I have been reading Bourget's "Idylle Tragique," which he very kindly sent me, and since then have been reading in Tolstoy's "War and Peace," which I never read before, strange to say. I must say that T. rather kills B., for my mind. B.'s moral atmosphere is anyhow so foreign to me, a lewdness so obligatory that it hardly seems as if it were part of a moral *donnée* at all; and then his overlabored descriptions, and excessive explanations.   But with it all an earnestness and enthusiasm for getting it said as well as possible, a richness of epithet, and a warmth of heart that makes you like him, in spite of the unmanliness of all the things he writes about.   I suppose there is a stratum in France to whom it is all manly and ideal, but he and I are, as Rosina says, a bad combination. . . .

Tolstoy is immense!

I am glad *you* are in a writing vein again, to go still higher up the scale!   I have abstained on principle from the "Atlantic" serial, wishing to get it all at once.   I am not going abroad; I can't afford it.   I have a chance to give $1500 worth of summer lectures here, which won't recur. I have a heavy year of work next year, and shall very likely *need* to go the following summer, which will anyhow be after a more becoming interval than this, so, *somme toute*, it is postponed.   If I went I should certainly enjoy seeing you at Rye more than in London, which I confess tempts me little now.   I love to *see* it, but staying there does n't seem to agree with me, and only suggests constraint and money-spending, apart from seeing you.   I wish you could see how comfortable our Cambridge house has got at last to be.   Alice who is upstairs sewing whilst I write below by the lamp — a great wood fire hissing in the fireplace — sings out her thanks and love to you. . . .

To Benjamin Paul Blood.

CHATHAM, MASS., *June* 28, 1896.

MY DEAR BLOOD,— Your letter was an "event," as anything always is from your pen — though of course I never expected any acknowledgment of my booklet.   Fear of life in one form or other is the great thing to exorcise; but it is n't reason that will ever do it. Impulse without reason is enough, and reason without impulse is a poor makeshift. I take it that no man is educated who has never dallied with the thought of suicide. Barely more than a year ago I was sitting at your table and dallying with the thought of publishing an anthology of your works. But, like many other projects, it has been postponed in indefinition. The hour never came last year, and pretty surely will not come next. Nevertheless I shall work for your fame some time! Count on W. J.[1] I wound up my "seminary" in speculative psychology a month ago by reading some passages from the "Flaw in Supremacy" — "game flavored as a hawk's wing." "Ever not quite" covers a deal of truth — yet it seems a very simple thing to have said. "There is no *Absolute*," were my last words. Whereupon a number of students asked where they could get "that pamphlet" and I distributed nearly all the copies I had from you. I wish you would keep on writing, but I see you are a man of discontinuity and insights, and not a philosophic pack-horse, or pack-mule. . . .

I rejoice that ten hours a day of toil makes you feel so hearty. Verily Mr. Rindge says truly. He is a Cambridge boy, who made a fortune in California, and then gave a lot of public buildings to his native town. Unfortunately he insisted on bedecking them with "mottoes" of his own composition, and over the Manual Training School near my house one reads: *"Work is one of our greatest blessings. Every man should have an honest occupation"* — which, if not lapidary in style, is at least what my father once said

[1] In 1910 — during his final illness, in fact — James fulfilled this promise. See "A Pluralistic Mystic," included in *Memories and Studies;* also letter of June 25, 1910, p. 348 *infra.*

Swedenborg's writings were, viz., "insipid with veracity," as your case now again demonstrates. Have you read Tolstoy's "War and Peace"? I am just about finishing it. It is undoubtedly the greatest novel ever written — also insipid with veracity. The man is infallible — and the anesthetic revelation [1] plays a part as in no writer. You have very likely read it. If you have n't, sell all you have and buy the book, for I know it will speak to your very gizzard. Pray thank Mrs. Blood for her appreciation of my "booklet" (such things encourage a writer!), and believe me ever sincerely yours,

WM. JAMES.

In July, 1896, James delivered, in Buffalo and at the Chautauqua Assembly, the substance of the lectures that were later published as "Talks to Teachers." His impressions of Chautauqua were so characteristic and so lively that they must be included here, even though they duplicate in some measure a well-known passage in the essay called "A Certain Blindness in Human Beings."

To Mrs. James.

CHAUTAUQUA, *July* 23, 1896.

... The audience is some 500, in an open-air auditorium where (strange to say) everyone seems to hear well; and it is very good-looking — mostly teachers and women, but they make the best impression of any audience of that sort that I have seen except the Brooklyn one. So here I go again! ...

July 24, 9.30 P.M.

... X—— departed after breakfast — a good inarticulate man, farmer's boy, four years soldier from private to major,

---

[1] *Cf.* William James's unsigned review of Blood's *Anæsthetic Revelation* in the *Atlantic Monthly*, 1874, vol. XXXIV, p. 627.

business man in various States, great reader, editor of a
"Handbook of Facts," full of swelling and bursting *Welt-schmerz* and religious melancholy, yet no more flexibility or
self-power in his mind than in a boot-jack. Altogether,
what with the teachers, him and others whom I've met,
I'm put in conceit of college training. It certainly gives
glibness and flexibility, if it does n't give earnestness and
depth. I've been meeting minds so earnest and helpless
that it takes them half an hour to get from one idea to its
immediately adjacent next neighbor, and that with infinite
creaking and groaning. And when they've got to the
next idea, they lie down on it with their whole weight and
can get no farther, like a cow on a door-mat, so that you
can get neither in nor out with them. Still, glibness is not
all. Weight is something, even cow-weight. Tolstoy feels
these things so — I am still in "Anna Karenina," volume I, a
book almost incredible and supernatural for veracity. I
wish we were reading it aloud together. It has rained at
intervals all day. Young Vincent, a powerful fellow, took
me over and into the whole vast college side of the institution this A.M. I have heard 4½ lectures, including the one
I gave myself at 4 o'clock, to about 1200 or more in the vast
open amphitheatre, which seats 6000 and which has very
good acoustic properties. I think my voice sufficed. I
can't judge of the effect. Of course I left out all that gossip about my medical degree, etc. But I don't want any
more sporadic lecturing — I must stick to more inward
things.

July 26, 12:30 P.M.

. . . 'T is the sabbath and I am just in from the amphitheatre, where the Rev. —— has been chanting, calling and
bellowing his hour-and-a-quarter-long sermon to 6000
people at least — a sad audition. The music was bully, a

chorus of some 700, splendidly drilled, with the audience to help. I have myself been asked to lead, or, if not to lead, at least to do something prominent — I declined so quick that I did n't fully gather what it was — in the exercise which I have marked on the program I enclose. Young Vincent, whom I take to be a splendid young fellow, told me it was the characteristically "Chautauquan" event of the day. I would give anything to have you here. I did n't write yesterday because there is no mail till tomorrow. I went to four lectures, in whole or in part. All to hundreds of human beings, a large proportion unable to get seats, who transport themselves from one lecture-room to another *en masse*. One was on bread-making, with practical demonstrations. One was on *walking*, by a graceful young Delsartian, who showed us a lot. One was on telling stories to children, the psychology and pedagogy of it. The audiences interrupt and ask questions occasionally in spite of their size. There is hardly a pretty woman's face in the lot, and they seem to have little or no humor in their composition. No *epicureanism* of any sort!

Yesterday was a beautiful day, and I sailed an hour and a half down the Lake again to "Celoron," "America's greatest pleasure resort," — in other words popcorn and peep-show place. A sort of Midway-Pleasance in the wilderness — supported Heaven knows how, so far from any human habitation except the odd little Jamestown from which a tramway leads to it. Good monkeys, bears, foxes, etc. Endless peanuts, popcorn, bananas, and soft drinks; crowds of people, a ferris wheel, a balloon ascension, with a man dropping by a parachute, a theatre, a vast concert hall, and all sorts of peep-shows. I feel as if I were in a foreign land; even as far east as this the accent of everyone is terrific. The "Nation" is no more known than the

London "Times." I see no need of going to Europe when such wonders are close by. I breakfasted with a Methodist parson with 32 false teeth, at the X's table, and discoursed of demoniacal possession. The wife said she had my portrait in her bedroom with the words written under it, "I want to bring a balm to human lives"!!!!! Supposed to be a quotation from me!!! After breakfast an extremely interesting lady who has suffered from half-possessional insanity gave me a long account of her case. Life *is* heroic indeed, as Harry wrote. I shall stay through tomorrow, and get to Syracuse on Tuesday. . . .

July 27.

. . . It rained hard last night, and today a part of the time. I took a lesson in roasting, in Delsarte, and I made with my own fair hands a beautiful loaf of graham bread with some rolls, long, flute-like, and delicious. I should have sent them to you by express, only it seemed unnecessary, since I can keep the family in bread easily after my return home. Please tell this, with amplifications, to Peggy and Tweedy. . . .

BUFFALO, N.Y., *July* 29.

. . . The Chautauqua week, or rather six and a half days, has been a real success. I have learned a lot, but I'm glad to get into something less blameless but more admiration-worthy. The flash of a pistol, a dagger, or a devilish eye, anything to break the unlovely level of 10,000 good people — a crime, murder, rape, elopement, anything would do. I don't see how the younger Vincents stand it, because they are people of such spirit. . . .

SYRACUSE, N.Y., *July* 31.

. . . Now for Utica and Lake Placid by rail, with East Hill in prospect for tomorrow. You bet I rejoice at the outlook — I long to escape from tepidity. Even an Armenian massacre, whether to be killer or killed, would seem an agreeable change from the blamelessness of Chautauqua as she lies soaking year after year in her lakeside sun and showers. Man wants to be *stretched* to his utmost, if not in one way then in another! . . .

To Miss Rosina H. Emmet.

BURLINGTON, VT., *Aug.* 2, 1896.

. . . I have seen more women and less beauty, heard more voices and less sweetness, perceived more earnestness and less triumph than I ever supposed possible. Most of the American nation (and probably all nations) is white-trash, — but Tolstoy has borne me up — and I say unto *you:* "*Smooth out your voices* if you want to be saved"!! . . .

To Charles Renouvier.

BURLINGTON, VT., *Aug.* 4, 1896.

DEAR MR. RENOUVIER,— My wife announces to me from Cambridge the reception of two immense volumes from you on the Philosophy of History. I thank you most heartily for the gift, and am more and more amazed at your intellectual and moral power — physical power, too, for the nervous energy required for your work has to be extremely great.

My own nervous energy is a small teacup-full, and is more than consumed by my duties of teaching, so that almost none is left over for writing. I sent you a "New World" the other day, however, with an article in it called "The Will to Believe," in which (if you took the trouble to glance at it) you probably recognized how completely I am still your disciple. In this point perhaps more fully than in any other; and this point is central!

I have to lecture on general "psychology" and "morbid

psychology," "the philosophy of nature" and the "philosophy of Kant," thirteen lectures a week for half the year and eight for the rest. Our University moreover inflicts a monstrous amount of routine business on one, faculty meetings and committees of every sort,[1] so that during term-time one can do no continuous reading at all — reading of books, I mean. When vacation comes, my brain is so tired that I can read nothing serious for a month. During the past month I have only read Tolstoy's two great novels, which, strange to say, I had never attacked before. I don't like his fatalism and semi-pessimism, but for infallible veracity concerning human nature, and absolute simplicity of method, he makes all the other writers of novels and plays seem like children.

All this proves that I shall be slow in attaining to the reading of your book. I have not yet read Pillon's last *Année* except some of the book notices and Danriac's article. How admirably clear P. is in style, and what a power of reading he possesses.

[1] James always did a reasonable share of college committee work, especially for the committee of his own department. But although he had exercised a determining influence in the selection of every member of the Philosophical Department who contributed to its fame in his time (except Professor Palmer, who was his senior in service), he never consented to be chairman of the Department. He attended the weekly meetings of the whole Faculty for any business in which he was concerned; otherwise irregularly. He spoke seldom in Faculty. Occasionally he served on special committees. He usually formed an opinion of his own quite quickly, but his habitual tolerance in matters of judgment showed itself in good-natured patience with discussion — this despite the fact that he often chafed at the amount of time consumed. "Now although I happen accidentally to have been on all the committees which have had to do with the proposed reform, and have listened to the interminable Faculty debates last winter, I disclaim all powers or right to speak in the *name* of the majority. Members of our dear Faculty have a way of discovering reasons fitted exclusively for their idiosyncratic use, and though voting with their neighbors, will often do so on incommunicable grounds. This is doubtless the effect of much learning upon originally ingenious minds; and the result is that the abundance of different points and aspects which a simple question ends by presenting, after a long Faculty discussion, beggars both calculation beforehand and enumeration after the fact." — "The Proposed Shortening of the College Course." *Harvard Monthly*, Jan., 1891.

I hope, dear Mr. Renouvier, that the years are not weighing heavily upon you, and that this letter will find you well in body and in mind.   Yours gratefully and faithfully,

WM. JAMES.

To Theodore Flournoy.

LAKE GENEVA, WISCONSIN, *Aug.* 30, 1896.

MY DEAR FLOURNOY,— You see the electric current of sympathy that binds the world together — I turn towards you, and the place I write from repeats the name of your Lake Leman. I was informed yesterday, however, that the lake here was named after Lake Geneva *in the State of New York!* and *that* Lake only has Leman for its Godmother. Still you see how dependent, whether immediately or remotely, America is on Europe. I was at Niagara some three weeks ago, and bought a photograph as souvenir and addressed it to you after getting back to Cambridge. Possibly Madame Flournoy will deign to accept it. I have thought of you a great deal without writing, for truly, my dear Flournoy, there is hardly a human being with whom I feel as much sympathy of aims and character, or feel as much "at home," as I do with you. It is as if we were of the same stock, and I often mentally turn and make a remark to you, which the pressure of life's occupations prevents from ever finding its way to paper.

I am hoping that you may have figured, or at any rate *been*, at the Munich "Congress" — that apparently stupendous affair. If they keep growing at this rate, the next Paris one will be altogether too heavy. I have heard no details of the meeting as yet. But whether you have been at Munich or not, I trust that you have been having a salubrious and happy vacation so far, and that Mrs. Flournoy and the young people are all well. I will venture to suppose that your illness of last year has left no bad effects whatever behind. I myself have had a rather busy and instructive, though possibly not very hygienic summer, making money (in moderate amounts) by lecturing on psychology to teachers at different "summer schools" in this land. There is a great fermentation in "pædagogy" at present in the U.S., and my wares come in for their share of patronage. But although I learn a good deal and become a better American for having all the travel and social experience, it has ended by being too tiresome; and when I give the lectures at Chicago, which I begin tomorrow, I shall have them stenographed and very likely published in a very small volume, and so remove from myself the temptation ever to give them again.

Last year was a year of hard work, and before the end of the term came, I was in a state of bad neurasthenic fatigue, but I got through outwardly all right. I have definitely given up the laboratory, for which I am more and more unfit, and shall probably devote what little ability I may hereafter have to purely "speculative" work. My inability to read troubles me a good deal: I am in arrears of several years with psychological literature, which, to tell the truth, does grow now at a pace too rapid for anyone to follow. I was engaged to review Stout's new book (which I fancy is very good) for "Mind," and after keeping it two months had to back out, from sheer inability to read it, and to ask permission to hand it over to my colleague Royce. Have you seen the colossal Renouvier's two vast volumes on the philosophy of history?— that will be another thing worth reading no doubt, yet very difficult to read. I give a course in Kant for the first time in my life (!) next year, and at present and for many months to come shall have to put most of my reading to the service of that overgrown subject. . . .

Of course you have read Tolstoy's "War and Peace" and "Anna Karenina." I never had that exquisite felicity before this summer, and now I feel as if I knew *perfection* in the representation of human life. Life indeed seems less real than his tale of it. Such infallible veracity! The impression haunts me as nothing literary ever haunted me before.

I imagine you lounging on some steep mountainside, with those demoiselles all grown too tall and beautiful and proud to think otherwise than with disdain of their elderly *commensal* who spoke such difficult French when he took walks with them at Vers-chez-les-Blanc. But I hope that they are happy as they were then. Cannot we all pass some summer near each other again, and can't it next time be in Tyrol rather than in Switzerland, for the purpose of increasing in all of us that "knowledge of the world" which is so desirable? I think it would be a splendid plan. At any rate, wherever you are, take my most affectionate regards for yourself and Madame Flournoy and all of yours, and believe me ever sincerely your friend,

                                        WM. JAMES.

To Dickinson S. Miller.

LAKE GENEVA, WISCONSIN, *Aug.* 30, 1896.

DEAR MILLER,— Your letter from Halle of June 22nd came duly, but treating of things eternal as it did, I thought it called for no reply till I should have caught up with more temporal matters, of which there has been no lack to press on my attention. To tell the truth, regarding you as my most penetrating critic and intimate enemy, I was greatly relieved to find that you had nothing worse to say about "The Will to Believe." You say you are no "rationalist," and yet you speak of the "sharp" distinction between beliefs

based on "inner evidence" and beliefs based on "craving."
I can find *nothing* sharp (or susceptible of schoolmaster's
codification) in the different degrees of "liveliness" in hypotheses concerning the universe, or distinguish *a priori* between legitimate and illegitimate cravings. And when an
hypothesis *is* once a live one, one *risks* something in one's
practical relations towards truth and error, *whichever* of the
three positions (affirmation, doubt, or negation) one may
take up towards it. *The individual himself is the only right-
ful chooser of his risk.* Hence respectful toleration, as the
only law that logic can lay down.

You don't say a word against my *logic*, which seems to
me to cover your cases entirely in its compartments. I
class you as one to whom the religious hypothesis is *von
vornherein* so dead, that the risk of error in espousing it now
far outweighs for you the chance of truth, so you simply
stake your money on the field as against it. If you *say*
this, of course I can, as logician, have no quarrel with you,
even though my own choice of risk (determined by the
irrational impressions, suspicions, cravings, senses of direction in nature, or what not, that make religion for me a
more live hypothesis than for you) leads me to an opposite
methodical decision.

Of course if any one comes along and says that men at
large don't need to have facility of faith in their inner convictions preached to them, [that] they have only too much
readiness in that way already, and the one thing needful to
preach is that they should hesitate with their convictions,
and take their faiths out for an airing into the howling
wilderness of nature, I should also agree. But my paper
was n't addressed to mankind at large but to a limited set
of studious persons, badly under the ban just now of certain
authorities whose simple-minded faith in "naturalism" also

is sorely in need of an airing — and an airing, as it seems to me, of the sort I tried to give.

But all this is unimportant; and I still await criticism of my *Auseinandersetzung* of the *logical situation* of man's mind *gegenüber* the Universe, in respect to the risks it runs.

I wish I could have been with you at Munich and heard the deep-lunged Germans roar at each other. I care not for the matters uttered, if I only could hear the voice. I hope you met [Henry] Sidgwick there. I sent him the American Hallucination-Census results, after considerable toil over them, but S. never acknowledges or answers anything, so I'll have to wait to hear from someone else whether he "got them off." I have had a somewhat unwholesome summer. Much lecturing to teachers and sitting up to talk with strangers. But it is instructive and makes one patriotic, and in six days I shall have finished the Chicago lectures, which begin tomorrow, and get straight to Keene Valley for the rest of September. My conditions just now are materially splendid, as I am the guest of a charming elderly lady, Mrs. Wilmarth, here at her country house, and in town at the finest hotel of the place. The political campaign is a bully one. Everyone outdoing himself in sweet reasonableness and persuasive argument — hardly an undignified note anywhere. It shows the deepening and elevating influence of a big topic of debate. It is difficult to doubt of a people part of whose life such an experience is. But imagine the country being saved by a McKinley! If only Reed had been the candidate! There have been some really splendid speeches and documents. . . .

Ever thine,

W. J.

To Henry James.

BURLINGTON, VT., *Sept.* 28, 1896.

DEAR HENRY,— The summer is over! alas! alas! I left Keene Valley this A.M. where I have had three life-and-health-giving weeks in the forest and the mountain air, crossed Lake Champlain in the steamer, not a cloud in the sky, and sleep here tonight, meaning to take the train for Boston in the A.M. and read Kant's Life all day, so as to be able to lecture on it when I first meet my class. School begins on Thursday — this being Monday night. It has been a rather cultivating summer for me, and an active one, of which the best impression (after that of the Adirondack woods, or even before it) was that of the greatness of Chicago. It needs a Victor Hugo to celebrate it. But as you won't appreciate it without demonstration, and I can't give the demonstration (at least not now and on paper), I will say no more on that score! Alice came up for a week, but went down and through last night. She brought me up your letter of I don't remember now what date (after your return to London, about Wendell Holmes, Baldwin and Royalty, etc.) which was very delightful and for which I thank. But don't take your epistolary duties hard! Letter-writing becomes to me more and more of an affliction, I get so many business letters now. At Chicago, I tried a stenographer and type-writer with an alleviation that seemed almost miraculous. I think that I shall have to go in for one some hours a week in Cambridge. It just goes "whiff" and six or eight long letters are *done*, so far as you 're concerned. I hear great reports of your "old things," and await the book. My great literary impression this summer has been Tolstoy. On the whole his atmosphere absorbs me into it as no one's else has ever done, and even his religious and melancholy stuff, his insanity, is probably more significant than the sanity of men who have n't been through that phase at all.

But I am forgetting to tell you (strange to say, since it has hung over me like a cloud ever since it happened) of dear old Professor Child's death. We shall never see his curly head and thickset figure more. He had aged greatly in the past three years, since being thrown out of a carriage, and went to the hospital in July to be treated surgically. He never recovered and died in three weeks, after much suffering, his family not being called down from the country till the last days. He had a moral delicacy and a richness of heart that I never saw and never expect to see equaled.[1] The children bear it well, but I fear it will be a bad blow for dear Mrs. Child. She and Alice, I am glad to say, are great friends. . . . Good-night. *Leb' wohl!*

W. J.

[1] "I *loved* Child more than any man I know." Sept. 12, '96.

XII

1893–1899 (CONTINUED)

The Will to Believe — Talks to Teachers — Defense of Mental Healers — Excessive Climbing in the Adirondacks

To Theodore Flournoy.

[Dictated]

CAMBRIDGE, *Dec.* 7, 1896.

MY DEAR FLOURNOY,— Your altogether precious and delightful letter reached me duly, and you see I am making a not altogether too dilatory reply. In the first place, we congratulate you upon the new-comer, and think if she only proves as satisfactory a damsel as her charming elder sisters, you will never have any occasion to regret that she is not a boy. I hope that Madame Flournoy is by this time thoroughly strong and well, and that everything is perfect with the baby. I should like to have been at Munich with you; I have heard a good many accounts of the jollity of the proceedings there, but on the whole I did a more wholesome thing to stay in my own country, of which the dangers and dark sides are singularly exaggerated in Europe.

Your lamentations on your cerebral state make me smile, knowing, as I do, under all your subjective feelings, how great your vigor is. Of course I sympathize with you about the laboratory, and advise you, since it seems to me you are in a position to make conditions rather than have them imposed on you, simply to drop it and teach what you prefer. Whatever the latter may be, it will be as good for the students as if they had something else from you in its place, and I see no need in this world, when there is someone provided somewhere to do everything, for anyone of us to do what he does least willingly and well.

I have got rid of the laboratory forever, and should resign my place immediately if they reimposed its duties upon me. The results that come from all this laboratory work seem to me to grow more and more disappointing and trivial. What is most needed is new ideas. For every man who has one of them one may find a hundred who are willing to drudge patiently at some unimportant experiment. The atmosphere of your mind is in an extraordinary degree sane and balanced on philosophical matters. That is where your forte lies, and where your University ought to see that its best interests lie in having you employed. Don't consider this advice impertinent. Your temperament is such that I think you need to be strengthened from without in asserting your right to carry out your true vocation.

Everything goes well with us here. The boys are developing finely; both of them taller than I am, and Peggy healthy and well. I have just been giving a course of public lectures of which I enclose you a ticket to amuse you.[1] The audience, a thousand in number, kept its numbers to the last. I was careful not to tread upon the domains of psychical research, although many of my hearers were eager that I should do so. *I am teaching Kant for the first time in*

[1] Eight lectures on "Abnormal Mental States" were delivered at the Lowell Institute in Boston, but were never published. Their several titles were "Dreams and Hypnotism," "Hysteria," "Automatisms," "Multiple Personality," "Demoniacal Possession," "Witchcraft," "Degeneration," "Genius." In a letter to Professor Howison (Apr. 5, 1897) James said, "In these lectures I did not go into psychical research so-called, and although the subjects were decidedly morbid, I tried to shape them towards optimistic and hygienic conclusions, and the audience regarded them as decidedly anti-morbid in their tone."

my life, and it gives me much satisfaction. I am also sending a collection of old essays through the press, of which I will send you a copy as soon as they appear; I am sure of your sympathy in advance for much of their contents. But I am afraid that what you never will appreciate is their wonderful English style! Shakespeare is a little streetboy in comparison!

Our political crisis is over, but the hard times still endure. Lack of confidence is a disease from which convalescence is not quick. I doubt, notwithstanding certain appearances, whether the country was ever morally in as sound a state as it now is, after all this discussion. And the very silver men, who have been treated as a party of dishonesty, are anything but that. They very likely are victims of the economic delusion, but their intentions are just as good as those of the other side. . . .

If you meet my friend Ritter, please give him my love. I shall write to you again ere long *eigenhändig*. Meanwhile believe me, with lots of love to you all, especially to *ces demoiselles*, and felicitations to their mother, Always yours,

WM. JAMES.

My wife wishes to convey to Madame Flournoy her most loving regards and hopes for the little one.

James had already been invited to deliver a course of "Gifford Lectures on Natural Religion" at the University of Edinburgh. He had not yet accepted for a definite date; but he had begun to collect illustrative material for the proposed lectures. A large number of references to such material were supplied to him by Mr. Henry W. Rankin of East Northfield.

To Henry W. Rankin.

NEWPORT, R.I., *Feb.* 1, 1897.

DEAR MR. RANKIN,— A pause in lecturing, consequent upon our midyear examinations having begun, has given me a little respite, and I am paying a three-days' visit upon an old friend here, meaning to leave for New York tomorrow where I have a couple of lectures to give. It is an agreeable moment of quiet and enables me to write a letter or two which I have long postponed, and chiefly one to you, who have given me so much without asking anything in return.

One of my lectures in New York is at the Academy of Medicine before the Neurological Society, the subject being "Demoniacal Possession." I shall of course duly advertise the Nevius book.[1] I am not as positive as you are in the belief that the obsessing agency is really demonic individuals. I am perfectly willing to adopt that theory if the facts lend themselves best to it; for who can trace limits to the hierarchies of personal existence in the world? But the lower stages of mere automatism shade off so continuously into the highest supernormal manifestations, through the intermediary ones of imitative hysteria and "suggestibility," that I feel as if no *general theory* as yet would cover all the facts. So that the most I shall plead for before the neurologists is the recognition of demon possession as a regular "morbid-entity" whose commonest homologue today is the "spirit-control" observed in test-mediumship, and which tends to become the more benignant and less alarming, the less pessimistically it is regarded. This last remark seems certainly to be true. Of course I shall not ignore the sporadic cases of old-fashioned malignant possession which still occur today. I am convinced that we stand

[1] *Demon Possession and Allied Themes,* by John C. Nevius.

with all these things at the threshold of a long inquiry, of which the end appears as yet to no one, least of all to myself. And I believe that the best theoretic work yet done in the subject is the beginning made by F. W. H. Myers in his papers in the S. P. R. Proceedings. The first thing is to start the medical profession out of its idiotically *conceited ignorance* of all such matters — matters which have everywhere and at all times played a vital part in human history.

You have written me at different times about conversion, and about miracles, getting as usual no reply, but not because I failed to heed your words, which come from a deep life-experience of your own evidently, and from a deep acquaintance with the experiences of others. In the matter of conversion I am quite willing to believe that a new truth may be supernaturally revealed to a subject when he really *asks*. But I am sure that in many cases of conversion it is less a new truth than a new power gained over life by a truth always known. It is a case of the conflict of two *self-systems* in a personality up to that time heterogeneously divided, but in which, after the conversion-crisis, the higher loves and powers come definitively to gain the upper-hand and expel the forces which up to that time had kept them down in the position of mere grumblers and protesters and agents of remorse and discontent. This broader view will cover an enormous number of cases *psychologically*, and leaves all the *religious importance* to the result which it has on any other theory.

As to true and false miracles, I don't know that I can follow you so well, for in any case the notion of a miracle as a mere attestation of superior power is one that I cannot espouse. A miracle must in any case be an expression of personal purpose, but the demon-purpose of antagonizing

God and winning away his adherents has never yet taken hold of my imagination. I prefer an open mind of inquiry, first *about the facts*, in all these matters; and I believe that the S. P. R. methods, if pertinaciously stuck to, will eventually do much to clear things up.— You see that, although religion is the great interest of my life, I am rather hopelessly non-evangelical, and take the whole thing too impersonally.

But my College work is lightening in a way. Psychology is being handed over to others more and more, and I see a chance ahead for reading and study in other directions from those to which my very feeble powers in that line have hitherto been confined. I am going to give all the fragments of time I can get, after this year is over, to religious biography and philosophy. Shield's book, Steenstra's, Gratry's, and Harris's, I don't yet know, but can easily get at them.

I hope your health is better in this beautiful winter which we are having. I am very well, and so is all my family. Believe me, with affectionate regards, truly yours,

WM. JAMES.

To Benjamin Paul Blood.

CAMBRIDGE, *Apr.* 28, 1897.

DEAR BLOOD,— Your letter is delectable. From your not having yet acknowledged the book,[1] I began to wonder whether you had got it, but this acknowledgment is almost too good. Your thought is obscure — lightning flashes darting gleams — but that 's the way truth is. And altho' I "put pluralism in the place of philosophy," I do it only so far as philosophy means the articulate and the scientific. Life and mysticism exceed the articulable, and if there is

---

[1] *The Will to Believe and Other Essays in Popular Philosophy* had just appeared.

a *One* (and surely men will never be weaned from the idea
of it), it must remain only mystically expressed.

I have been roaring over and quoting some of the passages of your letter, in which my wife takes as much delight
as I do. As for your strictures on my English, I accept
them humbly. I have a tendency towards too great col-
loquiality, I know, and I trust your sense of English better
than any man's in the country. I have a fearful job on
hand just now: an address on the unveiling of a military
statue. Three thousand people, governor and troops, etc.
Why they fell upon me, God knows; but being challenged,
I could not funk. The task is a mechanical one, and the
result somewhat of a school-boy composition. If I thought
it would n't bore you, I should send you a copy for you to
go carefully over and correct or rewrite as to the English.
I should probably adopt every one of your corrections.
What do you say to this? Yours ever,

WM. JAMES.

P.S. Please don't betitle *me!*

The "copy" which was offered for correction with so
much humility was the "Oration" on the unveiling of St.
Gaudens's monument to Colonel Robert Gould Shaw of the
54th Massachusetts Infantry (the first colored regiment).
James was quite accustomed to lecturing from brief notes
and to reading from a complete manuscript; but on this
occasion he thought it necessary to commit his address to
memory. He had never done this before and he never
tried to do it again. He memorized with great difficulty,
found himself placed in an entirely unfamiliar relation to
his audience, and felt as much nervous trepidation as any
inexperienced speaker.[1]

[1] The Address has been reprinted in *Memories and Studies.*

To Henry James.

CAMBRIDGE, *June* 5, 1897.

DEAR H.,— Alice wrote you (I think) a brief word after the crisis of last Monday. It took it out of me nervously a good deal, for it came at the end of the month of May, when I am always fagged to death; and for a week previous I had almost lost my voice with hoarseness. At nine o'clock the night before I ran in to a laryngologist in Boston, who sprayed and cauterized and otherwise tuned up my throat, giving me pellets to suck all the morning. By a sort of miracle I spoke for three-quarters of an hour without becoming perceptibly hoarse. But it is a curious kind of physical effort to fill a hall as large as Boston Music Hall, unless you are trained to the work. You have to shout and bellow, and you seem to yourself wholly unnatural. The day was an extraordinary occasion for sentiment. The streets were thronged with people, and I was toted around for two hours in a barouche at the tail end of the procession. There were seven such carriages in all, and I had the great pleasure of being with St. Gaudens, who is a most charming and modest man. The weather was cool and the skies were weeping, but not enough to cause any serious discomfort. They simply formed a harmonious background to the pathetic sentiment that reigned over the day. It was very peculiar, and people have been speaking about it ever since —the last wave of the war breaking over Boston, everything softened and made poetic and unreal by distance, poor little Robert Shaw erected into a great symbol of deeper things than he ever realized himself,— "the tender grace of a day that is dead,"— etc. We shall never have anything like it again. The monument is really superb, certainly one of the finest things of this century. Read the darkey [Booker T.]

Washington's speech, a model of elevation and brevity. The thing that struck me most in the day was the faces of the old 54th soldiers, of whom there were perhaps about thirty or forty present, with such respectable old darkey faces, the heavy animal look entirely absent, and in its place the wrinkled, patient, good old darkey citizen.

As for myself, I will never accept such a job again. It is entirely outside of my legitimate line of business, although my speech seems to have been a great success, if I can judge by the encomiums which are pouring in upon me on every hand. I brought in some mugwumpery at the end, but it was very difficult to manage it. . . . Always affectionately yours,

WM. JAMES.

Letters to Ellen and Rosina Emmet, which now enter the series, will be the better understood for a word of reminder. "Elly" Temple, one of the Newport cousins referred to in the very first letters, had married, and gone with her husband, Temple Emmet, to California. But in 1887, after his death, she had returned to the East to place her daughters in a Cambridge school. In 1895 and 1896 Ellen and Rosina had made several visits to the house in Irving Street; and thus the comradely cousinship of the sixties had been maintained and reëstablished with the younger generation. At the date now reached, Ellen, or "Bay" as she was usually called, was studying painting. She and Rosina had been in Paris during the preceding winter. Now they and their mother were spending the summer on the south coast of England, at Iden, quite close to Rye, where Henry James was already becoming established.

To Miss Ellen Emmet (Mrs. Blanchard Rand).

BAR HARBOR, ME., *Aug.* 11, 1897.

DEAR OLD BAY (and DEAR ROSINA),— For I have letters
from both of you and my heart inclines to both so that I
can't write to either without the other — I hope you are
enjoying the English coast. A rumor reached me not long
since that my brother Henry had given up his trip to the
Continent in order to be near to you, and I hope for the
sakes of all concerned that it is true. He will find in you
both that eager and vivid artistic sense, and that direct
swoop at the vital facts of human character from which I
am sure he has been weaned for fifteen years at least. And
I am sure it will rejuvenate him again. It is more Celtic
than English, and when joined with those faculties of
soul, conscience, or whatever they be that make England
rule the waves, as they are joined in you, Bay, they leave
no room for any anxiety about the creature's destiny. But
Rosina, who is all senses and intelligence, alarms me by
her recital of midnight walks on the Boulevard des Ital-
iens with bohemian artists. . . . You can't live by gaslight
and excitement, nor can naked intelligence run a *jeune
fille's* life. Affections, pieties, and prejudices must play
their part, and only let the intelligence get an occasional
peep at things from the midst of their smothering embrace.
That again is what makes the British nation so great.
Intelligence does n't flaunt itself there quite naked as in
France.

As for the MacMonnies Bacchante,[1] I only saw her faintly
looming through the moon-light one night when she was
sub judice, so can frame no opinion. The place certainly
calls for a lightsome capricious figure, but the solemn Boston

[1] For a short while MacMonnies's Bacchante stood in the court of the Boston
Public Library.

mind declared that anything but a solemn figure would be desecration. As to her immodesty, opinions got very hot. My knowledge of MacMonnies is confined to one statue, that of Sir Henry Vane, also in our Public Library, an impressionist sketch in bronze (I think), sculpture treated like painting — and I must say I don't admire the result *at all*. But you *know;* and I wish I could see other things of his also. How I wish I could *talk* with Rosina, or rather hear her talk, about Paris, *talk in her French* which I doubt not is by this time admirable. The only book she has vouchsafed news of having read, to me, is the d'Annunzio one, which I have ordered in most choice Italian; but of Lemaître, France, etc., she writes never a word. Nor of V. Hugo. She ought to read "La Légende des Siècles." For the picturesque pure and simple, go there! laid on with a trowel so generous that you really get your glut. But the things in French literature that I have gained most from — the next most to Tolstoy, in the last few years — are the whole cycle of Geo. Sand's life: her "Histoire," her letters, and now lately these revelations of the de Musset episode. The whole thing is beautiful and uplifting — an absolute "liver" harmoniously leading her own life and *neither* obedient nor defiant to what others expected or thought.

We are passing the summer very quietly at Chocorua, with our bare feet on the ground. Children growing up bullily, a pride to the parental heart. . . . Alice and I have just spent a rich week at North Conway, at a beautiful "place," the Merrimans'. I am now here at a really grand place, the Dorrs'— tell Rosina that I went to a domino party last night but was so afraid that some one of the weird and sinister sisters would speak to me that I came home at 12 o'clock, when it had hardly begun. I am so sensitive!

Tell her that a lady from Michigan was recently shown the sights of Cambridge by one of my Radcliffe girls. She took her to the Longfellow house, and as the visitor went into the gate, said, "I will just wait here." To her surprise, the visitor went up to the house, looked in to one window after the other, then rang the bell, and the door closed upon her. She soon emerged, and said that the servant had shown her the house. "I'm so sensitive that at first I thought I would only peep in at the windows. But then I said to myself, 'What 's the use of being so sensitive?' So I rang the bell."

Pray be happy this summer. I see nothing more of Rosina's in the papers. How is that sort of thing going on? . . . As for your mother, give her my old-fashioned love. For some unexplained reason, I find it very hard to write to her — probably it is the same reason that makes it hard for her to write to me — so we can sympathize over so strange a mystery. Anyhow, give her my best love, and with plenty for yourself, old Bay, and for Rosina, believe me, yours ever,

WM. JAMES.

To E. L. Godkin.

CHOCORUA, *Aug.* 17, 1897.

DEAR GODKIN,— Thanks for your kind note *in re* "Will to Believe." I suppose you expect as little a reply to it as I expected one from you to the book; but since you ask what I *du* mean by Religion, and add that until I define that word my essay cannot be effective, I can't forbear sending you a word to clear up that point. I mean by religion for a man *anything* that for *him* is a live hypothesis in that line, altho' it may be a dead one for anyone else. And what I try to show is that whether the man believes, disbelieves, or doubts his hypothesis, the moment he does either, on principle and methodically, he runs a risk of one sort or the other from his own point of view. There is no escaping the risk; why not then admit that one's human function is to run it? By settling down on that basis, and respecting each other's choice of risk to run, it seems to me that we should be in a clearer-headed condition than we now are in, postulating as most all of us do a rational certitude which does n't exist and disowning the semi-voluntary mental action by which we continue in our own severally characteristic attitudes of belief. Since our willing natures are active here, why not face squarely the fact without humbug and get the benefits of the admission?

I passed a day lately with the [James] Bryces at Bar Harbor, and we spoke — not altogether unkindly — of you. I hope you are enjoying, both of you, the summer. All goes well with us. Yours always truly,

WM. JAMES.

To F. C. S. Schiller [Corpus Christi, Oxford].

CAMBRIDGE, *Oct. 23, 1897.*

DEAR SCHILLER,— Did you ever hear of the famous international prize fight between Tom Sayers and Heenan the Benicia Boy, or were you too small a baby in 1857 [1860?] The "Times" devoted a couple of pages of report and one or more eulogistic editorials to the English champion, and the latter, brimming over with emotion, wrote a letter to the "Times" in which he touchingly said that he would live in future as one who had been once deemed worthy of commemoration in its leaders. After reading your review of me in the October "Mind" (which only reached me two days ago) I feel as the noble Sayers felt, and think I ought to write to Stout to say I will try to live up to such a character.   My past has not deserved such words, but my future shall.   Seriously, your review has given me the keenest possible pleasure.   This philosophy must be thickened up most decidedly — your review represents it as something to rally to, so we must fly a banner and start a school. Some of your phrases are bully: "reckless rationalism," "pure science is pure bosh," "infallible *a priori* test of truth to screen us from the consequences of our choice," etc., etc.   Thank you from the bottom of my heart!

The enclosed document [a returned letter addressed to Christ Church] explains itself.   The Church and the Body of Christ are easily confused and I have n't a scholarly memory.   I wrote you a post-card recently to the same address, patting you on the back for your article on Immortality in the "New World."   A staving good thing.   I am myself to give the "Ingersoll Lecture on Human Immortality" here in November — the second lecturer on the foundation. I treat the matter very inferiorly to you, but use your conception of the brain as a sifting agency, which explains my question in the letter.   Young [R. B.] Merriman is at Balliol and a really good fellow in all possible respects.   Pray be good to him if he calls on you.   I hope things have a peacock hue for you now that term has begun.   They are all going well here.   Yours always gratefully,

W. J.

To James J. Putnam.

CAMBRIDGE, *Mar.* 2, 1898.

DEAR JIM,— On page 7 of the "Transcript" tonight you will find a manifestation of me at the State House, protesting against the proposed medical license bill.

If you think I *enjoy* that sort of thing you are mistaken. I never did anything that required as much moral effort in my life. My vocation is to treat of things in an all-round manner and not make *ex-parte* pleas to influence (or seek to) a peculiar jury. *Aussi*, why do the medical brethren force an unoffending citizen like me into such a position? Legislative license is sheer humbug — mere abstract paper thunder under which every ignorance and abuse can still go on. Why this mania for more laws? Why seek to stop the really extremely important experiences which these peculiar creatures are rolling up?

Bah! I'm sick of the whole business, and I well know how all my colleagues at the Medical School, who go only by the label, will view me and my efforts. But if Zola and Col. Picquart can face the whole French army, can't I face their disapproval? — Much more easily than that of my own conscience!

You, I fancy, are not one of the fully disciplined demanders of more legislation. So I write to you, as on the whole my dearest friend hereabouts, to explain just what my state of mind is. Ever yours,

W. J.

James was not indulging in empty rhetoric when he said that his conscience drove him to face the disapproval of his medical colleagues. Some of them never forgave him, and to this day references to his "appearance" at the State House in Boston are marked by partisanship rather than understanding.

What happened cannot be understood without recalling that thirty-odd years ago the licensing of medical practitioners was just being inaugurated in the United States. Today it is evident that everyone must be qualified and licensed before he can be permitted to write prescriptions, to sign statements upon which public records, inquests, and health statistics are to be based, and to go about the community calling himself a doctor. On the other hand, experience has proved that those people who do not pretend to be physicians, who do not use drugs or the knife, and who attempt to heal only by mental or spiritual influence, cannot be regulated by the clumsy machinery of the criminal law. But either because the whole question of medical registration was new, or because professional men are seldom masters of the science of lawmaking, the sponsors of the bills proposed to the Massachusetts Legislature in 1894 and 1898 ignored these distinctions. James did not name them, although his argument implied them and rested upon them. The bills included clauses which attempted to abolish the faith-curers by requiring them to become Doctors of Medicine. The "Spiritualists" and Christian Scientists were a numerous element in the population and claimed a religious sanction for their beliefs. The gentlemen who mixed an anti-spiritualist program in their effort to have doctors examined and licensed by a State Board were either innocent of political discretion or blind to the facts. For it was idle to argue that faith-curers would be able to continue in their own ways as soon as they had passed the medical examinations of the State Board, and that accordingly the proposed law could not be said to involve their suppression. Obviously, medical examinations were barriers which the faith-curers could not climb over. This was the feature of the proposed law which roused James to opposition, and led him to take sides for the moment with all the spokesmen of all the -isms and -opathies.

"I will confine myself to a class of diseases" (he wrote to the Boston "Transcript" in 1894) "with which my occupation has made me somewhat conversant. I mean the diseases of the nervous system and the mind. . . . Of all the new agencies that our day has seen, there is but one that tends steadily to assume a more and more commanding importance, and that is the agency of the patient's mind itself. Whoever can produce effects there holds the key of the situation in a number of morbid conditions of which we do not yet know the extent; for systematic experiments in this direction are in their merest infancy. They began in Europe fifteen years ago, when the medical world so tardily admitted the facts of hypnotism to be true; and in this country they have been carried on in a much bolder and more radical fashion by all those 'mind-curers' and 'Christian Scientists' with whose results the public, and even the profession, are growing gradually familiar.

"I assuredly hold no brief for any of these healers, and must confess that my intellect has been unable to assimilate their theories, so far as I have heard them given. But their *facts* are patent and startling; and anything that interferes with the multiplication of such facts, and with our freest opportunity of observing and studying them, will, I believe, be a public calamity. The law now proposed will so interfere, simply because the mind-curers will not take the examinations. . . . Nothing would please some of them better than such a taste of imprisonment as might, by the public outcry it would occasion, bring the law rattling down about the ears of the mandarins who should have enacted it.

"And whatever one may think of the narrowness of the mind-curers, their logical position is impregnable. They are proving by the most brilliant new results that the therapeutic relation may be what we can at present describe only as a relation of one person to another person; and they are consistent in resisting to the uttermost any legislation that would make 'examinable' information the root of medical virtue, and hamper the free play of personal force and affinity by mechanically imposed conditions."

James knew as well as anyone that in the ranks of the healers there were many who could fairly be described as preying on superstition and ignorance. "X—— personally is a rapacious humbug" was his privately expressed opinion of one of them who had a very large following. He had no reverence for the preposterous theories with which their minds were befogged; but "every good thing like *science* in medicine," as he once said, "has to be imitated and grimaced by a rabble of people who would be at the required height; and the folly, humbug and mendacity is pitiful." Furthermore he saw a quackery quite as odious and much more dangerous than that of the "healers" in the patent-medicine business, which was allowed to advertise its lies and secret nostrums in the newspapers and on the bill-boards, and which flourished behind the counter of every apothecary and village store-keeper at that time. (The Federal Pure Food and Drug Act was still many years off.)

The spokesmen of the medical profession were ignoring what he believed to be instructive phenomena. "What the real interests of medicine require is that mental therapeutics should *not* be stamped out, but studied, and its laws ascertained. For that the mind-curers must at least be suffered to make their experiments. If they cannot interpret their results aright, why then let the orthodox M.D.'s follow up their facts, and study and interpret them? But to force the mind-curers to a State examination is to kill the experiments outright." But instead of the open-minded attitude which he thus advocated, he saw doctors who "had no more exact science in them than a fox terrier" [1] invoking the

---

[1] These words were not employed in public, but were once applied to a well-known professor in a private letter.

holy name of Science and blundering ahead with an air of moral superiority.

"One would suppose," he exclaimed again in the 1898 hearing, "that any set of sane persons interested in the growth of medical truth would rejoice if other persons were found willing to push out their experiences in the mental-healing direction, and provide a mass of material out of which the conditions and limits of such therapeutic methods may at last become clear. One would suppose that our orthodox medical brethren might so rejoice; but instead of rejoicing they adopt the fiercely partisan attitude of a powerful trades-union, demanding legislation against the competition of the 'scabs.' . . . The mind-curers and their public return the scorn of the regular profession with an equal scorn, and will never come up for the examination. Their movement is a religious or quasi-religious movement; personality is one condition of success there, and impressions and intuitions seem to accomplish more than chemical, anatomical or physiological information. . . . Pray do not fail, Mr. Chairman, to catch my point. You are not to ask yourselves whether these mind-curers do really achieve the successes that are claimed. It is enough for you as legislators to ascertain that a large number of our citizens, persons as intelligent and well-educated as yourself, or I, persons whose number seems daily to increase, are convinced that they do achieve them, are persuaded that a valuable new department of medical experience is by them opening up. Here is a purely medical question, regarding which our General Court, not being a well-spring and source of medical virtue, not having any private test of therapeutic truth, must remain strictly neutral under penalty of making the confusion worse. . . . Above all things, Mr. Chairman, let us not be infected with the Gallic spirit of regulation and reglementation for their own abstract sakes. Let us not grow hysterical about law-making. Let us not fall in love with enactments and penalties because they are so logical and sound so pretty, and look so nice on paper." [1]

To James J. Putnam.

CAMBRIDGE, *Mar.* [3?] 1898.

DEAR JIM,— Thanks for your noble-hearted letter, which makes me feel warm again. I am glad to learn that you feel positively *agin* the proposed law, and hope that you will express yourself freely towards the professional brethren to that effect.

Dr. Russell Sturgis has written me a similar letter.

Once more, thanks!

W. J.

P.S. *March* 3. The "Transcript" report, I am sorry to say, was a good deal cut. I send you another copy, to keep and use where it will do most good. The rhetorical problem with me was to say things to the Committee that might neutralize the influence of their medical advisers, who, I supposed, had the inside track, and all the *prestige*. I being banded with the spiritists, faith-curers, magnetic healers, etc., etc. Strange affinities! [2]

W. J.

---

[1] A full report of the speech made at the Legislative hearing was printed in the *Banner of Light*, Mar. 12, 1898. The letter to the Boston *Transcript* in 1894 appeared in the issue of Mar. 24.

[2] *James J. Putnam to William James*

BOSTON, *Mar.* 9, 1898.

DEAR WILLIAM,— We have thought and talked a good deal about the subject of your speech in the course of the last week. I prepared with infinite labor a letter intended for the *Transcript* of last Saturday, but it was not a weighty contribution and I am rather glad it was too late to get in. I think it is generally felt among the best doctors that your position was the liberal one, and that it would be a mistake to try to exact an examination of the mind-healers and Christian Scientists. On the other hand, I am afraid most of the doctors, even including myself, do not have any great feeling of fondness for them, and we are more in the way of

To François Pillon.

CAMBRIDGE, *June* 15, 1898.

MY DEAR PILLON,— I have just received your pleasant letter and the *Année*, volume 8, and shall immediately proceed to read the latter, having finished reading my examinations yesterday, and being now free to enjoy the vacation, but excessively tired. I grieve to learn of poor Mrs. Pillon's continued ill health. How much patience both of you require. I think of you also as spending most of the summer in Paris, when the country contains so many more elements that are good for body and soul.

How much has happened since I last heard from you! To say nothing of the Zola trial, we now have the Cuban War! A curious episode of history, showing how a nation's ideals can be changed in the twinkling of an eye, by a succession of outward events partly accidental. It is quite possible that, without the explosion of the Maine, we should still be at peace, though, since the *basis* of the whole American attitude is the persuasion on the part of the people that the cruelty and misrule of Spain in Cuba call for her expulsion (so that in that sense our war is just what a war of "the powers" against Turkey for the Armenian atrocities would have been), it is hardly possible that peace could have been maintained indefinitely longer, unless Spain had gone out — a consummation hardly to be expected by peaceful means. The actual declaration of war by Congress, however, was a case of *psychologie des foules*, a genuine hysteric stampede at the last moment, which shows how

seeing the fanatical spirit in which they proceed and the harm that they sometimes do than you are. Of course they do also good things which would remain otherwise not done, and that is the important point, and sincere fanatics are almost always, and in this case I think certainly, of real value.

Always affectionately,
JAMES J. P.

unfortunate that provision of our written constitution is which takes the power of declaring war from the Executive and places it in Congress. Our Executive has behaved very well. The European nations of the Continent cannot believe that our pretense of humanity, and our disclaiming of all ideas of conquest, is sincere. It has been *absolutely* sincere! The self-conscious feeling of our people has been entirely based in a sense of philanthropic duty, without which not a step would have been taken. And when, in its ultimatum to Spain, Congress denied any project of conquest in Cuba, it genuinely meant every word it said. But here comes in the psychologic factor: once the excitement of action gets loose, the taxes levied, the victories achieved, etc., the old human instincts will get into play with all their old strength, and the ambition and sense of mastery which our nation has will set up new demands. We shall never take Cuba; I imagine that to be very certain — unless indeed after years of unsuccessful police duty there, for that is what we have made ourselves responsible for. But Porto Rico, and even the Philippines, are not so sure. We had supposed ourselves (with all our crudity and barbarity in certain ways) a better nation morally than the rest, safe at home, and without the old savage ambition, destined to exert great international influence by throwing in our "moral weight," etc. Dreams! Human Nature is everywhere the same; and at the least temptation all the old military passions rise, and sweep everything before them. It will be interesting to see how it will end.

But enough of this! — It all shows by what short steps progress is made, and it confirms the "criticist" views of the philosophy of history. I am going to a great popular meeting in Boston today where a lot of my friends are to protest against the new "Imperialism."

In August I go for two months to California to do some lecturing. As I have never crossed the continent or seen the Pacific Ocean or those beautiful *parages*, I am very glad of the opportunity. The year after next (*i.e.* one year from now) begins a new year of absence from my college duties. I *may* spend it in Europe again. In any case I shall hope to see you, for I am appointed to give the "Gifford Lectures" at Edinburgh during 1899–1901 — two courses of 10 each on the philosophy of religion. A great honor.— I have also received the honor of an election as "Correspondent" of the Académie des Sciences Morales et Politiques. Have I *your* influence to thank for this? Believe me, with most sympathetic regards to Mrs. Pillon and affectionate greetings to yourself, yours most truly

WM. JAMES.

Before starting for California, James went to the Adirondack Lodge to snatch a brief holiday. One episode in this holiday can best be described by an extract from a letter to Mrs. James.

To Mrs. James.

ST. HUBERT'S INN,
KEENE VALLEY, *July* 9, 1898.

. . . I have had an eventful 24 hours, and my hands are so stiff after it that my fingers can hardly hold the pen. I left, as I informed you by post-card, the Lodge at seven, and five hours of walking brought us to the top of Marcy — I carrying 18 lbs. of weight in my pack. As usual, I met two Cambridge acquaintances on the mountain top — "Appalachians" from Beede's. At four, hearing an axe below, I went down (an hour's walk) to Panther Lodge Camp, and there found Charles and Pauline Goldmark, Waldo Adler

and another schoolboy, and two Bryn Mawr girls — the
girls all dressed in boys' breeches, and cutaneously dese-
crated in the extreme from seven of them having been
camping without a male on Loon Lake to the north of this.
My guide had to serve for the party, and quite unexpectedly
to me the night turned out one of the most memorable of
all my memorable experiences. I was in a wakeful mood
before starting, having been awake since three, and I may
have slept a little during this night; but I was not aware of
sleeping at all. My companions, except Waldo Adler,
were all motionless. The guide had got a magnificent provision of firewood, the sky swept itself clear of every trace
of cloud or vapor, the wind entirely ceased, so that the
fire-smoke rose straight up to heaven. The temperature
was perfect either inside or outside the cabin, the moon
rose and hung above the scene before midnight, leaving only
a few of the larger stars visible, and I got into a state of
spiritual alertness of the most vital description. The influences of Nature, the wholesomeness of the people round
me, especially the good Pauline, the thought of you and
the children, dear Harry on the wave, the problem of the
Edinburgh lectures, all fermented within me till it became
a regular Walpurgis Nacht. I spent a good deal of it in
the woods, where the streaming moonlight lit up things
in a magical checkered play, and it seemed as if the Gods
of all the nature-mythologies were holding an indescribable meeting in my breast with the moral Gods of the
inner life. The two kinds of Gods have nothing in common — the Edinburgh lectures made quite a hitch ahead.
The intense significance of some sort, of the whole scene,
if one could only *tell* the significance; the intense inhuman
remoteness of its inner life, and yet the intense *appeal* of it;
its everlasting freshness and its immemorial antiquity and

decay; its utter Americanism, and every sort of patriotic
suggestiveness, and you, and my relation to you part and
parcel of it all, and beaten up with it, so that memory and
sensation all whirled inexplicably together; it was indeed
worth coming for, and worth repeating year by year, if
repetition could only procure what in its nature I suppose
must be all unplanned for and unexpected. It was one of
the happiest lonesome nights of my existence, and I understand now what a poet is. He is a person who can feel the
immense complexity of influences that I felt, and make some
partial tracks in them for verbal statement. In point of
fact, I can't find a single word for all that significance, and
don't know what it was significant of, so there it remains,
a mere boulder of *impression*. Doubtless in more ways
than one, though, things in the Edinburgh lectures will be
traceable to it.

In the morning at six, I shouldered my undiminished pack
and went up Marcy, ahead of the party, who arrived half
an hour later, and we got in here at eight [P.M.] after 10½
hours of the solidest walking I ever made, and I, I think,
more fatigued than I have been after any walk. We
plunged down Marcy, and up Bason Mountain, led by
C. Goldmark, who had, with Mr. White, blazed a trail the
year before; [1] then down again, away down, and up the
Gothics, not counting a third down-and-up over an intermediate spur. It was the steepest sort of work, and,
as one looked from the summits, seemed sheer impossible,
but the girls kept up splendidly, and were all fresher than I.
It was true that they had slept like logs all night, whereas
I was "on my nerves." I lost my Norfolk jacket at the
last third of the course — high time to say good-bye to that
possession — and staggered up to the Putnams to find

---

[1] That is, there was here no path to follow, only "blazes" on the trees.

Hatty Shaw [1] taking me for a tramp. Not a soul was there, but everything spotless and ready for the arrival today. I got a bath at Bowditch's bath-house, slept in my old room, and slept soundly and well, and save for the unwashable staining of my hands and a certain stiffness in my thighs, am entirely rested and well. But I don't believe in keeping it up too long, and at the Willey House will lead a comparatively sedentary life, and cultivate sleep, if I can. . . .

W. J.

The intense experience which James thus described had consequences that were not foreseen at the time. He had gone to the Adirondacks at the close of the college term in a much fatigued condition. He had been sleeping badly for some weeks, and when he started up Mount Marcy he had neuralgia in one foot; but he had characteristically determined to ignore and "bully" this ailment. Under such conditions the prolonged physical exertion of the two days' climb, aggravated by the fact that he carried a pack all the second day, was too much for a man of his years and sedentary occupations. As the summer wore on, pain or discomfort in the region of his heart became constant. He tried to persuade himself that it signified nothing and would pass away, and concealed it from his wife until mid-winter. To Howison — who was himself a confessed heart case — he wrote, "My heart has been kicking about terribly of late, stopping, and hurrying and aching and so forth, but I do not propose to give up to it too much." The fact was that the strain of the two days' climb had caused a valvular lesion that was irreparable, although not great enough seriously to curtail his activities if he had given heed to

[1] The housekeeper at the Putnam-Bowditch "shanty."

his general condition and avoided straining himself again.

In August James went to California to give the lectures which have already been mentioned in a letter to Pillon. Again, these lectures were in substance the "Talks to Teachers." The next letter, written just before he left Cambridge, answers a request to him to address the Philosophical Club at the University of California.

To G. H. Howison.

CAMBRIDGE, *July* 24, 1898.

DEAR HOWISON,— Your kind letter greeted me on my arrival here three days ago — but I have waited to answer it in order to determine just what my lecture's title should be. I wanted to make something entirely popular, and as it were emotional, for technicality seems to me to spell "failure" in philosophy. But the subject in the margin of my consciousness failed to make connexion with the centre, and I have fallen back on something less vital, but still, I think, sufficiently popular and practical, which you can advertise under the rather ill-chosen title of "Philosophical Conceptions and Practical Results," if you wish.

I am just back from a month of practical idleness in the Adirondacks, but such is the infirmity of my complexion that I am not yet in proper working trim. You ask me, like an angel, in what form I like to take my sociability. The spirit is willing to take it in any form, but the flesh is weak, and it runs to destruction of nerve-tissue and madness in me to go to big stand-up receptions where the people scream and breathe in each other's faces. But I know my duties; and one such reception I will gladly face. For the rest, I should infinitely prefer a chosen few at dinner. But this enterprise is going, my friend, to give you and Mrs. Howison a heap of trouble. My purpose is to arrive on

the eve of the 26th. I will telegraph you the hour and train.
When the lectures to the teachers are over, I will make for
the Yosemite Valley, where I want to spend a fortnight if I
can, and come home. . . . Yours ever truly,

WM. JAMES.

To Henry James.

OCCIDENTAL HOTEL,
SAN FRANCISCO, Aug. 11, 1898.

DEAR OLD HENRY,—You see I have worked my way
across the Continent, and, full of the impressions of this
queer place, I must overflow for a page or two to you. I
saw some really grand and ferocious scenery on the Canadian Pacific, and wish I could go right back to see it again.
But it does n't mean much, on the whole, for human habitation, and the British Empire's investment in Canada is
in so far forth but *scenic*. It is grand, though, in its vastness and simplicity. In Washington and Oregon the whole
foreground consisted of desolation by fire. The magnificent coniferous forests burnt and burning, as they have
been for years and years back. Northern California one
pulverous earth-colored mass of hills and heat, with green
spots produced by irrigation hardly showing on the background. I drove through a wheatfield at Harry's Uncle
Christopher's on a machine, drawn by 26 mules, which cut
a swathe 18 feet wide through the wheat and threw it out
in bags to be taken home, as fast as the leisurely mules
could walk. It is like Egypt. Down here, splendid air,
and a city so indescribably odd and unique in its suggestions that I have been saying to myself all day that *you*
ought to have taken it in when you were under 30 and
added it to your portraits of places. So remote and terminal, so full of the sea-port nakedness, yet so new and

American, with its queer suggestions of a history based on the fifties and the sixties. But at my age those impressions are curiously weak to what they once were, and the time to travel is between one's 20th and 30th year. This hotel — an old house cleaned into newness — is redolent of '59 or '60, when it must have been built. Hideous vast stuccoed thing, with long undulating balustrades and wells and lace curtains. The fare is very good, but the servants all Irish, who seem cowed in the dining-room, and go about as if they had corns on their feet and for that reason had given up the pick and shovel. . . . Tomorrow, in spite of drouth and dust, I leave for the Yosemite Valley, with a young Californian philosopher, named [Charles M.] Bakewell, as companion. On the whole I prefer the works of God to those of man, and the alternative, a trip down the coast, beauties as it would doubtless show, would include too much humanity. . . .

To his Son Alexander.

BERKELEY, CAL., *Aug.* 28, 1898.

DARLING OLD CHERUBINI,—See how brave this girl and boy are in the Yosemite Valley![1] I saw a moving sight the other morning before breakfast in a little hotel where I slept in the dusty fields. The young man of the house had shot a little wolf called a coyote in the early morning. The heroic little animal lay on the ground, with his big furry ears, and his clean white teeth, and his jolly cheerful little body, but his brave little life was gone. It made me think how brave all these living things are. Here little coyote was, without any clothes or house or books or anything, with nothing but his own naked self to pay his way

[1] Photograph of a boy and girl standing on a rock which hangs dizzily over a great precipice above the Yosemite Valley.

with, and risking his life so cheerfully — and losing it — just to see if he could pick up a meal near the hotel. He was doing his coyote-business like a hero, and you must do your boy-business, and I my man-business bravely too, or else we won't be worth as much as that little coyote. Your mother can find a picture of him in those green books of animals, and I want you to copy it. Your loving

DAD.

To Miss Rosina H. Emmet.

MONTEREY, *Sept.* 9, 1898.

DEAR OLD ROSINA,— I have seen your native state and even been driven by dear, good, sweet Hal Dibblee (who is turning into a perfectly ideal fellow) through the charming and utterly lovable place in which you all passed your child-hood. (How your mother must sometimes long for it again!) Of California and its greatness, the half can never be told. I have been on a ranch in the white, bare dry-ness of Siskiyou County, and reaped wheat with a swathe of 18 feet wide on a machine drawn by a procession of 26 mules. I've been to Yosemite, and camped for five days in the high Sierras; I've lectured at the two universities of the state, and seen the youths and maidens lounge together at Stanford in cloisters whose architecture is purer and more lovely than aught that Italy can show. I've heard Mrs. Dibblee read letter after letter from Anita concerning your life together; and even one letter to Anita from Bay, which the former enclosed. (Dear Bay!) All this, dear old Rosina, is a "summation of stimuli" which at last car-ries me over the dam that has so long obstructed all my epistolary efforts in your direction.

Over and over again I have been on the point of writing to you, more than once I have actually written a page or two, but something has always checked the flow, and arrested the current of the soul. What is it? I think it is this: I naturally tend, when "familiar" with what the authors of the beginning of the century used to call "a refined female," to indulge in chaffing personalities in writing to her. There is something in you that doubtfully enjoys the chaffing; and subtly feeling that, I stop. But some day, when experience shall have winnowed you with her wing; when the illusions and the hopes of youth alike are faded; when eternal principles of order are more to you than sensations that pass in a day, however exciting; when friends that know you and your roots and derivations are more satisfactory, however humdrum and hoary they be, than the handsome recent acquaintances that know nothing of you but the hour; when, in short, your being is mellowed, dulled and harmonized by time so as to be a grave, wise, deep, and discerning moral and intellectual unity (as mine is already from the height of my 40 centuries!), then, Rosina, we two shall be the most perfect of combinations, and I shall write to you every week of my life and you will be utterly unable to resist replying. That will not be, however, before you are forty years old. You are sure to come to it! For you see the truth, irrespective of persons, as few people see it; and after all, you care for that more than for anything else — and that means a rare and unusual destiny, and ultimate salvation.— But here I am, chaffing, quite against my intentions and altogether in spite of myself. The ruling passion is irresistible. Let me stop!

But still I must be personal, and not write merely of the climate and productions of California, as I have been doing to others for the past four weeks. How I do wish I could be dropped amongst you for but 24 hours! What talk I should hear! What perceptions of truth from you and Bay (and probably young Leslie) would pour into my receptive soul. How I *should* like to hear you hold forth about the French, their art, their literature, their nature, and all else about them! How I should like to hear you *talk* French! How I should like to note the changes wrought in you by all this experience, and take all sorts of excursions in your company! Don't come home for one more year if you can help it. Stay and let the impressions set and tie themselves in with a hard knot, so that they will be worth something and definitive.

I am so glad to hear that Bay is doing so well, and doubly glad (as Mrs. Dibblee tells me from Anita) that H. J. is going to sit to her for his portrait. I am a bit sorry that the youthful Harry did n't accept your invitation, but his time was after all so short that it has been perhaps good for him to get the massive English impression. What times we live in! Dreyfus, Cuba, and Khartoum! — I keep well, though fragile as a worker. You will have heard of my Edinburgh appointment and my election to the Institut de France as *Correspondant*. The latter is silly, but the former a serious scrape out of which I am praying all the gods to help me, as the time for preparation is so short. All Cambridge friends are well. You heard of dear Child's death, last summer, I suppose. Good-bye! Write to me, dear old Rosina. Kiss Bay and Leslie — even *effleurez* your own cheek, for me. Give my best love to your mother, and believe me always your affectionate

W. J.

To Dickinson S. Miller.

CAMBRIDGE, *Dec.* 3, 1898.

ILLUSTRIOUS FRIEND AND JOY OF MY LIVER,— I am much pleased to hear from you, for I have wished to know of your destinies, and Bakewell could n't give me a very precise account. I congratulate you on getting your review of me off your hands — you must experience a relief similar to that of Christian when he lost his bag of sin. I imagine your account of its unsatisfactoriness is a little hyperæsthetic, and that what you have brooded over so long will, in spite of anything in the accidents of its production, prove solid and deep, and reveal *ex pede* the Hercules. Of course, if you do not unconditionally subscribe to my "Will to Believe" essay, it shows that you still are groping in the darkness of misunderstanding either of my meaning or of the truth; for in spite of "the bludgeonings of fate," my head is "bloody but unbowed" as to the rightness of my contention there, in both its parts. But we shall see; and I hope you are now free for more distant flights.

I am extremely sorry to hear you have been not well again, even though you say you are so much better now. You ought to be *entirely* well and every inch a king. Remember that, *whenever* you need a change, your bed is made in this house for as many weeks as you care to stay. I know there will come feelings of disconsolateness over you occasionally, from being so out of the academic swim. But that is nothing! And while this time is on, you should think exclusively of its unique characteristics of blessedness, which will be irrecoverable when you are in the harness again.

I spent the first six weeks after term began in trying to clear my table of encumbering tasks, in order to get at my own reading for the Gifford lectures. In vain. Each day brought its cargo, and I never got at my own work, until a fortnight ago the brilliant resolve was communicated to me, by divine inspiration, of not doing anything for anybody else, not writing a letter or looking at a MS., on any day until I should have done at least one hour of work for *myself.* If you spend your time preparing to be ready, you *never* will be ready. Since that wonderful insight into the truth, despair has given way to happiness. I do my hour or hour and a half of free reading; and don't care what extraneous interest suffers. . . . Good-night, dear old Miller. Your ever loving,

W. J.

To Dickinson S. Miller.

CAMBRIDGE, *Jan.* 31, 1899.

. . . Your account of Josiah Royce is adorable — we have both gloated over it all day. The best intellectual character-painting ever limned by an English pen! Since teaching the "Conception of God," I have come to perceive what I did n't trust myself to believe before, that looseness of thought is R.'s *essential* element. He *wants* it. There is n't a tight joint in his system; not one. And yet I thought that a mind that could talk me blind and black and numb on mathematics and logic, and whose favorite recreation is works on those subjects, must necessarily conceal closeness and exactitudes of ratiocination that I had n't the wit to find out. But no! he is the Rubens of philosophy. Richness, abundance, boldness, color, but a sharp contour never, and never any *perfection.* But is n't fertility better than perfection? Deary me! Ever thine,

W. J.

To Henry Rutgers Marshall.

CAMBRIDGE [*Feb.* 7, 1899?].

DEAR MARSHALL,— I will hand your paper to Eliot, though I am sure that nothing will come of it in *this* University.

Moreover, it strikes me that no good will ever come to

Art as such from the analytic study of Æsthetics — harm rather, if the abstractions could in any way be made the basis of practice. We should get stark things done on system with all the intangible personal *je ne sçais quaw* left out. The difference between the first- and second-best things in art absolutely seems to escape verbal definition — it is a matter of a hair, a shade, an inward quiver of some kind — yet what miles away in point of preciousness! Absolutely the same verbal formula applies to the supreme success and to the thing that just misses it, and yet verbal formulas are all that your æsthetics will give.

Surely imitation in the concrete is better for results than any amount of gabble in the abstract. Let the rest of us philosophers gabble, but don't mix us up with the interests of the art department as such! Them's my sentiments.

Thanks for the "cudgels" you are taking up for the "Will to Believe." Miller's article seems to be based solely on my little catchpenny *title*. Where would he have been if I had called my article "a critique of pure faith" or words to that effect? As it is, he does n't touch a *single* one of my points, and slays a mere abstraction. I shall greedily read what you write.

I have been too lazy and hard pressed to write to you about your "Instinct and Reason," which contains many good things in the way of psychology and morals, but which — I tremble to say it before you — on the whole *does* disappoint me. The religious part especially seems to me to rest on too narrow a phenomenal base, and the formula to be too simple and abstract. But it is a good contribution to American scholarship all the same, and I hope the Philippine Islanders will be forced to study it.

Forgive my brevity and levity. Yours ever,

W. J.

To Henry Rutgers Marshall.

CAMBRIDGE, *Feb.* 8 [1899].

DEAR MARSHALL,— Your invitation was perhaps the finest "tribute" the Jameses have ever received, but it is plumb impossible that either of us should accept. Pinned down, by ten thousand jobs and duties, like two Gullivers by the threads of the Lilliputians.

I should "admire" to see the Kiplings again, but it is no go. Now that by his song-making power he is the mightiest force in the formation of the "Anglo-Saxon" character, I wish he would hearken a bit more to his deeper human self and a bit less to his shallower jingo self. If the Anglo-Saxon race would drop its sniveling cant it would have a good deal less of a "burden" to carry. We 're the most loathsomely canting crew that God ever made. Kipling knows perfectly well that our camps in the tropics are not college settlements or our armies bands of philanthropists, slumming it; and I think it a shame that he should represent us to ourselves in that light. I wish he would try a bit interpreting the savage *soul* to us, as he *could*, instead of using such official and conventional phrases as "half-devil and half-child," which leaves the whole insides out.

Heigh ho!

I have only had time to glance at the first ½ of your paper on Miller. I am delighted you are thus going for him. His whole paper is an *ignoratio elenchi*, and he does n't touch a single one of my positions.

Believe me with great regrets and thanks, yours ever,

WM. JAMES.

To Mrs. Henry Whitman.

CHOCORUA, *June* 7, 1899.

DEAR MRS. WHITMAN,— I got your penciled letter the day before leaving. The R.R. train seems to be a great stimulus to the acts of the higher epistolary activity and correspondential amicality in you — a fact for which I have (occasional) reason to be duly grateful. So here, in the cool darkness of my road-side "sitting-room," with no pen in the house, with the soft tap of the carpenter's hammer and the pensive scrape of the distant wood-saw stealing through the open wire-netting door, along with the fragrant air of the morning woods, I get stimulus responsive, and send you penciled return. Yes, the daylight that now seems shining through the Dreyfus case is glorious, and if the President only gets his back up a bit, and mows down the whole gang of Satan, or as much of it as can be touched, it will perhaps be a great day for the distracted France. I mean it may be one of those moral crises that become starting points and high-water marks and leave traditions and rallying cries and new forces behind them. One thing is certain, that no other alternative form of government possible to France in this century could have stood the strain as this democracy seems to be standing it.

Apropos of which, a word about Woodberry's book.[1] I did n't know him to be that kind of a creature at all. The essays are grave and noble in the extreme. I hail another American author. They can't be popular, and for cause. The respect of him for the Queen's English, the classic leisureliness and explicitness, which give so rare a dignity to his style, also take from it that which our generation seems to need, the sudden word, the unmediated transition, the flash of perception that makes reasonings unnecessary. Poor Woodberry, so high, so true, so good, so original in his total make-up, and yet so unoriginal if you take him spotwise — and therefore so ineffective. His paper on Democracy is very fine indeed, though somewhat too abstract.

[1] G. E. Woodberry: *The Heart of Man;* 1899.

I have n't yet read the first and last essays in the book, which I shall buy and keep, and even send a word of gratulation to the author for it.

As for me, my bed is made: I am against bigness and greatness in all their forms, and with the invisible molecular moral forces that work from individual to individual, stealing in through the crannies of the world like so many soft rootlets, or like the capillary oozing of water, and yet rending the hardest monuments of man's pride, if you give them time. The bigger the unit you deal with, the hollower, the more brutal, the more mendacious is the life displayed. So I am against all big organizations as such, national ones first and foremost; against all big successes and big results; and in favor of the eternal forces of truth which always work in the individual and immediately unsuccessful way, under-dogs always, till history comes, after they are long dead, and puts them on the top. — You need take no notice of these ebullitions of spleen, which are probably quite unintelligible to anyone but myself. Ever your

W. J.

When the College term ended in June, 1899, the sailing date of the European steamer on which James had taken passage for his wife and daughter and himself was still three weeks away. He turned again to the Adirondack Lodge and there persuaded himself, to his intense satisfaction, that if he walked slowly and alone, so that there was no temptation to talk while walking, or to keep on when he felt like stopping, he could still spend several hours a day on the mountain sides without inconvenience to his heart. But one afternoon he took a wrong path and did not discover his mistake until he had gone so far that it seemed safer to go on than to turn back. So he kept on. But the "trail" he was following was not the one he supposed it to be and led him farther and farther. He fainted twice; it grew dark; but having neither food, coat, nor matches, he stumbled along until at last he came out on the Keene Valley road and, at nearly eleven o'clock at night, reached a house where he could get food and a conveyance.

He ought to have avoided all exertion for weeks thereafter, but he tried again to make light of what had occurred, and, on getting back to Cambridge, spent a very active few days over final arrangements for his year of absence. When his boat had sailed and the stimulus which his last duties supplied had been withdrawn, he began to discover what condition he was in.

XIII

1899–1902

Two years of Illness in Europe — Retirement from Active Duty at Harvard — The First and Second Series of the Gifford Lectures

WHEN James sailed for Hamburg on July 15, he planned quite definitely to devote the summer to rest and the treatment of his heart, then to write out the Gifford Lectures during the winter, and to deliver them by the following spring; and, happily, could not foresee that he was to spend nearly two years in exile and idleness. For nearly six years he had driven himself beyond the true limits of his strength. Now it became evident that the strain of his second overexertion in the Adirondacks had precipitated a complete collapse. He had been advised during the winter to go to Nauheim for a course of baths. But when he got there, the eminent specialists who examined his heart ignored his nervous prostration. He was doubtless a difficult patient to diagnose or prescribe for. Matters went from bad to worse; little by little all his plans had to be abandoned. A year went by, and a return to regular work in Cambridge was unthinkable. He was no better in the summer of 1900 than when he landed in Germany in July of 1899. His daughter had been sent to school in England. The three other children remained in America. He and Mrs. James moved about between England, Nauheim, the south of France, Switzerland and Rome, consulting a specialist in one place or trying the baths or the climate in another—with how much homesickness, and with how much courage none the less, the letters will indicate.

His only systematic reading was a persistent, though frequently intermitted, exploration of religious biographies and the literature of religious conversion, in preparation for the Gifford Lectures. During the second year he managed to get one course of these lectures written out. Not until he had delivered them in Edinburgh, in May, 1901, did he know that he had turned the corner and feel as if he had begun to live again.

Every letter that came to him from his family and friends at home was comforting beyond measure, and he poured out a stream of acknowledgment in long replies, which he dictated to Mrs. James. His own writing was usually limited to jottings in a note-book and to post-cards. He always had a fountain-pen and a few post-cards in his pocket, and often, when sitting in a chair in the open air, or at a little table in one of the outdoor restaurants that abound in Nauheim and in southern Europe, he would compress more news and messages into one of these little missives than most men ever get into a letter. A few of his friends at home divined his situation, and were at pains to write him regularly and fully. Letters that follow show how grateful he was for such devotion.

In this state of enforced idleness he browsed through newspapers and journals more than he had before or than he ever did again, and so his letters contained more comments on daily events. It will be clear that what was happening did not always please him. He was an individualist and a liberal, both by temperament and by reason of having grown up with the generation which accepted the doctrines of the *laissez-faire* school in a thoroughgoing way. The Philip-

pine policy of the McKinley administration seemed to him
a humiliating desertion of the principles that America had
fought for in the Revolution and the War of Emancipation.
The military occupation of the Philippines, described by
the President as "benevolent assimilation," and what he
once called the "cold pot-grease of McKinley's eloquence"
filled him with loathing. He saw the Republican Party in
the light in which Mr. Dooley portrayed it when he represented its leaders as praying "that Providence might remain
under the benevolent influence of the present administration." When McKinley and Roosevelt were nominated by
the Republicans in 1900, he called them "a combination of
slime and grit, soap and sand, that ought to scour anything
away, even the moral sense of the country." He was ready
to vote for Bryan if there were no other way of turning out
the administration responsible for the history of our first
years in the Philippines, "although it would doubtless have
been a premature victory of a very mongrel kind of reform."
In the same way, the cant with which many of the sup-
porters of England's program in South Africa extolled the
Boer War in the British press provoked his irony. The up-
roar over the Dreyfus case was at its height. The "intellectuels," as they were called in France, the "Little Eng-
landers" as they were nicknamed in England, and the
Anti-Imperialists in his own country had his entire sympathy. The state of mind of a member of the liberal
minority, observing the phase of history that was disclosing
itself at the end of the century, is admirably indicated in
his correspondence.

Miss Pauline Goldmark, next addressed, and her family
were in the habit of spending their summers in Keene Valley,
where they had a cottage that was not far from the Putnam

Shanty. James had often joined forces with them for a day's climb when he was staying at the Shanty. The reader will recall that it was their party that he had joined on Mt. Marcy the year before.

To Miss Pauline Goldmark.

BAD-NAUHEIM, *Aug.* 12, 1899.

MY DEAR PAULINE,—I am afraid we are stuck here till the latter half of September. Once a donkey, always a donkey; at the Lodge in June, after some slow walks which seemed to do me no harm at all, I drifted one day up to the top of Marcy, and then (thanks to the Trail Improvement Society!) found myself in the Johns Brook Valley instead of on the Lodge trail back; and converted what would have been a three-hours' downward saunter into a seven-hours' scramble, emerging in Keene Valley at 10.15 P.M. This did me no good—quite the contrary; so I have come to Nauheim just in time. My carelessness was due to the belief that there was only one trail in the Lodge direction, so I did n't attend particularly, and when I found myself off the track (the trail soon stopped) I thought I was going to South Meadow, and did n't reascend. Anyhow I was an ass, and you ought to have been along to steer me straight. I fear we shall ascend no more acclivities together. "Bent is the tree that should have grown full straight!" You have no idea of the moral repulsiveness of this *Curort* life. Everybody fairly revelling in disease, and abandoning themselves to it with a sort of *gusto*. "Heart," "heart," "heart," the sole topic of attention and conversation. As a "phase," however, one ought to be able to live through it, and the extraordinary nerve-rest, crawling round as we do, is beneficial. Man is never satisfied! Perhaps I shall be when the baths, etc., have had their effect. We go then

straight to England.— I do hope that you are all getting
what you wish in Switzerland, and that for all of you the
entire adventure is proving golden. Mrs. James sends her
love, and I am, as always, yours most affectionately,

                                        WM. JAMES.

To Mrs. E. P. Gibbens.
              VILLA LUISE, BAD-NAUHEIM, *Aug.* 22, 1899.

DARLING BELLE-MÈRE,—The day seems to have come for
another letter to you, though my fingers are so cold that
I can hardly write. We have had a most conveniently
dry season — convenient in that it does n't coop us up in
the house — but a deal of cloud and cold. Today is sunny
but frigid — like late October. Altogether the difference
of weather is very striking. European weather is stagnant
and immovable. It is as if it got stuck, and needed a kick
to start it; and although it is doubtless better for the nerves
than ours, I find my soul thinking most kindly from this
distance of our glorious quick passionate American climate,
with its transparency and its impulsive extremes. This
weather is as if fed on solid pudding. We inhabit one
richly and heavily furnished bedroom, 21 x 14, with good
beds and a balcony, and are rapidly making up for all our
estrangement, locally speaking, in the past. It is a great
"nerve-rest," though the listlessness that goes with all
nerve-rest makes itself felt. Alice seems very well. . . .
The place has wonderful adaptation to its purposes in the
possession of a vast park with noble trees and avenues and
incessant benches for rest; restaurants with out-of-door
tables everywhere in sight; music morning, afternoon and
night; and charming points to go to out of town. Cab-
fare is cheap. But nothing else. . . . The Gifford lectures
are in complete abeyance. I have word from Seth that

under the circumstances the Academic Senate will be sure to grant me any delay or indulgence I may ask for; so this relieves tension. I can make nothing out yet about my heart. . . . So I *try* to take long views and not fuss about temporary feelings, though I dare say I keep dear Alice worried enough by the fuss I imagine myself *not* to make. It is a loathsome world, this medical world; and I confess that the thought of another six weeks here next year does n't exhilarate me, in spite of the decency of all our physical conditions. I still remain faithful to Irving St. (95 and 107),[1] Chocorua, Silver Lake, and Keene Valley!

We get almost no syllable of American news, in spite of the fact that we take the London "Chronicle." Pray send the "Nation" and the "Literary Digest." *Don't* send the "Sciences" as heretofore. Let them accumulate. I think that after reception of this you had better address us care of H. J., Rye, Sussex. We shall probably be off by the 10th or 12th of Sept. I hope that public opinion is gathering black against the Philippine policy — in spite of my absence! I hope that Salter will pitch in well in the fall. The still blacker nightmare of a Dreyfus case hangs over us; and there is little time in the day save for reading the "Figaro's" full reports of the trial. Like all French happenings, it is as if they were edited expressly for literary purpose. Every "witness" so-called has a power of statement equal to that of a first-class lawyer; and the various human types that succeed each other, exhibiting their several peculiarities in full blossom, make the thing like a novel. Esterhazy seems to me the *great* hero. How Shakespeare would have enjoyed such a fantastic scoundrel,— knowing all the secrets, saying what he pleases, mystifying all Europe, leading the whole French army

---

[1] James's house was number 95, his mother-in-law's number 107.

(except apparently Picquart) by the nose,— a regular Shake-spearean type of villain, with an insane exuberance of rhetoric and fancy about his vanities and hatreds, that literature has never given yet. It would seem incredible that the Court-Martial should condemn. Henry was evidently the spy, employed by Esterhazy, and afterwards Du Paty helped their machinations, in order not to stultify his own record at the original trial — at least this seems the plausible theory. The older generals seem merely to have been passive connivers, stupidly and obstinately holding to the original official mistake rather than surrender under fire. And such is the prestige of caste-opinion, such the solidity of the professional spirit, that, incredible as it may seem, it is still quite probable that the officers will obey the lead of their superiors, and condemn Dreyfus again. The President, Jouaust, who was supposed to be impartial, is showing an apparently bad animus against Picquart. P. is a real *hero* — a precious possession for any country. He ought to be made Minister of War; though that would doubtless produce a revolution. I suppose that Loubet will pardon Dreyfus immediately if he is recondemned. Then Dreyfus, and perhaps Loubet, will be assassinated by some Anti-Semite, and who knows what will follow? But before you get this, you will know far more about the trial than I can tell you.

We long for news from the boys — not a word from Billy since he left Tacoma. I am glad their season promises to be shorter! Enough is as good as a feast! What a scattered lot we are! I hope that Margaret will be happy in Montreal. As for you in your desolation, I could almost weep for you. My only advice is that you should cling to Aleck as to a life-preserver. I trust you got the $200 I told Higginson to send you. I am mortified beyond measure by that overdrawn bank account, and do not understand it at all.

Oceans of love from your affectionate son,

WILLIAM.

To William M. Salter.

BAD-NAUHEIM, *Sept.* 11, 1899.

DEAR MACKINTIRE,— The incredible has happened, and Dreyfus, without one may say a single particle of *positive* evidence that he was guilty, has been condemned again. The French Republic, which seemed about to turn the most dangerous corner in her career and enter on the line of political health, laying down the finest set of political precedents in her history to serve as standards for future imitation and habit, has slipped Hell-ward and all the forces of Hell in the country will proceed to fresh excesses of insolence. But I don't believe the game is lost. "Les intellectuels," thanks to the Republic, are now aggressively militant as they never were before, and will grow stronger and stronger; so we may hope. I have sent you the "Figaro" daily; but of course the reports are too long for you to have read through. The most grotesque thing about the whole trial is the pretension of awful holiness, of semi-divinity in the diplomatic documents and waste-paper-basket scraps from the embassies — a farce kept up to the very end — these same documents being, so far as they were anything (and most of them were nothing), mere records of treason, lying, theft, bribery, corruption, and every crime on the part of the diplomatic agents. Either the German and Italian governments will now publish or not publish all the details of their transactions — give the exact documents meant by the *bordereaux* and the exact names of the French traitors. If they do not, there will be only two possible explanations: either Dreyfus's guilt, or the pride of their own sacrosanct etiquette. As it is scarcely conceivable that Dreyfus can have been guilty, their silences will be due to the latter cause.   (Of course it can't be due to what they owe in honor to Esterhazy and whoever their other allies and servants may have been. E. is safe over the border, and a pension for his services will heal all his wounds. Any other person can quickly be put in similar conditions of happiness.) And they and Esterhazy will then be exactly on a par morally, actively conspiring to have an innocent man bear the burden of their own sins. By their carelessness with the documents they got Dreyfus accused, and now they abandon him, for the sake of their own divine etiquette.

The breath of the nostrils of all these big institutions is crime — that is the long and short of it. We must thank God for America; and hold fast to every advantage of our position. Talk about our corruption! It is a mere fly-speck of superficiality compared with the rooted and permanent forces of corruption that exist in the European states. The only serious permanent force of corruption in America is party spirit. All the other forces are shifting like the clouds, and have no partnerships with any permanently organized ideal. Millionaires and syndicates have their immediate cash to pay, but they have no intrenched prestige to work with, like the church sentiment, the army sentiment, the aristocracy and royalty sentiment, which here can be brought to bear in favor of every kind of individual and collective crime — appealing not only to the immediate pocket of the persons to be corrupted, but to the ideals of their imagination as well. . . . My dear Mack, we "intellectuals" in America must all work to keep our precious birthright of individualism, and freedom from these institutions. *Every* great institution is perforce a means of corruption — whatever good it may also do. Only in the free personal relation is full ideality to be found.— I have vomited all this out upon you in the hope that it may wake a responsive echo. One must do *something* to work off the effect of the Dreyfus sentence.

I rejoice immensely in the purchase [on our behalf] of the two pieces of land [near Chocorua], and pine for the day when I can get back to see them. If all the same to you, I wish that you would buy Burke's in your name, and Mother-in-law Forrest's in her name. But let this be exactly as each of you severally prefers.

We leave here in a couple of days, I imagine. I am better; but I can't tell how much better for a few weeks yet. I hope that you will smite the ungodly next winter. What a glorious gathering together of the forces for the great fight there will be. It seems to me as if the proper tactics were to pound McKinley — put the whole responsibility on him. It is he who by his purely drifting "non-entanglement" policy converted a splendid opportunity into this present necessity of a conquest of extermination. It is he who has warped us from our continuous national habit, which, if we repudiate him, it will not be impossible to resume.

Affectionately thine, Mary's, Aleck's, Dinah's, Augusta's,[1] and everyone's,

W. J.

P.S. Damn it, America does n't know the meaning of the word corruption compared with Europe! Corruption is so permanently organized here that it is n't thought of as such — it is so transient and shifting in America as to make an outcry whenever it appears.

[1] Augusta was the house-maid; Dinah, a bull-terrier.

To Miss Frances R. Morse.

BAD-NAUHEIM, *Sept.* 17, 1899.

. . . In two or three days more I shall be discharged (in very decent shape, I trust) and after ten days or so of rigorously prescribed "Nachkur" in the cold and rain of Switzerland (we have seen the sun only in short but entrancing glimpses since Sept. 1, and you know what bad weather is when it once begins in Europe), we shall pick up our Peggy at Vevey, and proceed to Lamb House, Rye, *über* Paris, with all possible speed. God bless the American climate, with its transparent, passionate, impulsive variety and headlong fling. There are deeper, slower tones of earnestness and moral gravity here, no doubt, but ours is more like youth and youth's infinite and touching promise. God bless America in general! *Conspuez* McKinley and the Republican party and the Philippine war, and the Methodists, and the voices, etc., as much as you please, but bless the innocence. Talk of corruption! We don't know what the word corruption means at home, with our improvised and shifting agencies of crude pecuniary bribery, compared with the solidly intrenched and permanently organized corruptive geniuses of monarchy, nobility, church, army, that penetrate the very bosom of the higher kind as well as the lower kind of people in all the European states (except Switzerland) and sophisticate their motives away from the impulse to straightforward handling of any simple case. *Temoin* the Dreyfus case! But no matter! Of all the forms of mental crudity, that of growing earnest over international comparisons is probably the most childish. Every nation has its ideals which are a dead secret to other nations, and it has to develop in its own way, in touch with them. It can only be judged by itself. If each of us does as well as he can in his own sphere at home, he will do all he *can* do; that is why I hate to remain so long abroad. . . .

We have been having a visit from an extraordinary Pole named Lutoslawski, 36 years old, author of philosophical writings in seven different languages,— "Plato's Logic," in English (Longmans) being his chief work,— and knower of several more, handsome, and to the last degree genial. He has a singular philosophy — the philosophy of friendship. He takes in dead seriousness what most people admit, but only half-believe, viz., that we are *Souls* (Zoolss, he pronounces it), that souls are immortal, and agents of the world's destinies, and that the chief concern of a soul is to get ahead by the help of other souls with whom it can establish confidential relations. So he spends most of his time writing letters, and will send 8 sheets of reply to a post-card — that is the exact proportion of my correspondence with him. Shall I rope you in, Fanny? He has a great chain of friends and correspondents in all the countries of Europe. The worst of them is that they think a secret imparted to one may at his or her discretion become, *de proche en proche*, the property of all. He is a *wunderlicher Mensch:* abstractly his scheme is divine, but there is something on which I can't yet just lay my defining finger that makes one feel that there is some need of the corrective and critical and arresting judgment in his manner of carrying it out. These Slavs seem to be the great radical livers-out of their theories. Good-bye, dearest Fanny. . . .

Your affectionate

W. J.

To Mrs. Henry Whitman.

LAMB HOUSE, RYE, *Oct. 5,* 1899.

DEAR MRS. WHITMAN,— You see where at last we have arrived, at the end of the first *étape* of this pilgrimage — the second station of the cross, so to speak — with the Continent over, and England about to begin. The land is bathed in greenish-yellow light and misty drizzle of rain. The little town, with its miniature brick walls and houses and nooks and coves and gardens, makes a curiously vivid and quaint picture, alternately suggesting English, Dutch, and Japanese effects that one has seen in pictures — all exceedingly tiny (so that one wonders how *families* ever could have been reared in most of the houses) and neat and *zierlich* to the last degree. *Refinement* in architecture certainly consists in narrow trim and the absence of heavy mouldings. Modern Germany is incredibly bad from that point of view — much worse, apparently, than America. But the German people are a good safe fact for great powers to be intrusted to — earnest and serious, and pleasant to be with, as we found them, though it was humiliating enough to find how awfully imperfect were one's powers of conversing in their language. French not much better. I remember nothing of this extreme mortification in old times, and am inclined to think that it is due less to loss of ability to speak, than to the fact that, as you grow older, you speak better English, and expect more of yourself in the way of accomplishment. I am sure *you* spoke no such English as now, in the seventies, when you came to Cambridge! And how could I, as yet untrained by conversation with you?

Seven mortal weeks did we spend at the *Curort*, Nauheim, for an infirmity of the heart which I contracted, apparently, not much more than a year ago, and which now must be borne, along with the rest of the white man's burden, until additional visits to Nauheim have removed it altogether for ordinary practical purposes. N. was a sweetly pretty spot, but I longed for more activity. A glorious week in Switzerland, solid in its sometimes awful, sometimes beefy beauty; two days in Paris, where I could gladly have stayed the winter out, merely for the fun of the sight of the intelligent and interesting streets; then hither, where H. J. has a real little *bijou* of a house and garden, and seems absolutely adapted to his environment, and very well and contented in the leisure to write and to read which the place affords.

In a few days we go almost certainly to the said H. J.'s apartment, still unlet, in London, where we shall in all probability stay till January, the world forgetting, by the world forgot, or till such later date as shall witness the completion of the awful Gifford job, at which I have not been able to write one line since last January. I long for the definitive settlement and ability to get to work. I am very glad indeed, too, to be in an English atmosphere again. Of course it will conspire better with my writing tasks, and after all it is more congruous with one's nature and one's inner ideals. Still, one loves America above all things, for her youth, her greenness, her plasticity, innocence, good intentions, friends, everything. Je veux que mes cendres reposent sur les bords du Charles, au milieu de ce bon peuple de Harvarr Squerre que j'ai tant aimé. That is what I say, and what Napoleon B. would have said, had his life been enriched by your and my educational and other experiences — poor man, he knew too little of life, had never even heard of us, whilst we have heard of him!

Seriously speaking, though, I believe that international comparisons are a great waste of time — at any rate, international judgments and passings of sentence are. Every nation has ideals and difficulties and sentiments which are an impenetrable secret to one not of the blood. Let them alone, let each one work out its own salvation on its own lines. They talk of the decadence of France. The hatreds, and the *coups de gueule* of the newspapers there are awful. But I doubt if the better ideals were ever so aggressively strong; and I fancy it is the fruit of the much decried republican régime that they have become so. My brother represents English popular opinion as less cock-a-whoop for war than newspaper accounts would lead one to imagine; but I don't know that he is in a good position for judging. I hope if they do go to war that the Boers will give them fits, and I heartily emit an analogous prayer on behalf of the Philippinos.

I have had pleasant news of Beverly, having had letters both from Fanny Morse and Paulina Smith. I hope that your summer has been a good one, that work has prospered and that Society has been less *énervante* and more nutritious for the higher life of the Soul than it sometimes is. *We* have met but one person of any accomplishments or interest all summer. But I have managed to read a good deal about religion, and religious people, and care less for accomplishments, except where (as in you) they go with a sanctified heart. Abundance of accomplishments, in an unsanctified heart, only make one a more accomplished devil.

Good bye, angelic friend! We both send love and best wishes, both to you and Mr. Whitman, and I am as ever yours affectionately,

W. J.

To Thomas Davidson.

34 DE VERE GARDENS,
LONDON, *Nov.* 2, 1899.

DEAR OLD T. D.,—A recent letter from Margaret Gibbens says that you have gone to New York in order to undergo a most "radical operation." I need not say that my thoughts have been with you, and that I have felt anxiety mixed with my hopes for you, ever since. I do indeed hope that, whatever the treatment was, it has gone off with perfect success, and that by this time you are in the durable enjoyment of relief, and nerves and everything upon the upward track. It has always seemed to me that, were I in a similar plight, I should choose a kill-or-cure operation rather than anything merely palliative — so poisonous to one's whole mental and moral being is the irritation and worry of the complaint. It would truly be a spectacle for the Gods to see you rising like a phœnix from your ashes again, and shaking off even the memory of disaster like dew-drops from a lion's mane, etc.— and I hope the spectacle will be vouchsafed to us men also, and that you will be presiding over Glenmore as if nothing had happened, different from the first years, save a certain softening of your native ferocity of heart, and gentleness towards the shortcomings of weaker people. Dear old East Hill![1] I shall never forget the beauty of the morning (it had rained the night before) when I took my bath in the brook, before driving down to Westport one day last June.

We got your letter at Nauheim, a sweet safe little place, made for invalids, to which it took long to reconcile me on that account. But nous en avons vu bien d'autres depuis, and from my present retirement in my brother's still unlet flat (he living at Rye), Nauheim seems to me like New York for bustle and energy. My heart, in short, has gone back upon me badly since I was there, and my doctor, Bezley Thorne, the first specialist here, and a man who inspires me with great confidence, is trying to tide me over the crisis, by great quiet, in addition to a dietary of the

---

[1] It will be recalled that Davidson had a summer School of Philosophy at his place called Glenmore on East Hill, and that East Hill is at one end of Keene Valley. See also James's essay on Thomas Davidson, "A Knight Errant of the Intellectual Life," in *Memories and Studies*.

strictest sort, and more Nauheim baths, *à domicile*. Provided I can only get safely out of the Gifford scrape, the deluge has leave to come.— Write, dear old T. D., and tell how you are, and let it be good news if possible. Give much love to the Warrens, and believe me always affectionately yours,

WM. JAMES.

The woman thou gavest unto me comes out strong as a nurse, and treats me much better than I deserve.

To John C. Gray.
[Dictated to Mrs. James]
LONDON, *Nov.* 23, 1899.

DEAR JOHN,— A week ago I learnt from the "Nation"— strange to have heard it in no directer way!— that dear old John Ropes had turned his back on us and all this mortal tragi-comedy. No sooner does one get abroad than that sort of thing begins. I am deeply grieved to think of never seeing or hearing old J. C. R. again, with his manliness, good-fellowship, and cheeriness, and idealism of the right sort, and can't hold in any longer from expression. You, dear John, seem the only fitting person for me to condole with, for you will miss him most tremendously. Pray write and tell me some details of the manner of his death. I hope he did n't suffer much. Write also of your own personal and family fortunes and give my love to the members of our dining club collectively and individually, when you next meet.

I have myself been shut up in a sick room for five weeks past, seeing hardly anyone but my wife and the doctor, a bad state of the heart being the cause. We shall be at West Malvern in ten days, where I hope to begin to mend. Hurrah for Henry Higginson and his gift[1] to the Uni-

---

[1] A gift which provided for building the "Harvard Union."

versity! I think the Club cannot fail to be useful if they make it democratic enough.

I hope that Roland is enjoying Washington, but not so far transubstantiated into a politician as to think that McKinley & Co. are the high-water mark of human greatness up to date.

John Ropes, more than most men, seems as if he would be natural to meet again.

Please give our love to Mrs. Gray, and believe me, affectionately yours,

WM. JAMES.

To Miss Frances R. Morse.

LAMB HOUSE, *Dec.* 23, 1899.

DEAREST FANNY,— About a week ago I found myself thinking a good deal about you.

I may possibly have begun by wondering how it came that, after showing such a spontaneous tendency towards that "clandestine correspondence" early in the season, you should recently, in spite of pathetic news about me, and direct personal appeals, be showing such great epistolary reserve. I went on to great lengths about you; and ended by realizing your existence, and its significance, as it were, very acutely. I composed a letter to you in my mind, whilst lying awake, dwelling in a feeling manner on the fact that human beings are born into this little span of life of which the best thing is its friendships and intimacies, and soon their places will know them no more, and yet they leave their friendships and intimacies with no cultivation, to grow as they will by the roadside, expecting them to "keep" by force of mere inertia; they contribute nothing empirical to the relation, treating it as something transcendental and metaphysical altogether; whereas in truth it deserves from hour to hour the most active care and nurture and devotion. "There's that Fanny," thought I, "the rarest and most precious, perhaps, of all the phenomena that enter into the circle of my experience. I take her for granted; I seldom see her — *she has never passed a night in our house!* [1] and yet of all things she is the one that probably deserves the closest and most unremitting attention on my part. This transcendental relation of persons to each other in the absolute won't do! I must write to Fanny and tell her, in spite of her deprecations, just how perfect and rare and priceless a fact I know her existence in this Universe eternally to be. This very morrow I will dictate such a letter to Alice." The morrow came, and several days succeeded, and brought each its impediment with it, so that letter does n't get written till today. And now Alice, who had suddenly to take Peggy (who is with us for ten days) out to see a neighbor's little girl, comes in; so I will give the pen to her.

[Remainder of letter dictated to Mrs. James]

Sunday, 24th.

Brother Harry and Peggy came in with Alice last evening, so my letter got postponed till this morning. What I was going to say was this. The day before yesterday we received in one bunch seven letters from you, dating from the 20th of October to the 8th of December, and showing that you, at any rate, had been alive to the duty of actively nourishing friendship by deeds. . . . Your letters were sent to Baring Brothers, instead of Brown, Shipley and Co., and it was a mercy that we ever got them at all. You are a great letter-writer inasmuch as your pen flows on, giving out easily such facts and feelings and thoughts as form the

[1] "You have never spent a night under our roof, or eaten a meal in our house!" This fictitious charge had become the recognized theme of frequent elaborations.

actual contents of your day, so that one gets a live impression of concrete reality. *My* letters, I find, tend to escape into humorisms, abstractions and flights of fancy, which are not nutritious things to impart to friends thousands of miles away who wish to realize the facts of your private existence. We are now received into the shelter of H. J.'s "Lamb House," where we have been a week, having found West Malvern (where the doctor sent me after my course of baths) rather too bleak a retreat for the drear-nighted December. (Heaven be praised! we have just lived down the solstice after which the year always seems a brighter, hopefuller thing.) Harry's place is a most exquisite collection of quaint little stage properties, three quarters of an acre of brick-walled English garden, little brick courts and out-houses, old-time kitchen and offices, paneled chambers and tiled fire-places, but all very simple and on a small scale. Its host, soon to become its proprietor, leads a very lonely life but seems in perfect equilibrium therewith, placing apparently his interest more and more in the operations of his fancy. His health is good, his face calm, his spirits equable, and he will doubtless remain here for many years to come, with an occasional visit to London. He has spoken of you with warm affection and is grateful for the letters which you send him in spite of the lapse of years. . . .

I have resigned my Gifford lectureship, but they will undoubtedly grant me indefinite postponement. I have also asked for a second year of absence from Harvard, which of course will be accorded. If I improve, I may be able to give my first Gifford course next year. I can do no work whatsoever at present, but through the summer and half through the fall was able to do a good deal of reading in religious biography. Since July, in fact, my only companions have been saints, most excellent, though sometimes rather lop-sided company. In a general manner I can see my way to a perfectly bully pair of volumes, the first an objective study of the "Varieties of Religious Experience," the second, my own last will and testament, setting forth the philosophy best adapted to normal religious needs. I hope I may be spared to get the thing down on paper. So far my progress has been rather downhill, but the last couple of days have shown a change which possibly may be the beginning of better things. I mean to take great care of myself from this time on. In another week or two we hope to move to a climate (possibly near Hyères) where I may sit more out of doors. Gathering some strength there, I trust to make for Nauheim in May. If I am benefited there, we shall stay over next winter; otherwise we return by midsummer. Were Alice not holding the pen, I should celebrate her unselfish devotion, etc., and were I not myself dictating, I should celebrate my own uncomplaining patience and fortitude. As it is, I leave you to imagine both. Both are simply beautiful!

. . . There, dear Fanny, this is all I can do today in return for your seven glorious epistles. Take a heartful of love and gratitude from both of us. Remember us most affectionately to your Mother and Mary. Write again soon, I pray you, but always to *Brown, Shipley and Co.* Stir up Jim Putnam to write when he can, and believe me, lovingly yours,

WM. JAMES.

To Mrs. Glendower Evans.
[Dictated to Mrs. James]
COSTEBELLE, HYÈRES, Jan. 17, 1900.

DEAR BESSIE,— Don't think that this is the first time that my spirit has turned towards you since our departure.

Away back in Nauheim I began meaning to write to you, and although that meaning was "fulfilled" long before you were born, in Royce's Absolute, yet there was a hitch about it in the finite which gave me perplexity. I think that the real reason why I kept finding myself able to dictate letters to other persons — not many, 't is true — and yet postponing ever until next time my letter unto you, was that my sense of your value was so much greater than almost anybody else's — though I would n't have anything in this construed prejudicial to Fanny Morse. Bowed as I am by the heaviest of matrimonial chains, ever dependent for expression on Alice here, how can my spirit move with perfect spontaneity, or "voice itself" with the careless freedom it would wish for in the channels of its choice? I am sure you understand, and under present conditions of communication anything more explicit might be imprudent.

She has told you correctly all the outward facts. I feel within a week past as if I might really be taking a turn for the better, and I know you will be glad.

I have, in the last days, gone so far as to read Royce's book [1] from cover to cover, a task made easy by the familiarity of the thought, as well as the flow of the style. It is a charming production — it is odd that the adjectives "charming" and "pretty" emerge so strongly to characterize my impression. R. has got himself much more organically together than he ever did before, the result being, in its *ensemble*, a highly individual and original *Weltanschauung*, well-fitted to be the storm-centre of much discussion, and to form a wellspring of suggestion and education for the next generation of thought in America. But it makes youthful anew the paradox of philosophy — so trivial and so ponderous at once. The book leaves a total effect on you like

---

[1] *The World and the Individual*, vol. i. Mrs. Evans was inclined to contend for Royce's philosophy.

a picture — a summary impression of charm and grace as light as a breath; yet to bring forth that light nothing less than Royce's enormous organic temperament and technical equipment, and preliminary attempts, were required. The book consolidates an impression which I have never before got except by glimpses, that Royce's system is through and through to be classed as a light production. It is a charming, romantic sketch; and it is only by handling it after the manner of a sketch, keeping it within sketch technique, that R. can make it very impressive. In the few places where he tries to grip and reason close, the effect is rather disastrous, to my mind. But I do think of Royce now in a more or less settled way as primarily a sketcher in philosophy. Of course the sketches of some masters are worth more than the finished pictures of others. But stop! if this was the kind of letter I meant to write to you, it is no wonder that I found myself unable to begin weeks ago. My excuse is that I only finished the book two hours ago, and my mind was full to overflowing.

Next Monday we are expecting to move into the neighboring Château de Carqueiranne, which my friend Professor Richet of Paris has offered conjointly to us and the Fred Myerses, who will soon arrive. A whole country house in splendid grounds and a perfect Godsend under the conditions. If I can only bear the talking to the Myerses without too much fatigue! But that also I am sure will come. Our present situation is enviable enough. A large bedroom with a balcony high up on the vast hotel façade; a terrace below it graveled with white pebbles containing beds of palms and oranges and roses; below that a downward sloping garden full of plants and winding walks and seats; then a wide hillside continuing southward to the plain below, with its gray-green olive groves bordered by

great salt marshes with salt works on them, shut in from
the sea by the causeways which lead to a long rocky island,
perhaps three miles away, that limits the middle of our
view due south, and beyond which to the East and West
appears the boundless Mediterranean.   But delightful as
this is, there is no place like home; Otis Place is better
than Languedoc and Irving Street than Provence.   And
I am sure, dear Bessie, that there is no maid, wife or widow
in either of these countries that is half as good as you.   But
here I must absolutely stop; so with a good-night and a
happy New Year to you, I am as ever, affectionately your
friend,

WM. JAMES.

To Dickinson S. Miller.

[Dictated to Mrs. James]
HOTEL D' ALBION,
COSTEBELLE, HYÈRES, *Jan.* 18, 1900.

DARLING MILLER,— Last night arrived your pathetically
sympathetic letter in comment on the news you had just
received of my dropping out for the present from the active
career.   I want you to understand how deeply I value
your unflagging feeling of friendship, and how much we
have been touched by this new expression of it. . . . My
strength and spirits are coming back to me with the open-
air life, and I begin to feel quite differently towards the
future.   Even if this amelioration does not develop fast,
it is a check to the deterioration, and shows that curative
forces are still there.   I look perfectly well at present, and
that of itself is a very favorable sign.   In a couple of weeks
I mean to begin the Gifford lectures, writing, say, a page
a day, and having all next year before me empty, am very
likely to get, at any rate, the first course finished.   A letter

from Seth last night told me that the Committee [on the Gifford Lectureship] had refused my resignation and simply shoved my appointment forward by one year. So be of good cheer, Miller; we shall yet fight the good fight, sometimes side by side, sometimes agin one another, as merrily as if no interruption had occurred. Show this to Harry, to whom his mother will write today.

We enjoyed Royce's visit very much, and yesterday I finished reading his book, which I find perfectly charming as a composition, though as far as cogent reasoning goes, it leaks at every joint. It is, nevertheless, a big achievement in the line of philosophic fancy-work, perhaps the most important of all except religious fancy-work. He has got himself together far more intricately than ever before, and ought, after this, to be recognized by the world according to the measure of his real importance. To me, however, the book has brought about a curious settlement in my way of classing Royce. In spite of the great technical freight he carries, and his extraordinary mental vigor, he belongs essentially among the lighter skirmishers of philosophy. A sketcher and popularizer, not a pile-driver, foundation-layer, or wall-builder. Within his class, of course, he is simply magnificent. It all goes with his easy temperament and rare good-nature in discussion. The subject is not really vital to him, it is just fancy-work. All the same I do hope that this book and its successor will prove a great ferment in our philosophic schools. Only with schools and living masters can philosophy *bloom* in a country, in a generation.

No more, dear Miller, but endless thanks. All you tell me of yourself deeply interests me. I am deeply sorry about the eyes. Are you sure it is not a matter for glasses? With much love from both of us. Your ever affectionate,

W. J.

To Francis Boott.

[Dictated to Mrs. James]

CHÂTEAU DE CARQUEIRANNE, *Jan.* 31, 1900.

DEAR OLD FRIEND,— Every day for a month past I have said to Alice, "Today we must get off a letter to Mr. Boott"; but every day the available strength was less than the call upon it. Yours of the 28th December reached us duly at Rye and was read at the cheerful little breakfast table. I must say that you are the only person who has caught the proper tone for sympathizing with an invalid's feelings. Everyone else says, "We are glad to think that you are by this time in splendid condition, richly enjoying your rest, and having a great success at Edinburgh" — this, where what one craves is mere pity for one's unmerited sufferings! *You* say, "it is a great disappointment, more I should think than you can well bear. I wish you could give up the whole affair and turn your prow toward home." That, dear Sir, is the proper note to strike — la voix du coeur qui seul au coeur arrive; and I thank you for recognizing that it is a case of agony and patience. I, for one, should be too glad to turn my prow homewards, in spite of all our present privileges in the way of simplified life, and glorious climate. What would n't I give at this moment to be partaking of one of your recherchés déjeuners à la fourchette, ministered to by the good Kate. From the bed on which I lie I can "sense" it as if present — the succulent roast pork, the apple sauce, the canned asparagus, the cranberry pie, the dates, the "To Kalon," [1] — above all the *rire en barbe* of the ever-youthful host. Will they ever come again?

Don't understand me to be disparaging our present meals which, cooked by a broadbuilt sexagenarian Pro-

---

[1] The name of an American claret which his correspondent had "discovered" and in which it also pleased James to find merit.

vençale, leave nothing to be desired. Especially is the fish good and the artichokes, and the stewed lettuce. Our *commensaux*, the Myerses, form a good combination. The house is vast and comfortable and the air just right for one in my condition, neither relaxing nor exciting, and floods of sunshine.

Do you care much about the war? For my part I think Jehovah has run the thing about right, so far; though on utilitarian grounds it will be very likely better if the English win. When we were at Rye an interminable controversy raged about a national day of humiliation and prayer. I wrote to the "Times" to suggest, in my character of traveling American, that both sides to the controversy might be satisfied by a service arranged on principles suggested by the anecdote of the Montana settler who met a grizzly so formidable that he fell on his knees, saying, "O Lord, I hain't never yet asked ye for help, and ain't agoin' to ask ye for none now. But for pity's sake, O Lord, don't help the bear." The solemn "Times" never printed my letter and thus the world lost an admirable epigram. You, I know, will appreciate it.

Mrs. Gibbens speaks with great pleasure of your friendly visits, and I should think you might find Mrs. Merriman good company. I hope you are getting through the winter without any bronchial trouble, and I hope that neither the influenza nor the bubonic plague has got to Cambridge yet. The former is devastating Europe. If you see dear Dr. Driver, give him our warmest regards. One ought to stay among one's own people. I seem to be mending — though very slowly, and the least thing knocks me down. This noon I am still in bed, a little too much talking with the Myerses yesterday giving me a strong pectoral distress which is not yet over. This dictation begins to hurt me, so I will stop. My spirits now are first-rate, which is a great point gained.

Good-bye, dear old man! We both send our warmest love and are, ever affectionately yours,

WM. JAMES.

To Hugo Münsterberg.

CARQUEIRANNE, *March* 13, 1900.

DEAR MÜNSTERBERG,— Your letter of the 7th "ult." was a most delightful surprise — all but the part of it which told of your being ill again — and of course the news of poor Solomons's death was a severe shock. . . . As regards Solomons, it is pathetically tragic, and I hope that you will send me full details. There was something so lonely and self-sustaining about poor little S., that to be snuffed out like this before he had fairly begun to live in the eyes of the world adds a sort of tragic dramatic unity to his young career. Certainly the *keenest* intellect we ever had, and one of the loftiest characters! But there was always a mysterious side to me about his mind: he appeared so critical and destructive, and yet kept alluding all the while to ethical and religious ideals of his own which he wished to live for, and of which he never vouchsafed a glimpse to anyone else. He was the only student I have ever had of whose criticisms I felt afraid: and that was partly because I never quite understood the region from which they came, and with the authority of which he spoke. His surface thoughts, however, of a scientific order, were extraordinarily *treffend* and clearly expressed; in fact, the way in which he went to the heart of a subject in a few words was masterly. Of course he must have left, apart from his thesis, a good deal of MS. fit for publication. I have not seen our philosophical periodicals since leaving home. Have any parts of his thesis already appeared? If not, the whole thing should be published as "Monograph Supplement" to the "Psychological Review," and his papers gone over to see what else there may be. An adequate obituary of him ought also to be written. Who knew him most intimately? I think the obituary and a portrait ought also to be posted in the laboratory. Can you send me the address of his mother? — I think his father is dead. I should also like to write a word about him to Miss S——, if you can give me her address. If we had foreseen this early end to poor little Solomons, how much more we should have made of him, and how considerate we should have been!

It pleases me much to think of so many other good young fellows, as you report them, in the laboratory this year. How many candidates for Ph.D.? How glad I am to be clear of those examinations, certainly the most disagreeable part of the year's work. . . .

To George H. Palmer.

CARQUEIRANNE, *Apr.* 2, 1900.

GLORIOUS OLD PALMER,— I had come to the point of feeling that my next letter *must* be to you, when in comes your delightful "favor" of the 18th, with all its news, its convincing clipping, and its enclosures from Bakewell and Sheldon. I have had many impulses to write to Bakewell, but they have all aborted — my powers being so small and so much *in Anspruch genommen* by correspondence already under way. I judge him to be well and happy. What think you of his wife? I suppose she is no relation of yours. I should n't think any of your three candidates would do for that conventional Bryn Mawr. She stoneth the prophets, and I wish she would get X—— and get stung. He made a *deplorable* impression on me many years ago. The

only comment *I* heard when I gave my address there lately
(the last one in my "Talks") was that A—— had hoped
for something more technical and psychological! Nevertheless, some good girls seem to come out at Bryn Mawr.
I am awfully sorry that Perry is out of place. Unless he
gets something good, it seems to me that we ought to get
him for a course in Kant. He is certainly the soundest,
most normal all-round man of our recent production. Your
list for next year interests me muchly. I am glad of Münsterberg's and Santayana's new courses, and hope they'll
be good. I'm glad you're back in Ethics and glad that
Royce has "Epistemology" — portentous name, and small
result, in my opinion, but a substantive *discipline* which
ought, *par le temps qui court*, to be treated with due for-
mality. I look forward with eagerness to his new volume.[1]
What a colossal feat he has performed in these two years —
all thrown in by the way, as it were.

Certainly Gifford lectures are a good institution for stimulating production. They have stimulated me so far to produce two lectures of wishy-washy generalities. What is that
for a "showing" in six months of absolute leisure? The second lecture used me up so that I must be off a good while
again.

No! dear Palmer, the best I can possibly hope for at Cambridge after my return is to be able to carry one half-course.
So make all calculations accordingly. As for Windelband,
how can I ascertain anything except by writing to him?
I shall see no one, nor go to any University environment.
My impression is that we must go in for budding genius,
if we seek a European. If an American, we can get a *som-
mité!* But who? in either case? Verily there is room at

[1] The second volume of *The World and the Individual*. (Gifford Lectures at the
University of Aberdeen.)

the top.   S —— seems to be the only Britisher worth thinking of.   I imagine we had better train up our own men.
A——, B——, C——, either would no doubt do, especially
A—— if his health improves.   D—— is our last card, from
the point of view of policy, no doubt, but from that of inner
organization it seems to me that he may have too many
points of coalescence with both Münsterberg and Royce,
especially the latter.

The great event in my life recently has been the reading
of Santayana's book.[1]   Although I absolutely reject the
platonism of it, I have literally squealed with delight at the
imperturbable perfection with which the position is laid down
on page after page; and grunted with delight at such a
thickening up of our Harvard atmosphere.   If our students
now could begin really to understand what Royce means
with his voluntaristic-pluralistic monism, what Münsterberg
means with his dualistic scientificism and platonism, what
Santayana means by his pessimistic platonism (I wonder if he
and Mg. have had any close mutually encouraging intercourse
in this line?), what I mean by my crass pluralism, what you
mean by your ethereal idealism, that these are so many
religions, ways of fronting life, and worth fighting for, we
should have a genuine philosophic universe at Harvard.
The best condition of it would be an open conflict and
rivalry of the diverse systems.   (Alas! that I should be out
of it, just as my chance begins!)   The world might ring with
the struggle, if we devoted ourselves exclusively to belabor-
ing each other.

I now understand Santayana, the man.   I never understood him before.   But what a perfection of rottenness in a
philosophy!   I don't think I ever knew the anti-realistic
view to be propounded with so impudently superior an air.

[1] *Interpretations of Poetry and Religion*.   New York, 1900.

It is refreshing to see a representative of moribund Latinity rise up and administer such reproof to us barbarians in the hour of our triumph. I imagine Santayana's *style* to be entirely spontaneous. But it has curious classic echoes. Whole pages of pure Hume in style; others of pure Renan. Nevertheless, how fantastic a philosophy! — as if the "world of values" *were* independent of existence. It is only as *being*, that one thing is better than another. The idea of darkness is as good as that of light, as ideas. There is more value in light's *being*. And the exquisite consolation, when you have ascertained the badness of all fact, in knowing that badness is inferior to goodness, to the end — it only rubs the pessimism in. A man whose egg at breakfast turns out always bad says to himself, "Well, bad and good are not the same, anyhow." That is just the trouble! Moreover, when you come down to the facts, what do your harmonious and integral ideal systems prove to be? in the concrete? Always things burst by the growing content of experience. Dramatic unities; laws of versification; ecclesiastical systems; scholastic doctrines. Bah! Give me Walt Whitman and Browning ten times over, much as the perverse ugliness of the latter at times irritates me, and intensely as I have enjoyed Santayana's attack. The barbarians are in the line of mental growth, and those who do insist that the ideal and the real are dynamically continuous are those by whom the world is to be saved. But I'm nevertheless delighted that the other view, always existing in the world, should at last have found so splendidly impertinent an expression among ourselves. I have meant to write to Santayana; but on second thoughts, and to save myself, I will just ask you to send him this. It saves him from what might be the nuisance of having to reply, and on my part it has the advantage of being more free-spoken and direct. He is certainly an *extraordinarily distingué* writer. Thank him for existing!

As a contrast, read Jack Chapman's "Practical Agitation." The other pole of thought, and a style all splinters — but a gospel for our rising generation — I hope it will have its effect.

Send me your Noble lectures. I don't see how you could risk it without a MS. If you did fail (which I doubt) you deserved to. Anyhow the printed page makes everything good.

I can no more! Adieu! How is Mrs. Palmer this winter? I hope entirely herself again. You are impartially silent of her and of my wife! The "Transcript" continues to bless us. We move from this hospitable roof to the hotel at Costebelle today. Thence after a fortnight to Geneva, and in May to Nauheim once more, to be reëxamined and sentenced by Schott. Affectionately yours,

W. J.

To Miss Frances R. Morse.

COSTEBELLE, *Apr.* 12, 1900.

DEAREST FANNY,— Your letters continue to rain down upon us with a fidelity which makes me sure that, however it may once have been, *now*, on the principle of the immortal Monsieur Perrichon, we must be firmly rooted in your affections. You can never "throw over" anybody for whom you have made such sacrifices. All qualms which I might have in the abstract about the injury we must be inflicting on so busy a Being by making her, through our complaints of poverty, agony, and exile, keep us so much "on her mind" as to tune us up every two or three days by a long letter to which she sacrifices all her duties to the family and state, disappear, moreover, when I consider the character of the letters themselves.   They are so easy, the facts are so much the immediate out-bubblings of the moment, and the delicious philosophical reflexions so much like the spontaneous breathings of the soul, that the *effort* is manifestly at the zero-point, and into the complex state of affection which necessarily arises in you for the objects of so much loving care, there enter none of those curious momentary arrows of impatience and vengefulness which might make others say, if they were doing what you do for us, that they wished we were dead or in some way put beyond reach, so that our eternal "appeal" might stop.   No, Fanny! we have no repinings and feel no responsibilites towards you, but accept you and your letters as the gifts you are.   The infrequency of our answering proves this fact; to which you in turn must furnish the correlative, if the occasion comes.   On the day when you temporarily hate us, or don't "feel like" the usual letter, don't let any thought of inconsistency with your past acts worry you about not taking up the pen. Let us go; though it be for weeks and months — I shall know you will come round again.   "Neither heat nor frost nor thunder shall ever do away, I ween, the marks of that which once hath been."   And to think that you should never have spent a night, and only once taken a meal, in our house! When we get back, we must see each other daily, and may the days of both of us be right long in the State of Massachusetts!   Bless her!

I got a letter from J. J. Chapman praising her strongly the other day.   And sooth to say the "Transcript" and the "Springfield Republican," the reception of whose "weeklies" has become one of the solaces of my life, do make a first-rate showing for her civilization.   One can't just say what "tone" consists in, but these papers hold their own excellently in comparison with the English papers.   There is far less alertness of mind in the general make-up of the latter; and the "respectability" of the English editorial columns, though it shows a correcter literary drill, is apt to be due to a remorseless longitude of commonplace conventionality that makes them deadly dull. (The "Spectator" appears to be the only paper with a nervous system, in England — that of a *carnassier* at present!) The English people seem to have positively a passionate hunger for this mass of prosy stupidity, never less than a column and a quarter long. The Continental papers of course are "nowhere." As for our yellow papers — every country has its criminal classes, and with us and in France, they have simply got into journalism as part of their professional evolution, and they must be got out. Mr. Bosanquet somewhere says that so far from the "dark ages" being over, we are just at the beginning of a new dark-age period. He means that ignorance and unculture, which then were merely brutal, are now articulate and possessed of a literary voice, and the fight is transferred from fields and castles and town walls to "organs of publicity"; but it is the same fight, of reason and goodness against stupidity and passions; and it must be fought through to the same kind of success. But it means the reëducating of perhaps twenty more generations; and by that time some altogether new kind of institutional opportunity for the Devil will have been evolved.

April 13th. I had to stop yesterday. . . . Six months ago, I should n't have thought it possible that a life deliberately founded on pottering about and dawdling through the day would be endurable or even possible. I have attained such skill that I doubt if my days ever at any time seemed to glide by so fast. But it corrodes one's soul nevertheless. I scribble a little in bed every morning, and have reached page 48 of my third Gifford lecture — though Lecture II, alas! must be rewritten entirely. The conditions don't conduce to an energetic grip of the subject, and I am afraid that what I write is pretty slack and not what it would be if my vital tone were different. The problem I have set myself is a hard one: *first*, to defend (against all the prejudices of my "class") "experience" against "philosophy" as being the real backbone of the world's religious life — I mean prayer, guidance, and all that sort of thing immediately and privately felt, as against high and noble general views of our destiny and the world's meaning; and *second*, to make the hearer or reader believe, what I myself invincibly do believe, that, although all the special manifestations of religion may have been absurd (I mean its creeds and theories), yet the life of it as a whole is mankind's most important function. A task well-nigh impossible, I fear, and in which I shall fail; but to attempt it is *my* religious act.

We got a visit the other day from [a Scottish couple here who have heard that I am to give the Gifford lectures]; and two days ago went to afternoon tea with them at their hotel, next door. *She* enclosed a tract (by herself) in the invitation, and proved to be a [mass] of holy egotism and conceit based on professional invalidism and self-worship. I wish my sister Alice were there to "react" on her with a description! Her husband, apparently weak, and the slave of her. No talk but evangelical talk. It seemed assumed that a Gifford lecturer must be one of Moody's partners, and it gave me rather a foretaste of what the Edinburgh atmosphere may be like. Well, I shall enjoy sticking a knife into its gizzard — if atmospheres have gizzards? Blessed be Boston — probably the freest place on earth, that is n't merely heathen and sensual.

I have been supposing, as one always does, that you "ran

in" to the Putnams' every hour or so, and likewise they to
No. 12. But your late allusion to the telephone and the
rarity of your seeing Jim [Putnam] reminded me of the
actual conditions — absurd as they are. (Really you and
we are nearer together now at this distance than we have
ever been.) Well, let Jim see this letter, if you care to,
flattering him by saying that it is more written for him than
for you (which it certainly has not been till this moment!),
and thanking him for existing in this naughty world. His
account of the Copernican revolution (studento-centric)
in the Medical School is highly exciting, and I am glad to
hear of the excellent little Cannon becoming so prominent
a reformer. Speaking of reformers, do you see Jack Chapman's "Political Nursery"? of which the April number
has just come. (I have read it and taken my bed-break-
fast during the previous page of this letter, though you may
not have perceived the fact.) If not, *do* subscribe to it; it
is awful fun. He just looks at things, and tells the truth
about them — a strange thing even to *try* to do, and he
does n't always succeed. Office 141 Broadway, $1.00 a
year.

Fanny, you won't be reading as far as this in this interminable letter, so I stop, though 100 pent-up things are
seeking to be said. The weather has still been so cold
whenever the sun is withdrawn that we have delayed our
departure for Geneva to the 22nd — a week later. We
make a short visit to our friends the Flournoys (a couple
of days) and then proceed towards Nauheim *via* Heidelberg,
where I wish to consult the great Erb about the advisability
of more baths in view of my nervous complications, before
the great Schott examines me again. I do wish I could
send for Jim for a consultation. Good-bye, dearest and
best of Fannys. I hope your Mother is wholly well again.

Much love to her and to Mary Elliot. It interested me to hear of Jack E.'s great operation. Yours ever,

W. J.

To his Son Alexander.

[GENEVA, *circa May 3,* 1900.]

DEAR FRANÇOIS,— Here we are in Geneva, at the Flournoys' — dear people and splendid children. I wish Harry could marry Alice, Billy marry Marguerite, and you marry Ariane-Dorothée — the absolutely jolliest and beautifullest 3-year old I ever saw. I am trying to get you engaged! I enclose pictures of the dog. Ariane-Dorothée r-r-r-olls her r-r-r's like fury. I got your picture of the elephant — very good. Draw everything you see, no matter how badly, trying to notice how the lines run — one line every day! — just notice it and draw it, no matter how badly, and at the end of the year you'll be s'prised to see how well you can draw. Tell Billy to get you a big blank book at the Coöp., and every day take one page, just drawing down on it some *thing*, or *dog*, or *horse*, or *man* or *woman*, or *part* of a man or woman, which you have looked at that day just for the purpose, to see how the lines run. I bet the last page of that book will be better than the first! Do this for my sake. Kiss your dear old Grandma. P'r'aps, we shall get home this summer after all. In two or three days I shall see a doctor and know more about myself. Will let you know. Keep motionless and listen as much as you can. Take in things without speaking — it'll make you a better man. Your Ma thinks you'll grow up into a filosopher like me and write books. It is easy enuff, all but the writing. You just get it out of other books, and write it down. Always your loving,

DAD.

At this time James's thirteen-year-old daughter was living with family friends — the Joseph Thatcher Clarkes — in Harrow, and was going to an English school with their children. She had been passing through such miseries as a homesick child often suffers, and had written letters which evoked the following response.

To his Daughter.

VILLA LUISE,
BAD-NAUHEIM, *May* 26, 1900.

DARLING PEG,— Your letter came last night and explained sufficiently the cause of your long silence. You have evidently been in a bad state of spirits again, and dissatisfied with your environment; and I judge that you have been still more dissatisfied with the inner state of trying to consume your own smoke, and grin and bear it, so as to carry out your mother's behests made after the time when you scared us so by your inexplicable tragic outcries in those earlier letters. Well! I believe you have been trying to do the manly thing under difficult circumstances, but one learns only gradually to do the *best* thing; and the best thing for you would be to write at least weekly, if only a post-card, and say just how things are going. If you are in bad spirits, there is no harm whatever in communicating that fact, and defining the character of it, or describing it as exactly as you like. The bad thing is to pour out the *contents* of one's bad spirits on others and leave them with it, as it were, on their hands, as if it was for them to do something about it. That was what you did in your other letter which alarmed us so, for your shrieks of anguish were so excessive, and so unexplained by anything you told us in the way of facts, that we did n't know but what you had suddenly gone crazy. That is the *worst* sort of thing you can do. The middle sort of thing is what you do this time — namely, keep silent for more than a fortnight, and when you do write, still write rather mysteriously about your sorrows, not being quite open enough.

Now, my dear little girl, you have come to an age when the inward life develops and when some people (and on the whole those who have most of a destiny) find that all is not a bed of roses. Among other things there will be waves of terrible sadness, which last sometimes for days; and dissatisfaction with one's self, and irritation at others, and anger at circumstances and stony insensibility, etc., etc., which taken together form a melancholy. Now, painful as it is, this is sent to us for an enlightenment. It always passes off, and we learn about life from it, and we ought to learn a great many good things if we react on it rightly. [*From margin.*] (For instance, you learn how good a thing your home is, and your country, and your brothers, and you may learn to be more considerate of other people, who, you now learn, may have their inner weaknesses and sufferings, too.) Many persons take a kind of sickly delight in hugging it; and some sentimental ones may even be proud of it, as showing a fine sorrowful kind of sensibility. Such persons make a regular habit of the luxury of woe. That is the worst possible reaction on it. It is usually a sort of disease, when we get it strong, arising from the organism having generated some poison in the blood; and we must n't submit to it an hour longer than we can help, but jump at every chance to attend to anything cheerful or comic or take part in anything active that will divert us from our mean, pining inward state of feeling. When it passes off, as I said, we know more than we did before. And we must try to make it last as short a time as possible. The worst of it often is that, while we are in it, we don't *want* to get out of it.   We hate it, and yet we prefer staying in it — that is a part of the disease.   If we find ourselves like that, we must make ourselves do something different, go with people, speak cheerfully, set ourselves to some hard work, make ourselves sweat, etc.; and that is the good way of reacting that makes of us a valuable character.   The disease makes you think of *yourself* all the time; and the way out of it is to keep as busy as we can thinking of *things* and of *other people* — no matter what's the matter with our self.

I have no doubt you are doing as well as you know how, darling little Peg; but we have to learn everything, and I also have no doubt that you'll manage it better and better if you ever have any more of it, and soon it will fade away, simply leaving you with more experience.   The great thing for you *now*, I should suppose, would be to enter as friendlily as possible into the interest of the Clarke children.   If you like them, or acted as if you liked them, you need n't trouble about the question of whether they like you or not.   They probably will, fast enough; and if they don't, it will be their funeral, not yours.   But this is a great lecture, so I will stop.   The great thing about it is that it is all true.

The baths are threatening to disagree with me again, so I may stop them soon.   Will let you know as quick as anything is decided.   Good news from home: the Merrimans have taken the Irving Street house for another year, and the Wambaughs (of the Law School) have taken Chocorua, though at a reduced rent.   The weather here is almost continuously cold and sunless.   Your mother is sleeping, and will doubtless add a word to this when she wakes.   Keep a merry heart — "time and the hour run through the roughest day" — and believe me ever your most loving

W. J.

To Miss Frances R. Morse.

[Post-card]

ALTDORF, LAKE LUZERN, *July* 20, [1900].

Your last letter was, if anything, a more unmitigated blessing than its predecessors; and I, with my curious inertia to overcome, sit *thinking of letters*, and of the soul-music with which they might be filled if my tongue could only utter the thoughts that arise in me to youward, the beauty of the world, the conflict of life and death and youth and age and man and woman and righteousness and evil, etc., and Europe and America! but it stays all caked within and gets no articulation, the power of speech being so non-natural a function of our race. We are staying above Luzern, near a big spruce wood, at "Gutsch," and today being hot and passivity advisable, we came down and took the boat, for a whole day on the Lake. The works both of Nature and of Man in this region seem too perfect to be credible almost, and were I not a bitter Yankee, I would, without a moment's hesitation, be a Swiss, and probably then glad of the change. The *goodliness* of this land is one of the things I ache to utter to you, but can't. Some day I will write, also to Jim P. My condition baffles me. I have lately felt better, but been bad again, and altogether can *do* nothing without repentance afterwards. We have just lunched in this bowery back verandah, water trickling, beautiful old convent sleeping up the hillside. Love to you all!

W. J.

To Miss Frances R. Morse.

BAD-NAUHEIM, *Sept.* 16, 1900.

DEAREST FANNY,— . . . Here I am having a little private picnic all by myself, on this effulgent Sunday morning —

real American September weather, by way of a miracle. I
ordered my bath-chair man to wheel me out to the "Hoch-
wald," where, he having been dismissed for three hours,
until two o'clock, I am lying in the said luxurious throne,
writing this on my knee, with nothing between but a number of Kuno Fischer's "Hegel's Leben, Werke und Lehre,"
now in process of publication, and the flexibility of which accounts for the poor handwriting. I am alone, save for the
inevitable restaurant which hovers on the near horizon,
in a beautiful grove of old oak trees averaging some 16 or
18 feet apart, through whose leaves the sunshine filters and
dapples the clear ground or grass that lies between them.
Alice is still in England, having finally at my command had
to give up her long-cherished plan of a run home to see her
mother, the children, you, and all the other *dulcissima
mundi nomina* that make of life a thing worth living for.
I *funked* the idea of being alone so long when I came to the
point. It is not that I am worse, but there will be cold
weather in the next couple of months; and, unable to sit
out of doors then, as here and now, I shall probably either
have to over-walk or over-read, and both things will be
bad for me.

As things are *now*, I get on well enough, for the bath
business (especially the "bath-chair") carries one through
a good deal of the day. The great Schott has positively
forbidden me to go to England as I did last year; so, early
in October, our faces will be turned towards Italy, and by
Nov. 1 we shall, I hope, be ensconced in a *pension* close
to the Pincian Garden in Rome, to see how long *that* resource
will last. I confess I am in the mood of it, and that there
is a suggestion of more richness about the name of Rome
than about that of Rye, which, until Schott's veto, was the
plan. How the Gifford lectures will fare, remains to be

"Damn the Absolute!"

Chocorua, September, 1903. One morning James and Royce
strolled into the road and sat down on a wall in earnest discussion. When James heard the camera click, as his daughter took
the upper snap-shot, he cried, "Royce, you 're being photo-
graphed! Look out! I say *Damn the Absolute!*"

seen. I have felt strong movings towards home this fall, but reflection says: "Stay another winter," and I confess that now that October is approaching, it feels like the home-stretch and as if the time were getting short and the limbs of "next summer" in America burning through the veil which seems to hide them in the shape of the second European winter months. Who knows? perhaps I may be spry and active by that time! I have still one untried card up my sleeve, that may work wonders. All I can say of this third course of baths is that so far it seems to be doing me no harm. That it will do me any substantial good, after the previous experiences, seems decidedly doubtful. But one must suffer some inconvenience to please the doctors! Just as in most women there is a wife that craves to suffer and submit and be bullied, so in most men there is a *patient* that needs to have a doctor and obey his orders, whether they be believed in or not. . . .

Don't take the Malwida book[1] too seriously. I sent it *faute de mieux*. I don't think I ever told you how much I enjoyed hearing the Lesley volume[2] read aloud by Alice. We were just in the exactly right condition for enjoying that breath of old New England. Good-bye, dearest Fanny. Give my love to your mother, Mary, J. J. P., and all your circle. *Leb' wohl* yourself, and believe me, your ever affectionate,

W. J.

To Josiah Royce.

NAUHEIM, *Sept.* 26, 1900.

BELOVED ROYCE,— Great was my, was *our* pleasure in receiving your long and delightful letter last night. Like

[1] *Memoiren einer Idealistin*, by Malvida von Meysenbug, Stuttgart, 1877.
[2] *Recollections of My Mother* [Anne Jean Lyman], by Susan I. Lesley, Boston, 1886.

the lioness in Æsop's fable, you give birth to one young one only in the year, but that one is a lion. I give birth mainly to guinea-pigs in the shape of post-cards; but despite such diversities of epistolary expression, the heart of each of us is in the right place. I need not say, my dear old boy, how touched I am at your expressions of affection, or how it pleases me to hear that you have missed me. I too miss you profoundly. I do not find in the hotel waiters, chambermaids and bath-attendants with whom my lot is chiefly cast, that unique mixture of erudition, originality, profundity and vastness, and human wit and leisureliness, by accustoming me to which during all these years you have spoilt me for inferior kinds of intercourse. You are still the centre of my gaze, the pole of my mental magnet. When I write, 't is with one eye on the page, and one on you. When I compose my Gifford lectures mentally, 't is with the design exclusively of overthrowing your system, and ruining your peace. I lead a parasitic life upon you, for my highest flight of ambitious ideality is to become your conqueror, and go down into history as such, you and I rolled in one another's arms and silent (or rather loquacious still) in one last death-grapple of an embrace. How then, O my dear Royce, can I forget you, or be contented out of your close neighborhood? Different as our minds are, yours has nourished mine, as no other social influence ever has, and in converse with you I have always felt that my life was being lived importantly. Our minds, too, are not different in the *Object* which they envisage. It is the whole paradoxical physico-moral-spiritual Fatness, of which most people single out some skinny fragment, which we both cover with our eye. We "aim at him generally"— and most others don't. I don't believe that we shall dwell apart forever, though our formulas may.

Home and Irving Street look very near when seen through these few winter months, and tho' it is still doubtful what I may be able to do in College, for social purposes I shall be available for probably numerous years to come. I have n't got at work yet — only four lectures of the first course written (strange to say) — but I am decidedly better today than I have been for the past ten months, and the matter is all ready in my mind; so that when, a month hence, I get settled down in Rome, I think the rest will go off fairly quickly. The second course I shall have to resign from, and write it out at home as a book. It must seem strange to you that the way from the mind to the pen should be as intraversable as it has been in this case of mine — you in whom it always seems so easily pervious. But Miller will be able to tell you all about my condition, both mental and physical, so I will waste no more words on that to me decidedly musty subject.

I fully understand your great aversion to letters and other off-writing. You have done a perfectly Herculean amount of the most difficult productive work, and I believe you to be much more tired than you probably yourself suppose or know. Both mentally and physically, I imagine that a long vacation, in other scenes, with no sense of duty, would do you a world of good. I don't say the full fifteen months — for I imagine that one summer and one academic half-year would perhaps do the business better — you could preserve the relaxed and desultory condition as long as that probably, whilst later you 'd begin to chafe, and *then* you 'd better be back in your own library. If *my* continuing abroad is hindering this, my sorrow will be extreme. Of course I must some time come to a definite decision about my own relations to the College, but I am reserving that till the end of 1900, when I shall write to Eliot in full. There is still a therapeutic card to play, of which I will say nothing just now, and I don't want to commit myself before that has been tried.

You say nothing of the second course of Aberdeen lectures, nor do you speak at all of the Dublin course. Strange omissions, like your not sending me your Ingersoll lecture! I assume that the publication of [your] Gifford Volume II will not be very long delayed. I am eager to read them. I can read philosophy now, and have just read the first three *Lieferungen* of K. Fischer's "Hegel." I must say I prefer the original text. Fischer's paraphrases always flatten and dry things out; and he gives no rich sauce of his own to compensate. I have been sorry to hear from Palmer that he also has been very tired. One can't keep going forever! P. has been like an archangel in his letters to me, and I am inexpressibly grateful. Well! everybody has been kinder than I deserve. . . .

To Miss Frances R. Morse.

ROME, *Dec. 25*, 1900.

. . . Rome is simply the most satisfying lake of picturesqueness and guilty suggestiveness known to this child. Other places have single features better than anything in Rome, perhaps, but for an *ensemble* Rome seems to beat the world. Just a FEAST for the eye from the moment you leave your hotel door to the moment you return. Those who say that beauty is all made up of suggestion are well disproved here. For the things the eyes most gloat on, the inconceivably corrupted, besmeared and ulcerated surfaces, and black and cavernous glimpses of interiors, have no suggestions save of moral horror, and their "tactile values," as Berenson would say, are pure gooseflesh. Nevertheless the sight of them delights. And then there is such a geologic stratification of history! I dote on the fine equestrian statue of Garibaldi, on the Janiculum, quietly bending his head with a look half-meditative, half-strategical, but wholly victorious, upon Saint Peter's and the Vatican. What luck for a man and a party to have opposed to it an enemy that stood up for *nothing* that was ideal, for *everything* that was mean in life. Austria, Naples, and the Mother of harlots here, were enough to deify anyone who defied them. What glorious things are some of these Italian inscriptions — for example on Giordano Bruno's statue: —

A BRUNO

il secolo da lui divinato

qui

dove il rogo arse.

—"here, where the faggots burned." It makes the tears come, for the poetic justice; though I imagine B. to have been a very pesky sort of a crank, worthy of little sympathy had not the "rogo" done its work on him. Of the awful corruptions and cruelties which this place suggests there is no end.

Our neighbors in rooms and *commensaux* at meals are the J. G. Frazers — he of the "Golden Bough," "Pausanias," and other three- and six-volume works of anthropological erudition, Fellow of Trinity College, Cambridge, and a sucking babe of humility, unworldliness and molelike sightlessness to everything except *print*. . . . He, after Tylor, is the greatest authority now in England on the religious ideas and superstitions of primitive peoples, and he knows nothing of psychical research and thinks that the trances, etc., of savage soothsayers, oracles and the like, are all *feigned!* Verily science is amusing! But he is conscience

incarnate, and I have been stirring him up so that I imagine
he will now proceed to put in big loads of work in the morbid
psychological direction.

Dear Fanny . . . I can write no more this morning.
I hope your Christmas is "merry," and that the new year
will be "happy" for you all. Pray take our warmest love,
give it to your mother and Mary, and some of it to the
brothers. I will write better soon. Your ever grateful
and affectionate

W. J.

Don't let up on your own writing, so say we both! Your
letters are pure blessings.

To James Sully.

ROME, *Mar.* 3, 1901.

DEAR SULLY,— Your letter of Feb. 8th arrived duly and
gave me much pleasure *qua* epistolary manifestation of
sympathy, but less *qua* revelation of depression on your own
part. I have been so floundering up and down, now above
and now below the line of bad nervous prostration, that I
have written no letters for three weeks past, hoping thereby
the better to accomplish certain other writing; but the
other writing had to be stopped so letters and post-cards
may begin.

I see you take the war still very much to heart, and I
myself think that the blundering way in which the Colonial
Office drove the Dutchmen into it, with no conception
whatever of the psychological situation, is only outdone by
our still more anti-psychological blundering in the Philippines. Both countries have lost their moral prestige — we
far more completely than you, because for our conduct
there is literally *no* excuse to be made except *absolute* stupidity, whilst you can make out a very fair case, as such

cases go. But we can, and undoubtedly shall, draw back, whereas that for an Empire like yours seems politically impossible. Empire anyhow is half crime by necessity of Nature, and to see a country like the United States, lucky enough to be born outside of it and its fatal traditions and inheritances, perversely rushing to wallow in the mire of it, shows how strong these ancient race instincts be. And that is my consolation! We are no worse than the best of men have ever been. We are simply not superhuman; and the loud reaction against the brutal business, in both countries, shows how the *theory* of the matter has really advanced during the last century.

Yes! H. Sidgwick is a sad loss, with all his remaining philosophic wisdom unwritten. I feel greatly F. W. H. Myers's loss also. He suffered terribly with suffocation, but bore it stunningly well. He died in this very hotel, where he had been not more than a fortnight. I don't know *how* tolerant (or intolerant) you are towards his pursuits and speculations. I regard them as fragmentary and conjectural — of course; but as most laborious and praiseworthy; and knowing how much psychologists as a rule have counted him out from their profession, I have thought it my duty to write a little tribute to his service to psychology to be read on March 8th, at a memorial meeting of the S. P. R. in his honor. It will appear, whether read or not, in the Proceedings, and I hope may not appear to you exaggerated. I seriously believe that the general problem of the subliminal, as Myers propounds it, promises to be one of the *great* problems, possibly even the greatest problem, of psychology. . . .

We leave Rome in three days, booked for Rye the first of April. I *must* get into the *country!* If I do more than just pass through London, I will arrange for a meeting. My

Edinburgh lectures begin early in May — after that I shall have freedom. Ever truly yours,

WM. JAMES.

To Miss Frances R. Morse.
[Post-card]
FLORENCE, *March* 18, 1901.

Thus far towards home, thank Heaven! after a week at Perugia and Assisi. Glorious air, memorable scenes. Made acquaintance of Sabatier, author of St. Francis's life — very jolly. Best of all, made acquaintance with Francis's retreat in the mountain. *Navrant!* — it makes one see medieval Christianity face to face. The lair of the individual wild animal, and that animal the saint! I hope you saw it. Thanks for your last letter to Alice. Lots of love.

W. J.

To F. C. S. Schiller.
RYE, *April* 13, 1901.

DEAR SCHILLER,— You are showering benedictions on me. I return the bulky ones, keeping the lighter weights. I think the parody on Bradley amazingly good — if I had his book here I would probably revive my memory of his discouraged style and scribble a marginal contribution of my own. He is, really, an extra humble-minded man, I think, but even more humble-minded about his reader than about himself, which gives him that false air of arrogance. How you concocted those epigrams, *à la* preface of B., I don't see. In general I don't see how an epigram, being a pure bolt from the blue, with no introduction or cue, ever gets itself writ. On the Limericks, as you call them, I set less store, much less. If everybody is to come in for a share of allusion, I am willing, but I don't want my name to figure in the ghostly ballet with but few companions. Royce wrote a *very* funny thing in pedantic German some years ago, purporting to be the proof by a distant-future professor that I was an habitual drunkard, based on passages culled from my writings. He may have it yet. If I ever get any animal spirits again, I may get warmed up, by your example, into making jokes, and may then contribute. But I beg you let this thing mull till you get a *lot* of matter — and then *sift*. It's the only way. But Oxford seems a better climate for epigram than is the rest of the world.

I shall stay here — I find myself much more comfortable thoracically already than when I came — until my Edinburgh lectures begin on May 16th, though I shall have to run up to London towards the end of the month to get some clothes made, and to meet my son who arrives from home. I much regret that it will be quite impossible for me to go either to Oxford or Cambridge — though, if things took an unexpectedly good turn, I might indeed do so after June 18th, when my lecture course ends. Do you meanwhile keep hearty and "funny"! I stopped at Gersau half a day and found it a sweet little place. Fondly yours,

W. J.

To Miss Frances R. Morse.

ROXBURGHE HOTEL,
EDINBURGH, *May* 15, 1901.

DEAREST FANNY,— You see where we are! I give *you* the first news of life's journey being so far advanced! It is a deadly enterprise, I'm afraid, with the social entanglements that lie ahead, and I feel a cake of ice in my epigastrium at the prospect, but *le vin est versé, il faut le boire,* and from the other point of view, that it is real life beginning once more, it is perfectly glorious, and I feel as if yesterday in leaving London I had said good-bye to a rather dreadful and death-bound segment of life. As regards the sociability, it is fortunately a time of year in which only the medical part of the University is present. The professors of the other faculties are already in large part scattered, I think,— at least the two Seths (who are the only ones I directly know) are away, and I have written to the Secretary of the Academic Senate, Sir Ludovic Grant of the Law Faculty, that I am unable to "dine out" or attend afternoon receptions, so we may be pretty well left alone. I always hated lecturing except as regular instruction to students, of whom there will probably be none now in the audience. But to compensate, there begins next week a big convocation here of all ministers in Scotland, and there will doubtless be a number of them present, which, considering the matter to be offered, is probably better.

We had a splendid journey yesterday in an American (almost!) train, first-class, and had the pleasure of some talk with our Cambridge neighbor, Mrs. Ole Bull, on her way to Norway to the unveiling of a monument to her husband. She was accompanied by an extraordinarily fine character and mind — odd way of expressing myself! — a young Englishwoman named Noble, who has Hinduized herself (converted by Vivekananda to his philosophy) and lives now for the Hindu people. These free individuals who live their own life, no matter what domestic prejudices have to be snapped, are on the whole a refreshing sight to me, who can do nothing of the kind myself. And Miss Noble [1] is a most deliberate and balanced person — no frothy enthusiast in point of character, though I believe her philosophy to be more or less false. Perhaps no more so than anyone else's!

[1] Sister Nivedita.

We are in one of those deadly respectable hotels where you have to ring the front-door-bell. Give me a cheerful, blackguardly place like the Charing Cross, where we were in London. The London tailor and shirtmaker, it being in the height of the Season, did n't fulfill their promises; and as I sloughed my ancient cocoon at Rye, trusting to pick up my iridescent wings the day before yesterday in passing through the metropolis, I am here with but two *chemises* at present (one of them now in the wash) and fear that tomorrow, in spite of tailors' promises to send, I may have to lecture in my pyjamas — that would give a cachet of American originality. The weather is fine — we have just finished breakfast.

Our son Harry . . . and his mother will soon sally out to explore the town, whilst I lie low till about noon, when I shall report my presence and receive instructions from my boss, Grant, and prepare to meet the storm. It is astonishing how pusillanimous two years of invalidism can make one. Alice and Harry both send love, and so do I in heaps and steamer-loads, dear Fanny, begging your mother to take of it as much as she requires for her share. I will write again — doubtless — tomorrow.

May 17.

It proved quite impossible to write to you yesterday, so I do it the first thing this morning. I have made my plunge and the foregoing chill has given place to the warm "reaction." The audience was more numerous than had been expected, some 250, and exceedingly sympathetic, laughing at everything, even whenever I used a polysyllabic word. I send you the "Scotsman," with a skeleton report which might have been much worse made. I am all right this morning again, so have no doubts of putting the job through, if only I don't have too much sociability. I have got a week free of invitations so far, and all things considered, fancy that we shan't be persecuted.

Edinburgh is surely the noblest city ever built by man. The weather has been splendid so far, and cold and bracing as the top of Mount Washington in early April. Everyone here speaks of it however as "hot." One needs fires at night and an overcoat out of the sun. The full-bodied air, half misty and half smoky, holds the sunshine in that way which one sees only in these islands, making the shadowy side of everything quite black, so that all perspectives and vistas appear with objects cut blackly against each other according to their nearness, and plane rising behind plane of flat dark relieved against flat light in ever-receding gradation. It is magnificent.

But I must n't become a Ruskin! — the purpose of this letter being merely to acquaint you with our well-being and success so far. We have found bully lodgings, spacious to one's heart's content, upon a cheerful square, and actually with a book-shelf fully two feet wide and two stories high, upon the wall, the first we have seen for two years! (There were of course book-cases enough at Lamb House, but all tight packed already.) We now go out to take the air. I feel as if a decidedly bad interlude in the journey of my life were closed, and the real honest thing gradually beginning again. Love to you all! Your ever affectionate

W. J.

To Miss Frances R. Morse.

EDINBURGH, *May* 30, 1901.

DEAREST FANNY,— . . . Beautiful as the spring is here, the words you so often let drop about American weather make me homesick for that article. It is blasphemous, however, to pine for anything when one is in Edinburgh in

May, and takes an open drive every afternoon in the surrounding country by way of a constitutional. The green is of the vividest, splendid trees and acres, and the air itself an *object*, holding watery vapor, tenuous smoke, and ancient sunshine in solution, so as to yield the most exquisite minglings and gradations of silvery brown and blue and pearly gray. As for the city, its vistas are magnificent.

We are *comblés* with civilities, which Harry and Alice are to a certain extent enjoying, though I have to hang back and spend much of the time between my lectures in bed, to rest off the aortic distress which that operation gives. I call it aortic because it feels like that, but I can get no information from the Drs., so I won't swear I 'm right. My heart, under the influence of that magical juice, tincture of digitalis,— only 6 drops daily,— is performing *beautifully* and gives no trouble at all. The audiences grow instead of dwindling, and in spite of rain, being about 300 and just crowding the room. They sit as still as death and then applaud magnificently, so I am sure the lectures are a success. Previous Gifford lectures have had audiences beginning with 60 and dwindling to 15. In an hour and a half (I write this in bed) I shall be beginning the fifth lecture, which will, when finished, put me half way through the arduous job. I know you will relish these details, which please pass on to Jim P. I would send you the reports in the "Scotsman," but they distort so much by their sham continuity with vast omission (the reporters get my MS.), that the result is caricature. Edinburgh is *spiritually* much like Boston, only stronger and with more temperament in the people. But we 're all growing into much of a sameness everywhere.

I have dined out once — an almost fatal experiment! I was introduced to Lord Somebody: "How often do you lecture?"— "Twice a week."— "What do you do between?

— play golf?" Another invitation: "Come at 6 — the dinner at 7.30 — and we can walk or play bowls till dinner so
as not to fatigue you"— I having pleaded my delicacy of
constitution.

I rejoice in the prospect of Booker W.'s [1] book, and thank
your mother heartily. My mouth had been watering for
just that volume. Autobiographies take the cake. I mean
to read nothing else. Strange to say, I am now for the first
time reading Marie Bashkirtseff. It takes hold of me tre-
menjus. I feel as if I had lived inside of her, and in spite
of her hatefulness, esteem and even like her for her incorruptible way of telling the truth. I have not seen Huxley's life yet. It must be delightful, only I can't agree to
what seems to be becoming the conventionally accepted
view of him, that he possessed the exclusive specialty of
living for the truth. A good deal of humbug about that!
— at least when it becomes a professional and heroic attitude.

Your base remark about Aguinaldo is clean forgotten,
if ever heard. I know you would n't harm the poor man,
who, unless Malay human nature is weaker than human
nature elsewhere, has pretty surely some surprises up his
sleeve for us yet. Best love to you all. Your affectionate

WM. JAMES.

To Henry W. Rankin.

EDINBURGH, *June* 16, 1901.

DEAR MR. RANKIN,— I have received all your letters
and missives, inclusive of the letter which you think I must
have lost, some months back. I professor-ed you because
I had read your name printed with that title in a newspaper
letter from East Northfield, and supposed that, by courtesy

[1] Booker T. Washington's *Up from Slavery.*

at any rate, that title was conferred on you by a public opinion to which I liked to conform.

I have given nine of my lectures and am to give the tenth tomorrow. They have been a success, to judge by the numbers of the audience (300-odd) and their non-diminution towards the end. No previous "Giffords" have drawn near so many. It will please you to know that I am stronger and tougher than when I began, too; so a great load is off my mind. You have been so extraordinarily brotherly to me in writing of your convictions and in furnishing me ideas, that I feel ashamed of my churlish and chary replies. You, however, have forgiven me. Now, at the end of this first course, I feel my "matter" taking firmer shape, and it will please you less to hear me say that I believe myself to be (probably) permanently incapable of believing the Christian scheme of vicarious salvation, and wedded to a more continuously evolutionary mode of thought. The reasons you from time to time have given me, never better expressed than in your letter before the last, have somehow failed to convince. In these lectures the ground I am taking is this: The mother sea and fountain-head of all religions lie in the mystical experiences of the individual, taking the word mystical in a very wide sense. All theologies and all ecclesiasticisms are secondary growths superimposed; and the experiences make such flexible combinations with the intellectual prepossessions of their subjects, that one may almost say that they have no proper *intellectual* deliverance of their own, but belong to a region deeper, and more vital and practical, than that which the intellect inhabits. For this they are also indestructible by intellectual arguments and criticisms. I attach the mystical or religious consciousness to the possession of an extended subliminal self, with a thin partition through which messages make irruption. We are thus made convincingly aware of the presence of a sphere of life larger and more powerful than our usual consciousness, with which the latter is nevertheless continuous. The impressions and impulsions and emotions and excitements which we thence receive help us to live, they found invincible assurance of a world beyond the sense, they melt our hearts and communicate significance and value to everything and make us happy. They do this for the individual who has them, and other individuals follow him. Religion in this way is absolutely indestructible. Philosophy and theology give their conceptual interpretations of this experiential life. The farther margin of the subliminal field being unknown, it can be treated as by Transcendental Idealism, as an Absolute mind with a part of which we coalesce, or by Christian theology, as a distinct deity acting on us. Something, not our immediate self, does act on our life! So I seem doubtless to my audience to be blowing hot and cold, explaining away Christianity, yet defending the more general basis from which I say it proceeds. I fear that these brief words may be misleading, but let them go! When the book comes out, you will get a truer idea.

Believe me, with profound regards, your always truly,

WM. JAMES.

To Charles Eliot Norton.

RYE, *June* 26, 1901.

DEAR CHARLES NORTON,— Your delightful letter of June 1st has added one more item to my debt of gratitude to you; and now that the Edinburgh strain is over, I can sit down and make you a reply a little more adequate than heretofore has been possible. The lectures went off most successfully, and though I got tired enough, I feel that I

am essentially tougher and stronger for the old familiar
functional activity. My *tone* is changed immensely, and
that is the main point. To be actually earning one's salt
again, after so many months of listless waiting and wondering whether such a thing will ever again become possible,
puts a new heart into one, and I now look towards the future
with aggressive and hopeful eyes again, though perhaps
not with quite the cannibalistic ones of the youth of the new
century.

Edinburgh is great. A strong broad city, and, in its
spiritual essence, almost exactly feeling to me like old Boston,
nuclear Boston, though on a larger, more important scale.
People were very friendly, but we had to dodge invitations
— *hoffentlich* I may be able to accept more of them next
year. The audience was extraordinarily attentive and
reactive — I never had an audience so keen to catch every
point. I flatter myself that by blowing alternately hot and
cold on their Christian prejudices I succeeded in baffling
them completely till the final quarter-hour, when I satisfied
their curiosity by showing more plainly my hand. Then,
I think, I permanently dissatisfied both extremes, and
pleased a mean numerically quite small. *Qui vivra verra.*
London seemed curiously profane and free-and-easy, not
exactly *shabby*, but go-as-you-please, in aspect, as we came
down five days ago. Since then I spent a day with poor
Mrs. Myers. . . . I mailed you yesterday a notice I wrote
in Rome of him.[1] He "looms" upon me after death more
than he did in life, and I think that his forthcoming book
about "Human Personality" will probably rank hereafter
as "epoch-making."

At London I saw Theodora [Sedgwick] and the W. Dar-

---

[1] "Frederick Myers's Services to Psychology." Reprinted in *Memories and Studies.*

wins. Theodora was as good and genial as ever, and Sara [Darwin] looked, I thought, wonderfully "distinguished" and wonderfully little changed considering the length of intervening years and the advance of the Enemy. I was too tired to look up Leslie Stephen, or anyone else save Mrs. John Bancroft when in London, although I wanted much to see L. S. The first volume of his "Utilitarians" seems to me a wonderfully spirited performance — I have n't yet got at the other two.

I am hoping to get off to Nauheim tomorrow, leaving Alice and Harry to follow a little later. I confess that the Continent "draws" me again. I don't know whether it be the essential identity of soul that expresses itself in English things, and makes them seem known by heart already and intellectually dead and unexciting, or whether it is the singular lack of visible *sentiment* in England, and absence of "charm," or the oppressive ponderosity and superfluity and prominence of the unnecessary, or what it is, but I'm blest if I ever wish to be in England again. Any continental country whatever stimulates and refreshes vastly more, in spite of so much strong picturesqueness here, and so beautiful a Nature. England is ungracious, unamiable and heavy; whilst the Continent is everywhere light and amiably quaint, even where it is ugly, as in many elements it is in Germany. To tell the truth, I long to steep myself in America again and let the broken rootlets make new adhesions to the native soil. A man coquetting with too many countries is as bad as a bigamist, and loses his soul altogether.

I suppose you are at Ashfield and I hope surrounded, or soon to be so, by more children than of late, and all well and happy. Don't feel too bad about the country. We 've thrown away our old privileged and prerogative position among the nations, but it only showed we were less sincere about it than we supposed we were. The eternal fight of liberalism has now to be fought by us on much the same terms as in the older countries. We have still the better chance in our freedom from all the corrupting influences from on top from which they suffer.— Good-bye and love from both of us, to you all. Yours ever faithfully,

WM. JAMES.

To Nathaniel S. Shaler.

[1901?]

DEAR SHALER,— Being a man of methodical sequence in my reading, which in these days is anyhow rather slower than it used to be, I have only just got at your book.[1] Once begun, it slipped along "like a novel," and I must confess to you that it leaves a good taste behind; in fact a sort of *haunting* flavor due to its individuality, which I find it hard to explain or define.

To begin with, it does n't seem exactly like you, but rather like some quiet and conscientious old passive contemplator of life, not bristling as you are with "points," and vivacity. Its light is dampened and suffused — and all the better perhaps for that. Then it is essentially a confession of faith and a religious attitude — which one does n't get so much from you upon the street, although even there 't is clear that you have that within which passeth show. The optimism and healthy-mindedness are yours through and through, so is the wide imagination. But the moderate and non-emphatic way of putting things is not; nor is the absence of any "American humor." So I don't know just when or where or how you wrote it. I can't

---

[1] *The Individual, A Study of Life and Death.* New York, 1900. This letter is reproduced from the *Autobiography* of N. S. Shaler, where it has already been published.

place it in the Museum or University Hall. Probably it
was in Quincy Street, and in a sort of Piperio-Armadan
trance! Anyhow it is a sincere book, and tremendously
impressive by the gravity and dignity and peacefulness with
which it suggests rather than proclaims conclusions on these
eternal themes. No more than you can I believe that
death is due to selection; yet I wish you had framed some
hypothesis as to the physico-chemical necessity thereof, or
discussed such hypotheses as have been made. I think
you deduce a little too easily from the facts the existence of
a general guiding tendency toward ends like those which
our mind sets. We never know what ends may have been
kept from realization, for the dead tell no tales. The surviving witness would in any case, and whatever he were,
draw the conclusion that the universe was planned to make
him and the like of him succeed, for it actually did so. But
your argument that it is millions to one that it did n't do
so by chance does n't apply. It would apply if the witness
had preëxisted in an independent form and framed his
scheme, and then the world had realized it. Such a coincidence would prove the world to have a kindred mind to his.
But there has been no such coincidence. The world has
come but once; the witness is there after the fact and simply approves, dependently. As I understand improbability,
it only exists where independents coincide. Where only
one fact is in question, there is no relation of "probability"
at all. I think, therefore, that the excellences we have
reached and now approve may be due to no general design
but merely to a succession of the short designs we actually
know of, taking advantage of opportunity, and adding
themselves together from point to point. We are all you
say we are, as heirs; we are a mystery of condensation, and
yet of extrication and individuation, and we must worship

the soil we have so wonderfully sprung from. Yet I don't think we are necessitated to worship it as the Theists do, in the shape of one all-inclusive and all-operative designing power, but rather like polytheists, in the shape of a collection of beings who have each contributed and are now contributing to the realization of ideals more or less like those for which we live ourselves. This more pluralistic style of feeling seems to me both to allow of a warmer sort of loyalty to our past helpers, and to tally more exactly with the mixed condition in which we find the world as to its ideals. What if we did come where we are by chance, or by mere fact, with no one general design? What is gained, is gained, all the same. As to what may have been lost, who knows of it, in any case? or whether it might not have been much better than what came? But if it might, that need not prevent *us* from building on what *we* have.

There are lots of impressive passages in the book, which certainly will live and be an influence of a high order. Chapters 8, 10, 14, 15 have struck me most particularly.

I gave at Edinburgh two lectures on "The Religion of Healthy-Mindedness," contrasting it with that of "the sick soul." I shall soon have to quote your book as a healthy-minded document of the first importance, though I believe myself that the sick soul must have its say, and probably carries authority too. . . . Ever yours,

WM. JAMES.

To Miss Frances R. Morse.

NAUHEIM, *July* 10, 1901.

DEAREST FANNY,— Your letter of June 28th comes just as I was working myself up to a last European farewell to you, anyhow, the which has far more instigative spur now, with your magnificent effusion in my hands. Dear Fanny, whatever you do, don't *die* before our return! In these two short years so many of my best friends have been mown down, that I feel uncertainty everywhere, and gasp till the interval is over. John Ropes, Henry Sidgwick, F. Myers, T. Davidson, Carroll Everett, Edward Hooper, John Fiske, all intimate and valuable, some of them extremely so, and the circle grows ever smaller and will grow so to the end of one's own life. Now comes Whitman, whom I never knew very well, but whom I always liked thoroughly, and wish I had known better. . . . It will be interesting to know what new turn it will give to S. W.'s existence. I have n't the least idea how it will affect her outward life. Doubtless she will be freer to come abroad; but I hope and trust she will not be taking to staying any time in London or Paris, in the brutal cynical atmosphere of which places her little eagerness and efflorescences and cordialities would receive no such sympathetic treatment as they do with us, until she had stayed long enough for people to know her thoroughly and conquered a position by living down the first impression. Nothing so *anti-English* as S. W.'s whole "sphere." So keep her at home — with occasional sallies abroad; and if she must ever winter abroad, let it be in delightful slipshod old Rome! All which, as you perceive, is somewhat confidential. I trust that the present failure of health with her is something altogether transient, and that she will keep swimming long after everyone else has put into shore.

Which simile reminds me of Mrs. Holmes's panel, with its superb inscription.[1] What a sense she has for such things!

[1] Mrs. O. W. Holmes had used the following translation of an epitaph in the Greek Anthology:—

A shipwrecked sailor buried on this coast
Bids thee take sail.
Full many a gallant ship, when we were lost,
Weathered the gale.

and how I thank you for quoting it! With your and her permission, I shall make a vital use of it in a future book. It sums up the attitude towards life of a good philosophic pluralist, and that is what, in my capacity of author of that book, I am to be. I thank you also for the reference to I Corinthians, 1, 28, etc.[1] I had never expressly noticed that text; but it will make the splendidest motto for Myers's two posthumous volumes, and I am going to write to Mrs. Myers to suggest the same. I thank you also for your sympathetic remarks about my paper on Myers. Fifty or a hundred years hence, people will know better than now whether his instinct for truth was a sound one; and perhaps will then pat me on the back for backing him. At present they give us the cold shoulder. We are righter, in any event, than the Münsterbergs and Jastrows are, because we don't undertake, as a condition of our investigating phenomena, to bargain with them that they shan't upset our "presuppositions."

It is a beautiful summer morning, and I write under an awning on the high-perched corner balcony of the bedroom in which we live, of a corner house on the edge of the little town, with houses on the west of us and the fertile country spreading towards the east and south. A lovely region, though a climate terribly *flat*. I expect to take my last bath today, and to get my absolution from the terrible Schott; whereupon we shall leave tomorrow morning for Strassburg and the Vosges, for a week of touring up in higher air, and thence, *über* Paris, as straight as may be for Rye. I keep in a state of subliminal excitement over our sailing on the 31st. It seems too good to be really possible. Yet the ratchet of time will work along its daily cogs, and

---

[1] "And base things of the world and things which are despised hath God chosen, yes, and things which are not, to bring to naught things that are."

doubtless bring it safe within our grasp. Last year I felt no distinctly beneficial effect from the baths. This year it is distinct. I have, in other words, continued pretty steadily getting better for four months past; so it is evident that I am in a genuinely ameliorative phase of my existence, of which the acquired momentum may carry me beyond any living man of my age. At any rate, I set no limits now!

When we return I shall go straight up to Chocorua to the Salters'. What I *crave* most is some wild American country. It is a curious organic-feeling need. One's social relations with European landscape are entirely different, everything being so fenced or planted that you can't lie down and sprawl. Kipling, alluding to the "bleeding raw" appearance of some of our outskirt settlements, says, "Americans don't mix much with their landscape as yet." But we mix a darned, sight more than Europeans, so far as our individual organisms go, with our camping and general wild-animal personal relations. Thank Heaven that our Nature is so much less "redeemed"! . . .

You see, Fanny, that we are in good spirits on the whole, although my poor dear Alice has long sick-headaches that consume a good many days — she is just emerging from a bad one. Happiness, I have lately discovered, is no positive feeling, but a negative condition of freedom from a number of restrictive sensations of which our organism usually seems to be the seat. When they are wiped out, the clearness and cleanness of the contrast is happiness. This is why anæsthetics make us so happy. But don't you take to drink on that account! Love to your mother, Mary, and all. Write to us no more. How happy *that* responsibility gone must make you! We both send warmest love,

W. J.

To Henry James.

[Post-card]

BAD-NAUHEIM, *July* 11, [1901].

Your letter and paper, with the shock of John Fiske's death, came yesterday. It is too bad, for he had lots of good work in him yet, and is a loss to American letters as well as to his family. Singularly simple, solid, honest creature, he will be hugely missed by many! Everybody seems to be going! *We* stay. Life here is absolutely monotonous, but very sweet. The country is so innocently pretty. I sit up here on a terrace-restaurant, looking down on park and town, with the leaves playing in the warm breeze above me, and the little Gothic town of Friedberg only a mile off, in the midst of the great fertile plain all chequer-boarded with the different tinted crops and framed in a far-off horizon of low hills and woods. Alice and Harry, kept in by the heat, come later. He went for a distant walk yesterday P.M. and, not returning till near eleven, we thought he might have got lost in the woods. Yale beat the University race, *but* Bill's four[-oared crew] beat the Yale four. On such things is human contentment based. The baths stir up my aortic feeling and make me depressed, but I've had 6 of them, and the rest will pass quickly. Love.

W. J.

To E. L. Godkin.

BAD-NAUHEIM, *July* 25, 1901.

DEAR GODKIN,— Yours of the 9th, which came duly, gave me great pleasure, first because it showed that your love for me had not grown cold, and, second, because it seemed to reveal in you tendencies towards sociability at large which are incompatible with a very alarming condition of health. Nothing can give us greater pleasure than to come and see you before we sail. We shall stick here, probably, for a fortnight longer, then go for a week to the Hartz mountains to brace up a little — the baths being very debilitating and the air of Nauheim sedative. Then straight to Rye until we sail — on August 31st. I hope that you enjoy the "New Forest" — the "Children" thereof, by Capt. Mayne Reid, I think, was one of my most mysteriously impressive books about the age of ten. But I fear that there is not much primeval forest to be seen there nowadays. Nauheim is a sweet little place. One never sees a soldier and would n't know that *Militarismus* existed. There are two policemen, one of them an old fellow of 70 who shuffles along to keep his weak knees from giving way. I went on business to the police office t' other day. The building stood in a fine cabbage garden, and over the first door one met on entering stood the word *Küche* [1] in large letters. Quite like the old idyllic pre-Sadowan German days. My heart is getting *well!* I made an excursion to Homburg yesterday, with J. B. Warner of Cambridge, counsellor at law, and general disputant. For about six hours we discussed the Philippine question, he damning the anti-Imperialists — yet my thoracic contents remained as solid as if cast in Portland cement. Six months ago I should have had the wildest commotion there. Congratulate me! Kindest regards to you both, in which my wife joins. Yours ever affectionately,

WM. JAMES.

It should perhaps be explained that E. L. Godkin had had a cerebral hemorrhage the year before. It had left him clear in mind, but a permanent invalid, with little power of locomotion. James spent several days with him at Castle

[1] Kitchen.

William James and Henry James posing for a Kodak in 1900.

Malwood near Stony Cross before he sailed for home; and when he was in England again the next year, he repeated the visit.

To E. L. Godkin.

LAMB HOUSE, *Aug.* 29, 1901.

MY DEAR GODKIN,— Just a line to bid you both farewell! We leave for London tomorrow morning and at four on Saturday we shall be ploughing the deep. All goes well, save that the wife has sprained her ankle, and with the "firmness" that characterizes her lovely sex insists on hobbling about and doing all the packing. I shan't be aisy till I see her in her berth.

After all, in spite of you and Henry, and all Americophobes, I 'm glad I 'm going back to my own country again. Notwithstanding its "humble"ness, its fatigues, and its complications, there 's no place like home — though I think the New Forest might come near it as a substitute. England in general is too padded and cushioned for my rustic taste.

The most elevating *moral* thing I 've seen during these two years abroad, after Myers's heroic exit from this world at Rome last winter, has been the gentleness and cheerful spirit with which you are still able to remain in it after such a blow as you have received. Who could suppose so much public ferocity to cover so much private sweetness? Seriously speaking, it is more edifying to us others, dear Godkin, than you yourself can understand it to be, and I for one have learned by the example. I pray that your winter problems may gradually solve themselves without perplexity, and that next spring may find you relieved of all this helplessness. It is a very slow progress, with many steps backwards, but if the length of the forward steps preponderates, one may be well content. Good-bye and bless you both. Affectionately yours,

WM. JAMES.

James returned to America in early September, in advance of the beginning of the College term. But from this time on he limited his teaching to one half-course during the year. His intention was to husband his strength for writing. The course which he offered during the first half of the College year was accordingly announced as a course on "The Psychological Elements of Religious Life." By the end of the winter, the second series of Gifford lectures, constituting the last half of the "Varieties," had been written out.

To Miss Pauline Goldmark.

SILVER LAKE, N. H., *Sept.* 14, 1901.

DEAR PAULINE,— Your kind letter (excuse pencil — pen won't write) appears to have reached London after our departure and has just followed us hither. I had hoped for a word from you, first at Nauheim, then on the steamer, then at Cambridge; but this makes everything right. How good to think of you as the same old loveress of woods and skies and waters, and of your Bryn-Mawr friends. May none of the lot of you ever grow insufficient or forsake each other! The sight of you sporting in Nature's bosom once lifted me into a sympathetic region, and made a better boy of me in ways which it would probably amuse and surprise you to learn of, so strangely are characters useful to each other, and so subtly are destinies intermixed. But with you on the mountain-tops of existence still, and me apparently destined to remain grubbing in the cellar, we seem far enough apart at present and may have to remain so.

Alas! how brief is life's glory, at the best. I can't get to Keene Valley this year, and [may] possibly never get there. Give a kindly thought, my friend, to the spectre who once for a few times trudged by your side, and who would do so again if he could. I 'm a "motor," and morally ill-adapted to the game of patience. I have reached home in pretty poor case, but I think it 's mainly "nerves" at present, and therefore remediable; so I live on the future, but keep my expectations modest. Two years away has been too long, and the "strangeness" which I dreaded (from past experience of it) covers all things American as with a veil. Pathetic and poverty-stricken is all I see! This will pass away, but I don't want good things to pass away also, so I beseech you, Pauline, to sit down and write me a good intimate letter telling me what your life and interest were in New York last winter.

I am very sorry to hear of your sister Susan's illness, and pray that the summer will set her right. Did you see much of Miller this summer? I hate to think of his having grown so delicate! Did you see Perry again? He was at the Putnam Camp? How is Adler after his *Cur?* — or is he not yet back? What have you read? What have you cared for? Be indulgent to me, and write to me here — I stay for 10 days longer — the family — all well — remain in Cambridge. I find letters a great thing to keep one from slipping out of life.

Love to you all! Your

W. J.

The next letter was written across the back of a circular invitation to join the American Philosophical Association, then being formed, of which Professor Gardiner was Secretary.

To H. N. Gardiner.

CAMBRIDGE, *Nov.* 14, 1901.

DEAR GARDINER,— I am still pretty poorly and can't "jine" anything — but, apart from that, I don't foresee much good from a Philosophical Society. Philosophical discussion proper only succeeds between intimates who have learned how to converse by months of weary trials and failure. The philosopher is a lone beast dwelling in his individual burrow.— Count me *out !* — I hope all goes well with you. I expect to get well, but it needs *patience.*

WM. JAMES.

On April 1, 1902, James sailed for England, to deliver the second "course" of his series of Gifford Lectures in Edinburgh.

To F. C. S. Schiller.

HATLEY ST. GEORGE,
TORQUAY, *Apr.* 20, 1902.

MY DEAR SCHILLER,— I could shed tears that you should have been so near me and yet been missed. I got your big envelope on Thursday at the hotel, and your two other missives here this morning. Of the Axioms paper I have only read a sheet and a half at the beginning and the superb conclusion which has just arrived. I shall fairly *gloat* upon the whole of it, and will write you my impressions and criticisms, if criticisms there be. It is an uplifting thought that truth is to be told at last in a radical and attention-compelling manner. I think I know, though, how the attention of many will find a way not to be compelled — their will is so set on having a technically and artificially and *professionally* expressed system, that all talk carried on as yours is on principles of common-sense activity is as remote and little worthy of being listened to as the slanging each other of boys in the street as we pass. Men disdain to notice that. It is only after our (*i.e.* your and my) general way of thinking gets organized enough to become a regular part of the *bureaucracy* of philosophy that we shall get a serious hearing. Then, I feel inwardly convinced, our day will have come. But then, you may well say, the brains will be out and the man will be dead. Anyhow, *vive* the Anglo-Saxon amateur, disciple of Locke and Hume, and *pereat* the German professional!

We are here for a week with the Godkins — poor old G., once such a power, and now an utter wreck after a stroke of paralysis three years ago. Beautiful place, southeast gale, volleying rain and streaming panes and volumes of soft sea-laden wind.

I hope you are not serious about an Oxford degree for your humble servant. If you are, pray drop the thought! I am out of the race for all such vanities. Write me a degree on parchment and send it yourself — in any case it would be but your award ! — and it will be cheaper and more veracious. I *had* to take the Edinburgh one, and accepted the Durham one to please my wife. Thank you, no coronation either! I am a poor New Hampshire rustic, in bad health, and long to get back, after four summers' absence, to my own cottage and children, and never come away again for lectures or degrees or anything else. It all depends on a man's age; and after sixty, if ever, one feels as if one ought to come to some sort of equilibrium with one's native environment, and by means of a regular life get one's small message to mankind on paper. That nowadays is my only aspiration. The Gifford lectures are all facts and no philosophy — I trust that you may receive the volume by the middle of June.

When, oh, when is your volume to appear? The sheet you send me leaves off just at the point where Boyle-Gibson begins to me to be most interesting! Ever fondly yours,

WM. JAMES.

Your ancient President, Schurman, was also at Edinburgh getting LL. D'd. He is conducting a campaign in favor of Philippino independence with masterly tactics, which reconcile me completely to him, laying his finger on just the right and telling points.

To Charles Eliot Norton.

LAMB HOUSE, RYE, *May* 4, 1902.

DEAR NORTON,— I hear with grief and concern that you have had a bad fall. In a letter received this morning you are described as better, so I hope it will have had no untoward consequences beyond the immediate shock. We need you long to abide with us in undiminished vigor and health. Our voyage was smooth, though cloudy, and we found Miss Ward a very honest and lovable girl. Henry D. Lloyd, whose name you know as that of a state-socialist writer, sat opposite to us, and proved one of the most "winning" men it was ever my fortune to know.

We went to Stratford for the first time. The absolute extermination and obliteration of every record of Shakespeare save a few sordid material details, and the general suggestion of narrowness and niggardliness which ancient Stratford makes, taken in comparison with the way in which the spiritual quantity "Shakespeare" has mingled into the soul of the world, was most uncanny, and I feel ready to believe in almost any mythical story of the authorship. In fact a visit to Stratford now seems to me the strongest appeal a Baconian can make. The country round about was exquisite. Still more so the country round about

Torquay, where we stayed with the Godkins for eight days — he holding his own, as it seemed to me, but hardly improving, she earning palms of glory by her strength and virtue. A regular little trump! They have taken for the next two months the most beautiful country place I ever saw, occupying an elbow of the Dart, and commanding a view up and down. We are here for but a week, my lectures beginning on the 13th. H. J. seems tranquil and happy in his work, though he has been much pestered of late by gout.

I suppose you are rejoicing as much as I in the public interest finally aroused in the Philippine conquest. A personal scandal, it seems, is really the only thing that will wake the ordinary man's attention up. It should be the first aim of every good leader of opinion to rake up one on the opposite side. It should be introduced among our Faculty methods!

Don't think, dear Norton, that you must answer this letter, which only your accident has made me write. We shall be home so soon that I shall see you face to face. The wife sends love, as I do, to you all. No warm weather whatever as yet — I am having chilblains!! Ever affectionately yours,

WM. JAMES.

To Mrs. Henry Whitman.

R.M.S. IVERNIA, *June* 18, 1902.

DEAR MRS. WHITMAN,— We ought to be off Boston tonight. After a cold and wet voyage, including two days of head-gale and heavy sea, and one of unbroken fog with lugubriously moo-ing fog-horn, the sun has risen upon American weather, a strong west wind like champagne, blowing out of a saturated blue sky right in our teeth, the sea all effervescing and sparkling with white caps and lace, the strong sun lording it in the sky, and hope presiding in the heart. What more natural than to report all this happy turn of affairs to you, buried as you probably still are in the blankets of the London atmosphere, beautiful opalescent blankets though they be, and (when one's vitals once are acclimated) yielding more wonderful artistic effects than anything to be seen in America. "C'est le pays de la couleur," as my brother is fond of saying in the words of Alphonse Daudet! But no matter for international comparisons, which are the least profitable of human employments. Christ died for us all, so let us all be as we are, save where we want to reform ourselves. (The only unpardonable crime is that of wanting to reform *one another*, after the fashion of the U. S. in the Philippines.) . . . Your sweet letter of several dates reached us just before we left Edinburgh — excuse the insipid adjective "sweet," which after all does express something which less simple vocables may easily miss — and gave an impression of harmony and inner health which it warms the heart to become sensible of. I understand your temptation to stay over, but I also understand your temptation to get back; and I imagine that more and more you will solve the problem by a good deal of alternation in future years. It is curious how utterly distinct the three countries of England, Ireland and Scotland are, which we so summarily lump together — Scotland so democratic and so much like New England in many respects. But it would be a waste of time for you to go there. Keep to the South and spend one winter in Rome, before you die, and a spring in the smaller Italian cities!

I hope that Henry will have managed to get you and Miss Tuckerman to Rye for a day — it is so curiously quaint and characteristic. I had a bad conscience about leaving him, for I think he feels lonely as he grows old, and friends pass over to the majority. He and I are so utterly different in all our observances and springs of action, that we can't rightly judge each other. I even feel great shrinking from urging him to pay us a visit, fearing it might yield him little besides painful shocks — and, after all, what besides pain and shock *is* the right reaction for anyone to make upon our vocalization and pronunciation? The careful consonants and musical cadences of the Scotchwomen were such a balm to the ear! I wish that you and poor Henry could become really intimate. He is at bottom a very tender-hearted and generous being! No more paper! so I cross! I wish when we once get settled again at Chocorua that we might enclose you under our roof, even if only for one night, on your way to or from the Merrimans. I should like to show you true simplicity. [*No signature.*]

The Gifford Lectures were published as "The Varieties of Religious Experience, a Study in Human Nature," in June, 1902. The immediate "popularity" of this psychological survey of man's religious propensities was great; and the continued sales of the book contributed not a little to relieve James of financial anxiety during the last years of his life.

The cordiality with which theological journals and private correspondents of many creeds greeted the "Varieties," as containing a fair treatment of facts which other writers had approached with a sectarian or anti-theological bias, was striking. James was amused at being told that the book had "supplied the protestant pulpits with sermons for a twelve-month." Regarding himself as "a most protestant protestant," as he once said, he was especially pleased by the manner in which it was received by Roman Catholic reviewers.

Certain philosophical conclusions were indicated broadly in the "Varieties" without being elaborated. The book was a survey, an examination, of the facts. James had originally conceived of the Gifford appointment as giving him "an opportunity for a certain amount of psychology and a certain amount of metaphysics," and so had thought of making the first series of lectures descriptive of man's religious propensities and the second series a metaphysical study of their satisfaction through philosophy. The psychological material had grown to unforeseen dimensions, and it ended by filling the book. The metaphysical study remained to be elaborated; and to such work James now turned.

XIV

1902–1905

The Last Period (I) — Philosophical Writing — Statements of Religious Belief

JAMES now limited his teaching in Harvard University, as has been said, to half a course a year and tried to devote his working energies to formulating a statement of his philosophical conceptions. For two years he published almost nothing; then the essays which were subsequently collected in the volumes called "Pragmatism," "The Pluralistic Universe," "The Meaning of Truth," and "Essays in Radical Empiricism," began to appear in the philosophic journals, or were delivered as special lectures. Whenever he accepted invitations to lecture outside the College, as he still did occasionally, it was with the purpose of getting these conceptions expressed and of throwing them into the arena of discussion. But demands which correspondents and callers from all parts of the globe now made on his time and sympathy were formidable, for he could not rid himself of the habit of treating the most trivial of these with consideration, or acquire the habit of using a secretary. In this way there continued to be a constant drain on his strength. "It is probably difficult [thus he wrote wearily to Mr. Lutoslawski, who had begged him to collaborate with him on a book in 1904] for a man whose cerebral machine works with such facility as yours does to imagine the kind of consciousness of men like Flournoy and myself. The background of my consciousness, so far as my own achievements go, is composed of a *sense of impossibility* — a sense well warranted by the facts. For instance, two years ago, the 'Varieties' being published, I decided that everything was cleared and that my duty was immediately to begin writing my meta-physical system. Up to last October, when the academic year began, I had written some 200 pages of *notes*, *i.e.* dis-connected *brouillons*. I hoped this year to write 400 or 500 pages of straight composition, and could have done so without the interruptions. As a matter of fact, with the best will in the world, I have written exactly 32 pages! For an academic year's work, that is not brilliant! You see that, when I refuse your request, it is, after a fashion, in order to save my own life. My working day is anyhow, *at best*, only three hours long — by working I mean writing and reading philosophy." This estimate of his "notes" was, as always, self-deprecatory; but there was no denying a great measure of truth to the statement. Frequently his health made it necessary for him to escape from Cambridge and his desk. These incidents will be noted separately wherever the context requires.

Yet in spite of these difficulties and notwithstanding his complaints of constant frustration, the spirit with which James still did his work emerges from the essays of this time as well as from his letters. It was as if the years that had preceded had been years of preparation for just what he was now doing. At the age of sixty-three he turned to the formulation of his empirical philosophy with the eagerness of a schoolboy let out to play. Misunderstanding disturbed him only momentarily, opposition stimulated him, he re-joiced openly in the controversies which he provoked, and engaged in polemics with the good humor and vigor that were the essence of his genius. His "truth" must prevail! the Absolute should suffer its death-blow! Flournoy, Bergson, Schiller, Papini, and others too were "on his side." He made merry at the expense of his critics, or bewailed the perversity of their opposition; but he always encouraged them to "lay on." The imagery of contest and battle appeared in the letters which he threw off, and he expressed himself as freely as only a man can who has outgrown the reserves of his youth.

To Henry L. Higginson.

CHOCORUA, *July* 3, 1902.

DEAR HENRY,— Thanks for your letter of the other day, etc. Alice tells me of a queer conversation you and she had upon the cars. I am not anxious about money, beyond wishing not to live on capital. . . . As I have frequently said, I mean to support you in your old age. In fact the hope of that is about all that I now live for, being surfeited with the glory of academic degrees just escaped, like this last one which, in the friendliness of its heart, your [Harvard] Corporation designed sponging upon me at Commencement.[1] Boil it and solder it up from the microbes, and it may do for another year, if I am not in prison! The friendliness of such recognition is a delightful thing to a man about to graduate from the season of his usefulness. "La renommé vient," as I have heard John La Farge quote, "à ceux qui ont la patience d'attendre, et s'accroit à raison de leur imbecillité." Best wishes to you all. Yours ever,

WM. JAMES.

To Miss Grace Norton.

CHOCORUA, *Aug.* 29, 1902.

MY DEAR GRACE,— Will you kindly let me know, by the method of effacement, on the accompanying post-card,

[1] Although James had received the usual hint that Harvard intended to confer an honorary degree upon him, he had absented himself from both the honors and fatigues of Commencement time. The next year he was present, and the LL.D. was conferred.

whether the box from Germany of which I wrote you some time ago has or has not yet been left at your house. I paid the express, over twenty dollars, on it three weeks ago, directing it to be left with you.

The ice being thus broken, let me ramble on! How do-ist thou? And how is the moist and cool summer suiting thee? I hope, well! It has certainly been a boon to most people. Our house has been full of company of which tomorrow the last boys will leave, and I confess I shall enjoy the change to no responsibility. The scourge of life is *responsibility* — always there with its scowling face, and when it ceases to someone else, it begins to yourself, or to your God, if you have one. Consider the lilies, how free they are from it, and yet how beautiful the expression of their face. Especially should those emerging from "nervous prostration" be suffered to be without it — they have trouble enough in any case. I am getting on famously, but for that drawback, on which my temper is liable to break; but I *walk* somewhat as in old times, and that is the main corner to have turned. The country seems as beautiful as ever — it is good that, when age takes away the zest from so many things, it seems to make no difference at all in one's capacity for enjoying landscape and the aspects of Nature. We are all well, and shall very soon be buzzing about Irving Street as of yore. Keep well yourself, dear Grace; and believe me ever your friend,

WM. JAMES.

To this word about enjoying the aspects of nature may be added a few lines from a letter to his son William, which James wrote from Europe in 1900: —

"Scenery seems to wear in one's consciousness better than any other element in life. In this year of much solemn and idle meditation, I have often been surprised to find what a predominant part in my own spiritual experience it has played, and how it stands out as almost the only thing the memory of which I should like to carry over with me beyond the veil, unamended and unaltered. From the midst of every thing else, almost, *surgit amari aliquid;* but from the days in the open air, never any bitter whiff, save that they are gone forever."

To Miss Frances R. Morse.

STONEHURST,
INTERVALE, N. H., *Sept.* 18, 1902.

DEAREST FANNY,— How long it is since we have exchanged salutations and reported progress! Happy the country which is without a history! *I* have had no history to communicate, and I hope that you have had none either, and that the summer has glided away as happily for you as it has for us. Now it begins to fade towards the horizon over which so many ancient summers have slipped, and our household is on the point of "breaking up" just when the season invites one most imperiously to stay. *Dang* all schools and colleges, say I. Alice goes down tomorrow (I being up here with the Merrimans only for one day) to start Billy for Europe — he will spend the winter at Geneva University — and to get "the house" ready for our general reception on the 26th. I may possibly make out to stay up here till the Monday following, and spend the interval of a few days by myself among the mountains, having stuck to the domestic hearth unusually tight all summer. . . .

We have had guests — too many of them, rather, at one time, for me — and a little reading has been done, mostly philosophical technics, which, by the strange curse laid upon Adam, certain of his descendants have been doomed to invent and others, still more damned, to learn. But I 've also read Stevenson's letters, which everybody ought to read just to know how charming a human being can be, and I 've read a good part of Goethe's *Gedichte* once again, which are also to be read, so that one may realize how absolutely healthy an organization may every now and then eventuate into this world. To have such a lyrical gift and to treat it with so little solemnity, so that most of the output consists of mere escape of the over-tension into bits of occasional verse, irresponsible, unchained, like smoke-wreaths! — it *du* give one a great impression of personal power. In general, though I 'm a traitor for saying so, it seems to me that the German race has been a more massive organ of expression for the travail of the Almighty than the Anglo-Saxon, though we did seem to have something more like it in Elizabethan times. Or are clearness and dapperness the absolutely final shape of creation? Good-bye! dear Fanny — you see how mouldy I am temporarily become. The moment I take my pen, I can write in no other way. Write thou, and let me know that things are greener and more vernal where you are. Alice would send much love to you, were she here. Give mine to your mother, brother, and sister-in-law, and all. Your loving,

W. J.

To Henry L. Higginson.

CAMBRIDGE, MASS., *Nov.* 1, 1902.

DEAR HENRY,— I am emboldened to the step I am taking by the consciousness that though we are both at least sixty years old and have known each other from the cradle, I have never but once (or possibly twice) traded on your well-known lavishness of disposition to swell any "subscription" which I was trying to raise.

Now the doomful hour has struck. The altar is ready, and I take the victim by the ear. I choose you for a victim because you still have some undesiccated human feeling about you and can think in terms of pure charity — for the love of God, without ulterior hopes of returns from the investment.

The subject is a man of fifty who can be recommended to no other kind of a benefactor. His story is a long one, but it amounts to this, that Heaven made him with no other power than that of thinking and writing, and he has proved by this time a truly pathological inability to keep body and soul together. He is abstemious to an incredible degree, is the most innocent and harmless of human beings, is n't propagating his kind, has never had a dime to spend except for vital necessities, and never has had in his life an hour of what such as *we* call freedom from care or of "pleasure" in the ordinary exuberant sense of the term. He is refinement itself mentally and morally; and his writings have all been printed in first-rate periodicals, but are too scanty to "pay." There 's no excuse for him, I admit. But God made him; and after kicking and cuffing and prodding him for twenty years, I have now come to believe that he ought to be treated in charity pure and simple (even though that be a vice) and I want to guarantee him $350 a year as a pension to be paid to the Mills Hotel in Bleecker Street, New York, for board and lodging and a few cents weekly over and above. I will put in $150. I have secured $100 more. Can I squeeze $50 a year out of you for such a non-public cause? If not, don't reply and forget this letter. If "ja" and you think you really can afford it, and it is n't wicked, let me know, and I will dun you regularly every year for the $50. Yours as ever,

Wm. James.

It is a great compliment that I address you. Most men say of such a case, "Is the man deserving?" Whereas the real point is, "Does he need us?" What is deserving nowadays?

The beneficiary of this appeal was that same unfulfilled promise of a metaphysician who appeared as "X" on page 292 of the first volume — a man upon whom, in Cicero's phrase, none but a philosopher could look without a groan. There were more parallels to X's case than it would be permissible to cite here. James did not often appeal to others to help such men with money, but he did things for them himself, even after it had become evident that they could give nothing to the world in return, and even when they had exhausted his patience. "Damn your half-successes, your imperfect geniuses!" he exclaimed of another who shall be called Z. "I'm tired of making allowances for them and propping them up. . . . Z has never constrained himself in his life. Selfish, conceited, affected, a monster of desultory intellect, he has become now a seedy, almost sordid, old man without even any intellectual residuum from his work that can be called a finished construction; only 'suggestions' and a begging old age." But Z, too, was helped to the end.

To Henri Bergson.

CAMBRIDGE, *Dec.* 14, 1902.

MY DEAR SIR,—I read the copy of your "Matière et Mémoire" which you so kindly sent me, immediately on receiving it, four years ago or more. I saw its great originality, but found your ideas so new and vast that I could not be sure that I fully understood them, although the *style*, Heaven knows, was lucid enough. So I laid the book aside for a second reading, which I have just accomplished, slowly and carefully, along with that of the "Données Immédiates," etc.

I think I understand the main lines of your system very well at present — though of course I can't yet trace its proper relations to the aspects of experience of which you do not treat. It needs much building out in the direction of Ethics, Cosmology and Cosmogony, Psychogenesis, etc., before one can apprehend it fully. That I should take it in so much more easily than I did four years ago shows that even at the age of sixty one's mind can grow — a pleasant thought.

It is a work of exquisite genius. It makes a sort of Copernican revolution as much as Berkeley's "Principles" or Kant's "Critique" did, and will probably, as it gets better and better known, open a new era of philosophical discussion. It fills *my* mind with all sorts of new questions and hypotheses and brings the old into a most agreeable liquefaction. I thank you from the bottom of my heart.

The *Hauptpunkt* acquired for me is your conclusive demolition of the dualism of object and subject in perception. I believe that the "transcendency" of the object will not recover from your treatment, and as I myself have been working for many years past on the same line, only with other general conceptions than yours, I find myself most agreeably corroborated. My health is so poor now that work goes on very slowly; but I am going, if I live, to write a general system of metaphysics which, in many of its fundamental ideas, agrees closely with what you have set forth, and the agreement inspires and encourages me more than you can well imagine. It would take far too many words to attempt any detail, but some day I hope to send you the book.[1]

How good it is sometimes simply to *break away* from all old categories, deny old worn-out beliefs, and restate things *ab initio*, making the lines of division fall into entirely new places!

I send you a little popular lecture of mine on immortality,[2]—no positive theory but merely an *argumentum ad hominem* for the ordinary cerebralistic objection,— in which it may amuse you to see a formulation like your own that the brain is an organ of *filtration* for spiritual life.

I also send you my last book, the "Varieties of Religious Experience," which may some time beguile an hour. Believe, dear Professor Bergson, the high admiration and regard with which I remain, always sincerely yours,

WM. JAMES.

To Mrs. Louis Agassiz.

CAMBRIDGE, *Dec.* 15, 1902.

DEAR MRS. AGASSIZ,— I never dreamed of your replying to that note of mine (of Dec. 5th). If you are replying to all the notes you received on that eventful day, it seems to me a rather heavy penalty for becoming an octogenarian.[3] But glad I am that you replied to mine, and so beautifully. Indeed I do remember the meeting of those two canoes, and the dance, over the river from Manaos; and many an-

[1] "I have been re-reading Bergson's books, and nothing that I have read in years has so excited and stimulated my thought. Four years ago I could n't understand him at all, though I felt his power. I am sure that that philosophy has a great future. It breaks through old *cadres* and brings things into a solution from which new crystals can be got." (From a letter to Flournoy, Jan. 27, 1902.)

[2] The Ingersoll Lecture on *Human Immortality*.

[3] There had been a celebration of Mrs. Agassiz's eightieth birthday at Radcliffe College, of which she was President.

other incident and hour of that wonderful voyage.[1] I remember your freshness of interest, and readiness to take hold of everything, and what a blessing to me it was to have one civilized lady in sight, to keep the memory of cultivated conversation from growing extinct. I remember my own folly in wishing to return home after I came out of the hospital at Rio; and my general greenness and incapacity as a naturalist afterwards, with my eyes gone to pieces. It was all because my destiny was to be a "philosopher" — a fact which then I did n't know, but which only means, I think, that, if a man is good for nothing else, he can at least teach philosophy. But I 'm going to write one book worthy of you, dear Mrs. Agassiz, and of the Thayer expedition, if I am spared a couple of years longer.

I hope you were not displeased at the *applause* the other night, as you went out. *I* started it; if I had n't, someone else would a moment later, for the tension had grown intolerable.

How delightful about the Radcliffe building!

Well, once more, dear Mrs. Agassiz, we both thank you for this beautiful and truly affectionate letter. Your affectionate,

WM. JAMES.

E. L. Godkin had recently died, and at the date of the next letter a movement was on foot to raise money for a memorial in commemoration of his public services. The money was soon subscribed and the Memorial took shape in the endowment of the Godkin Lectureship at Harvard. James had started discussion of the project at a meeting of the dinner Club and Henry L. Higginson had continued it in a letter to which the following replied.

[1] On the Amazon in 1865-66.

To Henry L. Higginson.

CAMBRIDGE, *Feb.* 8, 1903.

DEAR HENRY,— I am sorry to have given a wrong impression, and made you take the trouble of writing — nutritious though your letters be to receive. My motive in mentioning the Godkin testimonial was pure curiosity, and not desire to promote it. We were ten "liberals" together, and I wanted to learn how many of us had been alienated from Godkin by his temper in spite of having been influenced by his writing. I found that it was just about half and half. I never said — Heaven bear me witness — that I had learned more from G. than from anyone. I said I had got more *political* education from him. You see the "Nation" took me at the age of 22 — you were already older and wickeder. If you follow my advice now, you don't subscribe a cent to this memorial. *I* shall subscribe $100, for mixed reasons. Godkin's "home life" was very different from his life against the world. When a man differed in type from him, and consequently reacted differently on public matters, he thought him a preposterous monster, pure and simple, and so treated him. He could n't imagine a different kind of creature from himself in politics. But in private relations he was simplicity and sociability and affectionateness incarnate, and playful as a young opossum. I never knew his first wife well, but I admire the pluck and fidelity of the second, and I note your chivalrous remarks about the sex, including Mrs. W. J., to whom report has been made of them, making her blush with pleasure.

Don't subscribe, dear Henry. I am not trying to raise subscriptions. You left too early Friday eve. Ever affectionately yours,

W. J.

James's college class finished its work at the end of the first half of the academic year, and in early February he turned for a few days to the thought of a Mediterranean voyage, as a vacation and a means of escape from Cambridge during the bad weather of March. While considering this plan, he cabled M. Bergson to inquire as to the possibility of a meeting in Paris or elsewhere.

To Henri Bergson.

CAMBRIDGE, *Feb. 25*, 1903.

DEAR PROFESSOR BERGSON,— Your most obliging cablegram (with 8 words instead of four!) arrived duly a week ago, and now I am repenting that I ever asked you to send it, for I have been feeling so much less fatigued than I did a month ago, that I have given up my passage to the Mediterranean, and am seriously doubting whether it will be necessary to leave home at all. I *ought* not to, on many grounds, unless my health imperatively requires it. Pardon me for having so frivolously stirred you up, and permit me at least to pay the cost (as far as I can ascertain it) of the despatch which you were so liberal as to send.

There is still a bare possibility (for I am so strongly tempted) that I may, after the middle of March, take a cheaper vessel direct to England or to France, and spend ten days or so in Paris and return almost immediately. In that case, we could still have our interview. I think there must be great portions of your philosophy which you have not yet published, and I want to see how well they combine with mine. *Writing* is too long and laborious a process, and I would not inflict on you the task of answering my questions by letter, so I will still wait in the hope of a personal interview some time.

I am convinced that a philosophy of *pure experience*, such as I conceive yours to be, can be made to work, and will reconcile many of the old inveterate oppositions of the schools. I think that your radical denial (the manner of it at any rate) of the notion that the brain can be in any way the *causa fiendi* of consciousness, has introduced a very sudden clearness, and eliminated a part of the idealistic paradox. But your unconscious or subconscious permanence of memories is in its turn a notion that offers difficulties, seeming in fact to be the equivalent of the "soul" in another shape, and the manner in which these memories "insert" themselves into the brain action, and in fact the whole conception of the difference between the outer and inner worlds in your philosophy, still need to me a great deal of elucidation. But behold me challenging you to answer me *par écrit!*

I have read with great delight your article in the "Revue de Métaphysique" for January, agree thoroughly with all its critical part, and wish that I might see in your *intuition métaphysique* the full equivalent for a philosophy of concepts. *Neither* seems to be a full equivalent for the other, unless indeed the intuition becomes completely mystical (and that I am willing to believe), but I don't think that that is just what *you* mean. The *Syllabus* [1] which I sent you the other day is (I fear), from its great abbreviation, somewhat unintelligible, but it will show you the sort of lines upon which I have been working. I think that a normal philosophy, like a science, must live by hypotheses — I think that the indispensable hypothesis in a philosophy of pure experience is that of many kinds of other experience than ours, that the question of $\begin{Bmatrix} \text{co-consciousness} \\ \text{conscious synthesis} \end{Bmatrix}$ (its conditions, etc.)

[1] An 8-page *Syllabus* printed for the use of his students in the course on the "Philosophy of Nature" which James was giving during the first half of the college year.

becomes a most urgent question, as does also the question of the relations of what is possible only to what is actual, what is past or future to what is present. These are all urgent matters in your philosophy also, I imagine. How exquisitely you do *write!* Believe me, with renewed thanks for the telegram, yours most sincerely,

WM. JAMES.

To Theodore Flournoy.

CAMBRIDGE, *Apr. 30,* 1903.

MY DEAR FLOURNOY,— I forget whether I wrote you my applause or not, on reading your chapter on religious psychology in the "Archives." I thought it a splendid thing, and well adapted to set the subject in the proper light before students. Abauzit has written to me for authorization to translate my book, and both he and W. J., Junior, have quoted you as assured of his competency. I myself feel confident of it, and have given him the authorization required. Possibly you may supply him with as much of your own translation as you have executed, so that the time you have spent on the latter may not be absolutely lost. "Billy" also says that you have executed a review of Myers's book,[1] finding it a more difficult task than you had anticipated. I am highly curious to see what you have found to say. I, also, wrote a notice of the volumes, and found it exceeding difficult to know how to go at the job. At last I decided just to skeletonize the points of his reasoning, but on correcting the proof just now, what I have written seems deadly flat and unprofitable and makes me wish that I had stuck to my original intention of refusing to review the book at all. The fact is, such a book need not be *criticized* at all at present. It is obviously too soon for it to be either refuted

[1] *Human Personality and its Survival of Bodily Death,* by F. W. H. Myers.

or established by mere criticism. It is a hypothetical construction of genius which must be kept hanging up, as it were, for new observations to be referred to. As the years accumulate these in a more favorable or in a more unfavorable sense, it will tend to stand or to fall. I confess that reading the volumes has given me a higher opinion than ever of Myers's constructive gifts, but on the whole a lower opinion of the objective solidity of the system. So many of the facts which form its pillars are still dubious.[1]

Bill says that you were again convinced by Eusapia,[2] but that the conditions were not satisfactory enough (so I understood) to make the experiments likely to convince absent hearers. Forever baffling is all this subject, and I confess that I begin to lose my interest. Believe me, in whatever difficulties your review of Myers may have occasioned you, you have my fullest sympathy!

Bill has had a perfectly splendid winter in Geneva, thanks almost entirely to your introductions, and to the generous manner in which you took him into your own family. I wish we could ever requite you by similar treatment of Henri, or of *ces demoiselles*. He seems to labor under an apprehension of not being able to make you all believe how appreciative and grateful he is, and he urges me to "Make you understand it" when I write. I imagine that you understand it anyhow, so far as he is concerned, so I simply assure you that *our* gratitude here is of the strongest and sincerest kind. I imagine that this has been by far the most profitable and educative winter of his life, and I rejoice exceedingly that he has obtained in so short a time so com-

---

[1] "The piles driven into the quicksand are too few for such a structure. But it is essential as a preliminary attempt at methodizing, and will doubtless keep a very honorable place in history." To F. C. S. Schiller, April 8, 1903.

[2] Eusapia Paladino, the Italian "medium." The physical manifestations which occurred during her trance had excited much discussion.

plete a sense of being at home in, and so lively an affection for, the Swiss people and country. (As for *your* family he has written more than once that the Flournoy family seems to be "the finest family" he has ever seen in his life.)

His experience is a good measure of the improvement in the world's conditions. Thirty years ago *I* spent nine months in Geneva — but in how inferior an "Academy," and with what inferior privileges and experiences! Never inside a private house, and only after three months or more familiar enough with other students to be admitted to Zofingue.[1] Ignorant of 1000 things which have come to my son and yours in the course of education. It *is* a more evolved world, and no mistake.

I find myself very tired and unable to work this spring, but I think it will depart when I get to the country, as we soon shall. I am neither writing nor lecturing, and reading nothing heavy, only Emerson's works again (divine things, some of them!) in order to make a fifteen-minute address about him on his centennial birthday. What I want to get at, and let no interruptions interfere, is (at last) my *system of tychistic and pluralistic philosophy of pure experience.*

I wish, and even more ardently does Alice wish, that you and Mrs. Flournoy, and all the children, or any of them, might pay us a visit. I don't *urge* you, for there is so little in America that pays one to come, except sociological observation. But in the big slow steamers, the voyage is always interesting — and once here, how happy we should be to harbor you. In any case, perhaps Henri and one of his sisters will come and spend a year. From the point of view of education, Cambridge is first-rate. Love to you all from us both.

WM. JAMES.

[1] The name of a student-society.

Late in April came a letter from Henry James in which he spoke, as if with many misgivings, of returning to America for a six months' visit. "I should wish," he said, "to write a book of 'impressions' and to that end get quite away from Boston and New York — really *see* the country at large. On the other hand I don't see myself prowling alone in Western cities and hotels or finding my way about by myself, and it is all darksome and tangled. Some light may break — but meanwhile next Wednesday (awful fact) is my 60th birthday." He had not been in America for more than twenty years, and had never known anything of the country outside of New England and New York.

To Henry James.

CAMBRIDGE, *May* 3, 1903.

. . . Your long and *inhaltsvoll* letter of April 10th arrived duly, and constituted, as usual, an "event." Theodora had already given us your message of an intended visit to these shores; and your letter made Alice positively overflow with joyous anticipations. On my part they are less unmixed, for I feel more keenly a good many of the *désagréments* to which you will inevitably be subjected, and imagine the sort of physical loathing with which many features of our national life will inspire you. It takes a long time to notice such things no longer. One thing, for example, which would reconcile *me* most easily to abandoning my native country forever would be the certainty of immunity, when traveling, from the sight of my fellow beings at hotels and dining-cars having their boiled eggs brought to them, broken by a negro, two in a cup, and eaten with butter. How irrational this dislike is, is proved both by logic, and by the pleasure taken in the custom by the élite of mankind over here. . . . Yet of such irrational sympathies and aversions (quite con-

ventional for the most part) does our pleasure in a country
depend, and in your case far more than in that of most men.
The *vocalization* of our countrymen is really, and not conventionally, so ignobly awful that the process of hardening
oneself thereto is very slow, and would in your case be impossible.　It is simply incredibly loathsome.　I should hate
to have you come and, as a result, feel that you had now
done with America forever, even in an ideal and imagina-
tive sense, which after a fashion you can still indulge in.
As far as your copyright interests go, could n't they be
even more effectually and just as cheaply or more cheaply
attended to by your [engaging an agent] over here.　Alice
foresees Lowell [Institute] lectures; but lectures have such
an awful side (when not academic) that I myself have fore-
sworn them — it is a sort of prostitution of one's person.
This is rather a throwing of cold water; but it is well to
realize both sides, and I think I can realize certain things
for you better than the sanguine and hospitable Alice does.

Now for the other side, there are things in the American
out-of-door nature, as well as comforts indoors that can't
be beat, and from which *I* get an infinite pleasure.　If you
avoided the *banalité* of the Eastern cities, and traveled far
and wide, to the South, the Colorado, over the Canadian
Pacific to that coast, possibly to the Hawaiian Islands, etc.,
you would get some reward, at the expense, it is true, of a
considerable amount of cash.　I think you ought to come
in March or April and stay till the end of October or into
November.　The hot summer months you could pass in
an absolutely quiet way — if you wished to — at Chocorua
with us, where you could do as much writing as you liked,
continuous, and undisturbed, and would (I am sure) grow
fond of, as you grew more and more intimate with, the sweet
rough country there.　After June, 1904, *I* shall be free, to

go and come as I like, for I have fully decided to resign, and nothing would please me so well (if I found then that I could afford it) as to do some of that proposed traveling along with you. I could take you into certain places that perhaps you would n't see alone. Don't come therefore, if you do come, before the spring of 1904!

I have been doing nothing in the way of work of late, and consequently have kept my fatigue somewhat at bay. The reading of the divine Emerson, volume after volume, has done me a lot of good, and, strange to say, has thrown a strong practical light on my own path. The incorruptible way in which he followed his own vocation, of seeing such truths as the Universal Soul vouchsafed to him from day to day and month to month, and reporting them in the right literary form, and thereafter kept his limits absolutely, refusing to be entangled with irrelevancies however urging and tempting, knowing both his strength and its limits, and clinging unchangeably to the rural environment which he once for all found to be most propitious, seems to me a moral lesson to all men who have any genius, however small, to foster. I see now with absolute clearness, that greatly as I have been helped and enlarged by my University business hitherto, the time has come when the remnant of my life must be passed in a different manner, contemplatively namely, and with leisure and simplification for the one remaining thing, which is to report in one book, at least, such impression as my own intellect has received from the Universe. This I mean to stick to, and am only sorry that I am obliged to stay in the University one other year. It is giving up the inessentials which have grown beyond one's powers, for the sake of the duties which, after all, are most essentially imposed on one by the nature of one's powers.

Emerson is exquisite! I think I told you that I have to hold forth in praise of him at Concord on the 25th — in company with Senator Hoar, T. W. Higginson, and Charles Norton — quite a *vieille garde*, to which I now seem to belong. You too have been leading an Emersonian life — though the environment differs to suit the needs of the different psychophysical organism which you present.

I have but little other news to tell you. Charles Peirce is lecturing here — queer being. . . . Boott is in good spirits, and as sociable as ever. Grace Norton ditto. I breakfasted this Sunday morning, as of yore, with Theodora [Sedgwick], who had a bad voyage in length but not in quality, though she lay in her berth the whole time. I can hardly conceive of being willing to travel under such conditions. Otherwise we are well enough, except Peggy, whose poor condition I imagine to result from influenza. Aleck has been regenerated through and through by "bird lore," happy as the day is long, and growing acquainted with the country all about Boston. All in consequence of a neighboring boy on the street, 14 years old and an ornithological genius, having taken him under his protection. Yesterday, all day long in the open air, from seven to seven, at Wayland, spying and listening to birds, counting them, and writing down their names!

I shall go off tomorrow or next day to the country again, by myself, joining Henry Higginson and a colleague at the end of the week, and returning by the 14th for Ph.D. examinations which I hate profoundly. H. H. has bought some five miles of the shore of Lake Champlain adjoining his own place there, and thinks of handing it over to the University for the surveying, engineering, forestry and mining school. He is as liberal-hearted a man as the Lord ever walloped entrails into. . . .

What a devil of a bore your forced purchase of the unnecessary neighboring land must have been. *I* am just buying 150 acres more at Chocorua, to round off our second estate there. Keep well and prolific — everyone speaks praise of your "Better Sort," which I am keeping for the country. . . .

To his Daughter.

FABYANS, N. H., *May 6, 1903.*

SWEET MARY,— Although I wrote to thy mother this P.M. I can't refrain from writing to thee ere I go up to bed. I left Intervale at 3.30 under a cloudy sky and slight rain, passing through the gloomy Notch to Crawford's and then here, where I am lodged in a house full of working men, though with a good clean bedroom. I write this in the office, with an enormous air-tight stove, a parrot and some gold-fish as my companions. I took a slow walk of an hour and a half before supper over this great dreary mountain plateau, pent in by hills and woods still free from buds. Although it is only 1500 feet high, the air is real mountain air, soft and strong at once. I wish that you could have taken that four-hour drive with Topsy [1] and me this morning. You would already be well — it had so healing an influence. Poverty-stricken this New Hampshire country may be — weak in a certain sense, shabby, thin, pathetic — say all that, yet, like "Jenny," it *kissed* me; and it is not *vulgar* — even H. J. can't accuse it of that — or of "stodginess," especially at this emaciated season. It remains pure, and clear and distinguished — Bless it! Once more, would thou hadst been along! I have just been reading Emerson's "Representative Men." What luminous truths he communicates about their home-life — for instance: "Nature

[1] The horse.

never sends a Great Man into the planet without confiding the secret to another soul" — namely your mother's! How he hits her off, and how I recognized whom he meant immediately. Kiss the dear tender-hearted thing.

Common men also have their advantages. I have seen all day long such a succession of handsome, stalwart, burnt-faced, out-of-door workers as made me glad to be, however degenerate myself, one of their tribe. Splendid, honest, good-natured fellows.

Good-night! I 'm now going to bed, to read myself to sleep with a tiptop novel sent me by one Barry, an old pupil of mine. 'T is called "A Daughter of Thespis." Is this the day of your mother's great and noble lunch? If so, I pray that it may have gone off well. Kisses to her, and all. Your loving

PAPA.

The next letter describes the Emerson Centenary at Concord. The Address which James delivered was published in the special volume commemorative of the proceedings, and also in "Memories and Studies."

To Miss Frances R. Morse.

CAMBRIDGE, *May 26, 1903.*

DEAREST FANNY,— On Friday I called at your house and to my sorrow found the blinds all down. I had not supposed that you would leave so soon, though I might well have done so if I had reflected. It has been a sorrow to me to have seen so little of you lately, but so goes the *train du monde.* Collapsed condition, absences, interruptions of all sorts, have made the year end with most of the desiderata postponed to next year. I meant to write to you on Friday evening, then on Saturday morning. But

I went to Lincoln on Saturday P.M. and stayed over the Emerson racket, without returning home, and have been packing and winding up affairs all day in order to get off to Chocorua tomorrow at 7.30. These windings up of unfinished years continue till the unfinished life winds up.

I wish that you had been at Concord. It was the most harmoniously æsthetic or æsthetically harmonious thing! The weather, the beauty of the village, the charming old meeting-house, the descendants of the grand old man in such profusion, the mixture of Concord and Boston heads, so many of them of our own circle, the allusions to great thoughts and things, and the old-time New England rusticity and rurality, the silver polls and ancient voices of the *vieille garde* who did the orating (including this 'yer child), all made a matchless combination, took one back to one's childhood, and made that rarely realized marriage of reality with ideality, that usually only occurs in fiction or poetry.

It was a sweet and memorable day, and I am glad that I had an active share in it. I thank you for your sweet words to Alice about my address. I let R. W. E. speak for himself, and I find now, hearing so much from others of him, that there are only a few things that *can* be said of him; he was so squarely and simply himself as to impress every one in the same manner. Reading the whole of him over again continuously has made me feel his real greatness as I never did before. He's really a critter to be thankful for. Good-night, dear Fanny. I shall be back here by Commencement, and somehow we must see you at Chocorua this summer.

Love to your mother as well as to yourself, from your ever affectionate

WM. JAMES.

heard a word about you since that day, but I hope that the times have treated you kindly, and that you have not been "overdoing" in your usual naughty way. I, with the exception of six days lately with the Merrimans, have been sitting solidly at home, and have found myself in much better condition than I was in last summer, and consequently better than for several years. It is pleasant to find that one's organism has such reparative capacities even after sixty years have been told out. But I feel as if the remainder could n't be very long, at least for "creative" purposes, and I find myself eager to get ahead with work which unfortunately won't allow itself to be done in too much of a hurry. I am convinced that the desire to formulate truths is a virulent disease. It has contracted an alliance lately in me with a feverish personal ambition, which I never had before, and which I recognize as an unholy thing in such a connexion. I actually dread to die until I have settled the Universe's hash in one more book, which shall be *epoch-machend* at last, and a title of honor to my children! Childish idiot — as if formulas about the Universe could ruffle its majesty, and as if the common-sense world and its duties were not eternally the really real! — I am on my way from Ashfield, where I was a guest at the annual dinner, to *feu* Davidson's "school" at Glenmore, where, in a sanguine hour, I agreed to give five discourses. Apparently they are having a good season there. Mrs. Booker Washington was the hero of the Ashfield occasion — a big hearty handsome natural creature, quite worthy to be her husband's mate. Fred Pollock made a tip-top speech. . . . Charles Norton appeared to great advantage as a benignant patriarch, and the place was very pretty. Have you read Loti's "Inde sans les Anglais"? If not, then begin. I seem to myself to have been doing some pretty good reading this summer, but when I try to recall it, nothing but philosophic works come up. Good-bye! and Heaven keep you! Yours affectionately,

                                        W. J.

To Miss Frances R. Morse.
                              CHOCORUA, *Sept.* 24, 1903.

DEAREST FANNY,— It is so long since we have held communion that I think it is time to recommence. Our summer is ending quietly enough, not only you, but Theodora and Mary Tappan, having all together conspired to leave us in September solitude, and some young fellows, companions of Harry and Billy, having just gone down. The cook goes tomorrow for a fortnight of vacation, but Alice and I, and probably both the older boys, hope to stay up here more or less until the middle of October. My "seminary" begins on Friday, October 2nd, and for the rest of the year Friday is my only day with a college exercise in it — an arrangement which leaves me extraordinarily free, and of which I intend to take advantage by making excursions. Hitherto, during the entire 30 years of my College service, I have had a midday exercise every day in the week. This has always kept me tied too tight to Cambridge. I am *vastly* better in nervous tone than I was a year ago, my work is simplified down to the exact thing I want to do, and I ought to be happy in spite of the lopping off of so many faculties of activity. The only thing to do, as with the process of the suns one finds one's faculties dropping away one by one, is to be good-natured about it, remember that the next generation is as young as ever, and try to live and have a sympathetic share in their activities. I spent three days lately (only three, alas!) at the "Shanty" [in Keene Valley], and was moved to admiration at the foundation for a consciousness that was being laid in the children by the bare-headed and bare-legged existence "close to nature" of which the memory was being stored up in them in these years. They lay around the camp-fire at night at the feet of their elders, in every attitude of soft recumbency, heads on stomachs and legs mixed up, happy and dreamy, just like the young of some prolific carnivorous species. The coming generation ought to reap the benefit of all this healthy animality. What would n't I give to have been educated in it! . . .

To Mrs. Henry Whitman.

CAMBRIDGE, *Oct.* 29, 1903.

MY DEAR "S. W.,"— On inquiry at your studio last Monday I was told that you would be in the country for ten days or a fortnight more. I confess that this pleased me much for it showed you both happy and prudent. Surely the winter is long enough, however much we cut off of this end — the city winter I mean; and the country this month has been little short of divine.

We came down on the 16th, and I have to get mine (my country, I mean) from the "Norton Woods." But they are very good indeed,— indeed, indeed!

I am better, both physically and morally, than for years past. The whole James family thrives; and were it not for one's "duties" one could be happy. But that things should give pain proves that something is being *effected*, so I take that consolation. I have the duty on Monday of reporting at a "Philosophical Conference" on the Chicago School of Thought. Chicago University has during the past six months given birth to the fruit of its ten years of gestation under John Dewey. The result is wonderful — a *real school*, and *real Thought*. Important thought, too!

Did you ever hear of such a city or such a University? Here we have thought, but no school. At Yale a school, but no thought. Chicago has both. . . . But this, dear Madam, is not intended as a letter — only a word of greeting and congratulation at your absence. I don't know why it makes me so happy to hear of anyone being in the country. I suppose *they* must be happy.

Your last letter went to the right spot — but I don't expect to hear from you now until I see you. Ever affectionately yours,

W. J.

To Henry James.

Newport, *Jan.* 20, 1904.

. . . I came down here the night before last, to see if a change of air might loosen the grip of my influenza, now in its sixth week and me still weak as a baby, almost, from its virulent effects. . . . Yesterday A.M. the thermometer fell to 4 below zero. I walked as far as Tweedy's (I am staying at a boarding-house, Mrs. Robinson's, Catherine St., close to Touro Avenue, Daisy Waring being the only other boarder) — the snow loudly creaking under foot and under teams however distant, the sky luminously white and dazzling, no distance, everything equally near to the eye, and the architecture in the town more huddled, discordant, cheap, ugly and contemptible than I had ever seen it. It brought back old times so vividly. So it did in the evening, when I went after sunset down Kay Street to the termination. That low West that I 've so often fed on, with a sombre but intense crimson vestige smouldering close to the horizon-line, economical but profound, and the western well of sky shading upward from it through infinite shades of transparent luminosity in darkness to the deep blue darkness overhead. It was purely American. You never see that western sky anywhere else. Solemn and wonderful. I should think you'd like to see it again, if only for the sake of shuddering at it! . . .

To François Pillon.

CAMBRIDGE, *June* 12, 1904.

DEAR PILLON,— Once more I get your faithful and indefatigable "Année" and feel almost ashamed of receiving it thus from you, year after year, when I make nothing of a return! So you are 75 years old — I had no idea of it, but thought that you were much younger. I am only(!) 62, and wish that I could expect another 13 years of such activity as you have shown. I fear I cannot. My arteries are senile, and none of my ancestors, so far as I know of them, have lived past 72, many of them dying much earlier. This is my last day in Cambridge; tomorrow I get away into the country, where "the family" already is, for my vacation. I shall take your "Année" with me, and shall be greatly interested in both Danriac's article and yours. What a mercy it is that your eyes, in spite of cataract-operations, are still good for reading. I have had a very bad winter for work — two attacks of influenza, one very long and bad, three of gout, one of erysipelas, etc., etc. I expected to have written at least 400 or 500 pages of my magnum opus,— a general treatise on philosophy which has been slowly maturing in my mind,— but I have written only 32 pages! That tells the whole story. I resigned from my professorship, but they would not accept my resignation, and owing to certain peculiarities in the financial situation of our University just now, I felt myself obliged in honor to remain.

My philosophy is what I call a radical empiricism, a

pluralism, a "tychism," which represents order as being gradually won and always in the making. It is theistic, but not *essentially* so. It rejects all doctrines of the Absolute. It is finitist; but it does not attribute to the question of the Infinite the great methodological importance which you and Renouvier attribute to it. I fear that you may find my system too *bottomless* and romantic. I am sure that, be it in the end judged true or false, it is essential to the evolution of clearness in philosophic thought that *someone* should defend a pluralistic empiricism radically. And all that I fear is that, with the impairment of my working powers from which I suffer, the Angel of Death may overtake me before I can get my thoughts on to paper. Life here in the University consists altogether of *interruptions*.

I thought much of you at the time of Renouvier's death, and I wanted to write; but I let that go, with a thousand other things that had to go. What a life! and what touching and memorable last words were those which M. Pratt published in the "Revue de Métaphysique" — memorable, I mean from the mere fact that the old man could dictate them at all. I have left unread his last publications, except for some parts of the "Monadologie" and the "Personalisme." He will remain a great figure in philosophic history; and the sense of his absence must make a great difference to your consciousness and to that of Madame Pillon. My own wife and children are well. . . . Ever affectionately yours,

WM. JAMES.

To Henry James.

CAMBRIDGE, *June* 28, 1904.

DEAR H.,— I came down from Chocorua yesterday A.M. to go to —

Mrs. Whitman's funeral!

She had lost ground steadily during the winter. The last time I saw her was five weeks ago, when at noon I went up to her studio thinking she might be there. . . . She told me that she was to go on the following day to the Massachusetts General Hospital, for a cure of rest and seclusion. There she died last Friday evening, having improved in her cardiac symptoms, but pneumonia supervening a week ago. It's a great mercy that the end was so unexpectedly quick. What I had feared was a slow deterioration for a year or more to come, with all the nameless misery — peculiarly so in her case — of death by heart disease. As it was, she may be said to have died standing, a thing she always wished to do. She went to every dinner-party and evening party last winter, had an extension, a sort of ball-room, built to her Mount Vernon house, etc. The funeral was beautiful both in Trinity Church and at the grave in Mt. Auburn. I was one of the eight pall-bearers — the others of whom you would hardly know. The flowers and greenery had been arranged in absolutely Whitmanian style by Mrs. Jack Gardner, Mrs. Henry Parkman, and Sally Fairchild. The scene at the grave was *beautiful*. She had no blood relatives, and all Boston — I mean the few whom we know — had gone out, and seemed swayed by an overpowering emotion which abolished all estrangement and self-consciousness. It was the sort of ending that would please her, could she know of it. An extraordinary and indefinable creature! I used often to feel coldly towards her on account of her way of taking people as a great society "business" proceeding, but now that her agitated life of tip-toe reaching in so many directions, of genuinest amiability, is over, pure tenderness asserts its own. Against that dark background of natural annihilation she seems to have been a pathetic little slender worm, writhing and curving blindly through its little day, expending such intensities of consciousness to terminate in that small grave.

She was a most peculiar person. I wish that you had known her whole life here more intimately, and understood its significance. You might then write a worthy article about her. For me, it is impossible to define her. She leaves a dreadful vacuum in Boston. I have often wondered whether I should survive her — and here it has come in the night, without the sound of a footstep, and the same world is here — but without her as its witness. . . .

To Charles Eliot Norton.

CAMBRIDGE, *June* 30, 1904.

DEAR CHARLES,— I have just read the July "Atlantic," and am so moved by your Ruskin letters that I can't refrain from overflowing. They seem to me immortal documents — as the clouds clear away he will surely take his stable place as one of the noblest of the sons of men. Mere sanity is the most philistine and (at bottom) unimportant of a man's attributes. The chief "cloud" is the bulk of "Modern Painters" and the other artistic writings, which have made us take him primarily as an art-connoisseur and critic. Regard all that as inessential, and his inconsistencies and extravagances fall out of sight and leave the Great Heart alone visible.

Do you suppose that there are many other correspondents of R. who will yield up their treasures in our time to the light? I wish that your modesty had not suppressed certain passages which evidently expressed too much regard for yourself. The point should have been *his* expression of that sort of thing — no matter to whom addressed! I understand and sympathize fully with his attitude about our war. Granted him and his date, that is the way he ought to have felt, and I revere him perhaps the more for it. . . .

S. W.'s sudden defection is a pathetic thing! It makes one feel like closing the ranks.

Affectionately — to all of you — including Theodora,

W. J.

To L. T. Hobhouse.

CHOCORUA, *Aug.* 12, 1904.

DEAR BROTHER HOBHOUSE,— Don't you think it a *tant soit peu* scurvy trick to play on me ('t is true that you don't name me, but to the informed reader the reference is transparent — I say nothing of poor Schiller's case) to print in the "Aristotelian Proceedings" (pages 104 *ff.*)[1] a beautiful duplicate of my own theses in the "Will to Believe" essay (which should have been called by the less unlucky title the *Right* to Believe) in the guise of an *alternative and substitute* for my doctrine, for which latter you, in the earlier pages of your charmingly written essay, *substitute a travesty* for which I defy any candid reader to find a single justification in my text? My essay hedged the license to indulge in private over-beliefs with so many restrictions and signboards of danger that the outlet was narrow enough. It made of tolerance the essence of the situation; it defined the permissible cases; it treated the faith-attitude as a necessity for individuals, because the total "evidence," which only the race can draw, has to include their experiments among its data. It tended to show only that faith could not be absolutely *vetoed*, as certain champions of "science" (Clifford, Huxley, etc.) had claimed it ought to be. It was a function that might lead, and probably does lead, into a wider world. You say identically the same things; only, from your special polemic point of view, you emphasize more the dangers;

[1] *Aristotelian Society Proceedings*, vol. IV, pp. 87-110.

while I, from *my* polemic point of view, emphasized more the right to run their risk.

Your essay, granting that emphasis and barring the injustice to me, seems to me exquisite, and, taking it as a unit, I subscribe unreservedly to almost every positive word. — I say "positive," for I doubt whether you have seen enough of the extraordinarily invigorating effect of mind-*cum*-philosophy on certain people to justify your somewhat negative treatment of that subject; and I say "almost" because your distinction between "spurious" and "genuine" courage (page 91) reminds me a bit too much of "true" and "false" freedom, and other sanctimonious come-offs.— Could you not have made an equally sympathetic reading of *me?*

I should n't have cared a copper for the misrepresentation were it not a "summation of stimuli" affair. I have just been reading Bradley on Schiller in the July "Mind," and A. E. Taylor on the Will to Believe in the "McGill Quarterly" of Montreal. Both are vastly worse than you; and I cry to Heaven to tell me of what insane root my "leading contemporaries" have eaten, that they are so smitten with blindness as to the meaning of printed texts. Or are we others absolutely incapable of making our meaning clear?

I imagine that there is neither insane root nor unclear writing, but that in these matters each man writes from out of a field of consciousness of which the bogey in the background is the chief object. Your bogey is superstition; my bogey is desiccation; and each, for his contrast-effect, clutches at any text that can be used to represent the enemy, regardless of exegetical proprieties.

In my essay the evil shape was a vision of "Science" in the form of abstraction, priggishness and sawdust, lording it over all. Take the sterilest scientific prig and cad you know, compare him with the richest religious intellect you know, and you would not, any more than I would, give the former the exclusive right of way. But up to page 104 of your essay he will deem you altogether on his side.

Pardon the familiarity of this epistle. I like and admire your theory of Knowledge so much, and you re-duplicate (I *don't* mean *copy*) my views so beautifully in this article, that I hate to let you go unchidden.

Believe me, with the highest esteem (plus some indignation, for you ought to know better!), Yours faithfully,

WM. JAMES.

To Edwin D. Starbuck

SALISBURY, CONN. *Aug.* 24, 1904.

DEAR STARBUCK,— . . . Of the strictures you make [in your review of my "Varieties"], the first one (undue emphasis on extreme case) is, I find, almost universally made; so it must in some sense be correct. Yet it would never do to study the passion of love on examples of ordinary liking or friendly affection, or that of homicidal pugnacity on examples of our ordinary impatiences with our kind. So here it must be that the extreme examples let us more deeply into the secrets of the religious life, explain why the tamer ones value their religion so much, tame though it be, because it is so continuous with a so much acuter ideal. But I have long been conscious that there is on this matter something to be said which neither my critics have said, nor I can say, and which I must therefore commit to the future.

The second stricture (in your paragraph 4 on pages 104 *ff.*) is of course deeply important, if true. At present I can see but vaguely just what sort of outer relations our inner organism might respond to, which our feelings and intellect interpret by religious thought. You ought to work your program for all it is worth in the way of growth in definiteness. I look forward with great eagerness to your forthcoming book, and meanwhile urge strongly that you should publish the advance article you speak of in Hall's new Journal. I can't see any possible risk. It will objectify a part of your material for you, and possibly, by arousing criticism, enable you to strengthen your points.

Your third stricture, about Higher Powers, is also very important, and I am not at all sure that you may not be right. I have frankly to confess that my "Varieties" carried "theory" as far as I could then carry it, and that I can carry it no farther today. I can't see clearly over that edge. Yet I am sure that tracks have got to be made there — I think that the fixed point with me is the conviction that our "rational" consciousness touches but a portion of the real universe and that our life is fed by the "mystical" region as well. I have no mystical experience of my own, but just enough of the germ of mysticism in me to recognize the region from which their voice comes when I hear it.

I was much disappointed in Leuba's review of my book in the "International Journal of Ethics." . . . I confess that the way in which he stamps out all mysticism whatever, using the common pathological arguments, seemed to me unduly crude. I wrote him an expostulatory letter, which evidently made no impression at all, and which he possibly might send you if you had the curiosity to apply.

I am having a happy summer, feeling quite hearty again. I congratulate you on being settled, though I know nothing of the place. I congratulate you and Mrs. Starbuck also on airy fairy Lilian, who makes, I believe, the third. Long may they live and make their parents proud. With best regards to you both, I am yours ever truly,

WM. JAMES.

The "expostulatory" letter to Professor Leuba began with a series of objections to statements which he had made, and continued with the passage which follows.

To James Henry Leuba.

CAMBRIDGE, *Apr.* 17, 1904.

. . . My personal position is simple. I have no living sense of commerce with a God. I envy those who have, for I know the addition of such a sense would help me immensely. The Divine, for my *active* life, is limited to abstract concepts which, as ideals, interest and determine me, but do so but faintly, in comparison with what a feeling of God might effect, if I had one. It is largely a question of intensity, but differences of intensity may make one's whole centre of energy shift. Now, although I am so devoid of *Gottesbewustsein* in the directer and stronger sense, yet there is *something in me* which *makes response* when I hear utterances made from that lead by others. I recognize the deeper voice. Something tells me, "*thither lies truth*" — and I am *sure* it is not old theistic habits and prejudices of infancy. Those are Christian; and I have grown so out of Christianity that entanglement therewith on the part of a mystical utterance has to be abstracted from and overcome, before I can listen. Call this, if you like, my mystical *germ*. It is a very common germ. It creates the rank and file of believers. As it withstands in my case, so it will withstand in most cases, all purely atheistic criticism, but *interpretative* criticism (not of the mere "hysteria" and "nerves" order) it can energetically combine with. Your criticism seems to amount to a pure *non possumus:* "Mystical deliverances must be infallible revelations in every particular, or nothing. Therefore they are *nothing*, for anyone else than their owner." Why may they not be *some*thing, although not everything?

Your only consistent position, it strikes me, would be a dogmatic atheistic naturalism; and, without any mystical germ in us, that, I believe, is where we all should *unhesitatingly* be today.

Once allow the mystical germ to influence our beliefs, and I believe that we are in my position. Of course the "subliminal" theory is an inessential hypothesis, and the question of pluralism or monism is equally inessential.

I am letting loose a deluge on you! Don't reply at length, or at all. *I* hate to reply to anybody, and will sympathize with your silence. But I had to restate my position more clearly. Yours truly,

WM. JAMES.

The following document is not a letter, but a series of answers to a questionnaire upon the subject of religious belief, which was sent out in 1904 by Professor James B. Pratt of Williams College, and to which James filled out a reply at an unascertained date in the autumn of that year.

QUESTIONNAIRE [1]

It is being realized as never before that religion, as one of the most important things in the life both of the community and of the individual, deserves close and extended study. Such study can be of value only if based upon the personal experiences of many individuals. If you are in sympathy with such study and are willing to assist in it, will you kindly write out the answers to the following questions and return them with this questionnaire, as soon as you conveniently can, to JAMES B. PRATT, 20 Shepard Street, Cambridge, Mass.

Please answer the questions at length and in detail. Do not give philosophical generalizations, but your own personal experience.

[1] James's answers are printed in italics.

1. What does religion mean to you personally? Is it
   (1) A belief that something exists? *Yes.*
   (2) An emotional experience? *Not powerfully so, yet a social reality.*
   (3) A general attitude of the will toward God or toward righteousness! *It involves these.*
   (4) Or something else?

If it has several elements, which is for you the most important? *The social appeal for corroboration, consolation, etc., when things are going wrong with my causes (my truth denied), etc.*

2. What do you mean by God? *A combination of Ideality and (final) efficacity.*
   (1) Is He a person — if so, what do you mean by His being a person? *He must be cognizant and responsive in some way.*
   (2) Or is He only a Force? *He must do.*
   (3) Or is God an attitude of the Universe toward you? *Yes, but more conscious. "God," to me, is not the only spiritual reality to believe in. Religion means primarily a universe of spiritual relations surrounding the earthly practical ones, not merely relations of "value," but agencies and their activities. I suppose that the chief premise for my hospitality towards the religious testimony of others is my conviction that "normal" or "sane" consciousness is so small a part of actual experience. What e'er be true, it is not true exclusively, as philistine scientific opinion assumes. The other kinds of consciousness bear witness to a much wider universe of experiences, from which our belief selects and emphasizes such parts as best satisfy our needs.*

How do you apprehend his relation to mankind and to you personally?

If your position on any of these matters is uncertain, please state the fact. ⎱ *Uncertain.*

3. Why do you believe in God? Is it
   (1) From some argument? *Emphatically, no.*
   Or (2) Because you have experienced His presence? *No, but rather because I need it so that it "must" be true.*
   Or (3) From authority, such as that of the Bible or of some prophetic person? *Only the whole tradition of religious people, to which something in me makes admiring response.*
   Or (4) From any other reason? *Only for the social reasons.*

If from several of these reasons, please indicate carefully the order of their importance.

4. Or do you not so much *believe* in God as want to *use* Him? *I can't use him very definitely, yet I believe.* Do you accept Him not so much as a real existent Being, but rather as an ideal to live by? *More as a more powerful ally of my own ideals.* If you should become thoroughly convinced that there was no God, would it make any great difference in your life — either in happiness, morality, or in other respects? *Hard to say. It would surely make some difference.*

5. Is God very real to you, as real as an earthly friend, though different? *Dimly [real]; not [as an earthly friend].*

Do you feel that you have experienced His presence? If so, please describe what you mean by such an experience. *Never.*

How vague or how distinct is it? How does it affect you mentally and physically?

If you have had no such experience, do you accept the testimony of others who claim to have felt God's presence directly? Please answer this question with special care and in as great detail as possible. *Yes! The whole line of testimony on this point is so strong that I am unable to pooh-pooh it away. No doubt there is a germ in me of something similar that makes response.*

6. Do you pray, and if so, why? That is, is it purely from habit, and social custom, or do you really believe that God hears your prayers? *I can't possibly pray — I feel foolish and artificial.*

Is prayer with you one-sided or two-sided — *i.e.*, do you sometimes feel that in prayer you receive something — such as strength or the divine spirit — from God? Is it a real communion?

7. What do you mean by "spirituality"? *Susceptibility to ideals, but with a certain freedom to indulge in imagination about them. A certain amount of "other worldly" fancy. Otherwise you have mere morality, or "taste."*

Describe a typical spiritual person. *Phillips Brooks.*

8. Do you believe in personal immortality? *Never keenly; but more strongly as I grow older.* If so, why? *Because I am just getting fit to live.*

9. Do you accept the Bible as *authority* in religious matters? Are your religious faith and your religious life based on it? If so, how would your belief in God and your life toward Him and your fellow men be affected by loss of faith in the *authority* of the

Bible? No. No. No. It is so human a book that I don't see how belief in its divine authorship can survive the reading of it.

10. What do you mean by a "religious experience"? Any moment of life that brings the reality of spiritual things more "home" to one.

To Miss Pauline Goldmark.

CHOCORUA, *Sept.* 21, 1904.

DEAR PAULINE,— Alice went off this morning to Cambridge, to get the house ready for the advent of the rest of us a week hence — viz., Wednesday the 28th. Having breakfasted at 6:30 to bid her God speed, the weather was so lordly fine (after a heavy rain in the night) that I trudged across lots to our hill-top, which you never saw, and now lie there with my back against a stone, scribbling you these lines at half-past nine. The vacation has run down with an appalling rapidity, but all has gone well with us, and I have been extraordinarily well and happy, and mean to be a good boy all next winter, to say nothing of remoter futures. My brother Henry stayed a delightful fortnight, and seemed to enjoy nature here intensely — found so much *sentiment* and feminine delicacy in it all. It is a pleasure to be with anyone who takes in things through the eyes. Most people don't. The two "savans" who were here noticed *absolutely nothing*, though they had never been in America before.

Naturally I have wondered what things your eyes have been falling on. Many views from hill-tops? Many magic dells and brooks? I hope so, and that it has all done you endless good. Such a green and gold and scarlet morn as this would raise the dead. I hope that your sister Susan has also got great good from the summer, and that the fair Josephine is glad to be at home again, and your mother reconciled to losing you. Perhaps even now you are pre-

paring to go down. I have only written as a *Lebenszeichen*
and to tell you of our dates. I expect no reply, till you
write a word to say when you are to come to Boston. Un-
happily we can't ask you to Irving St.,being mortgaged three
deep to foreigners. Ever yours,

W. J.

It will be recalled that the St. Louis Exposition had occurred shortly before the date of the last letter and had led
a number of learned and scientific associations to hold international congresses in America. James kept away from
St. Louis, but asked several foreign colleagues to visit him
at Chocorua or in Cambridge before their return to Europe.
Among them were Dr. Pierre Janet of Paris and his wife,
Professor C. Lloyd Morgan of Bristol, and Professor Harold
Höffding of Copenhagen.

To F. C. S. Schiller.
CAMBRIDGE, *Oct.* 26, 1904.

DEAR SCHILLER,— . . . Last night the Janets left us — a
few days previous, Lloyd Morgan. I am glad to possess
my soul for a while alone. Make much of dear old Höffding,
who is a good pluralist and irrationalist. I took to him immensely and so did everybody. Lecturing to my class, he
told against the Absolutists an anecdote of an "American"
child who asked his mother if God made the world in six
days. "Yes." — "The whole of it?" — "Yes."— "Then it
is finished, all done?" — "Yes."— "Then in what business
now is God?" If he tells it in Oxford you must reply:
"Sitting for his portrait to Royce, Bradley, and Taylor."

Don't return the "McGill Quarterly"! — I have another
copy. Good-bye!

W. J.

To F. J. E. Woodbridge.

CAMBRIDGE, *Feb.* 6, 1905.

DEAR WOODBRIDGE,— I appear to be growing into a graphomaniac. Truth boils over from my organism as muddy water from a Yellowstone Geyser. Here is another contribution to my radical empiricism, which I send hot on the heels of the last one. I promise that, with the possible exception of one post-scriptual thing, not more than eight pages of MS. long, I shall do no more writing this academic year. So if you accept this,[1] you have not much more to fear. . . . I think, on the whole, that though the present article directly hitches on to the last words of my last article, "The Thing and Its Relations," the article called the "Essence of Humanism" had better appear before it. . . . Always truly yours

WM. JAMES.

To Edwin D. Starbuck.

CAMBRIDGE, *Feb.* 12, 1905.

DEAR STARBUCK,— I have read your article in No. 2 of Hall's Journal with great interest and profit. It makes me eager for the book, but pray take great care of your style in that — it seems to me that this article is less well written than your "Psychology of Religion" was, less clear, more involved, more technical in language — probably the result of rapidity. Our American philosophic literature is dreadful from a literary point of view. Pierre Janet told me he thought it was much worse than German stuff — and I begin to believe so; technical and semi-technical language, half-clear thought, fluency, and no composition! Turn your face resolutely the other way! But I did n't start to

---

[1] "How Two Minds Can Know One Thing," *Journal of Philosophy, Psychology, and Scientific Methods*, 1905, vol. II, p. 176.

say this.   Your thought in this article is both important and original, and ought to be worked out in the clearest possible manner. . . . Your thesis needs to be worked out with great care, and as concretely as possible.   It is a difficult one to put successfully, on account of the vague character of all its terms.   One point you should drive home is that the anti-religious attitudes (Leuba's, Huxley's, Clifford's), so far as there is any "pathos" in them, obey exactly the same logic.   The real crux is when you come to define objectively the ideals to which feeling reacts.   "God is a Spirit" — *darauf geht es an* — on the last available definition of the term Spirit.   It may be very abstract.

Love to Mrs. Starbuck.   Yours always truly,

WM. JAMES.

To F. J. E. Woodbridge.

[*Feb.* 22, 1905.]

DEAR WOODBRIDGE,— Here's another!   But I solemnly swear to you that this shall be my very last offense for some months to come.   This is the "postscriptual" article [1] of which I recently wrote you, and I have now cleaned up the pure-experience philosophy from all the objections immediately in sight. . . . Truly yours,

WM. JAMES.

[1] "Is Radical Empiricism Solipsistic?" *Journal of Philosophy, Psychology; and Scientific Methods*, 1905, vol. II, p. 235.

XV

The Last Period (II) — Italy and Greece — Philosophical
Congress in Rome — Stanford University — The
Earthquake — Resignation of Professorship

In the spring of 1905 an escape from influenza, from Cambridge duties, and from correspondents, became impera-
tive. James had long wanted to see Athens with his own
eyes, and he sailed on April 3 for a short southern holiday.
During the journey he wrote letters to almost no one except
his wife. On his way back from Athens he stopped in Rome
with the purpose of seeing certain young Italian philosophers. A Philosophical Congress was being held there at
the time; and James, though he had originally declined the
invitation to attend it, inevitably became involved in its
proceedings and ended by seizing the occasion to discuss his
theory of consciousness. It was obvious that the appro-
priate language in which to address a full meeting of the
Congress would be French, and so he shut himself up in
his hotel and composed "La Notion de Conscience." His
experience in writing this paper threw an instructive side-
light on his process of composition. Ordinarily — when he
was writing in English — twenty-five sheets of manuscript,
written in a large hand and corrected, were a maximum
achievement for one day. The address in Rome was not
composed in English and then translated, but was written
out in French. When he had finished the last lines of one
day's work, James found to his astonishment that he had
completed and corrected over forty pages of manuscript.

The inhibitions which a habit of careful attention to points of style ordinarily called into play were largely inoperative when he wrote in a language which presented to his mind a smaller variety of possible expressions, and thus imposed limits upon his self-criticism.

In the following year (1906), James took leave of absence from Harvard in January and accepted an invitation from Stanford University to give a course during its spring term. He planned the course as a general introduction to Philosophy. Had he not been interrupted by the San Francisco earthquake, he would have rehearsed much of the projected "Introductory Textbook of Philosophy," in which he meant to outline his metaphysical system. But the earthquake put an end to the Stanford lectures in April, as the reader will learn more fully. In the ensuing autumn and winter (1907), James made the same material the basis of a half-year's work with his last Harvard class.

In November, 1906, the lectures which compose the volume called "Pragmatism" were written out and delivered in November at the Lowell Institute in Boston. In January, 1907, they were repeated at Columbia University, and then James published them in the spring.

The time had now come for him to stop regular teaching altogether. He had been continuing to teach, partly in deference to the wishes of the College; but it had become evident that he must have complete freedom to use his strength and time for writing when he could write, for special lectures, like the series on Pragmatism, when such might serve his ends, and for rest and change when recuperation became necessary. So, in February, 1907, he sent his resignation to the Harvard Corporation. The last meeting of his class ended in a way for which he was quite unprepared. His undergraduate students presented him with a silver loving-cup, the graduate students and assistants with an inkwell. There were a couple of short speeches, and words were spoken by which he was very much moved. Unfortunately there was no record of what was said.

To Mrs. James.

AMALFI, *Mar.* 30, 1905.

. . . It is good to get something in full measure, without haggling or stint, and today I have had the picturesque ladled out in buckets full, heaped up and running over. I never realized the beauties of this shore, and forget (in my habit of never noticing proper names till I have been there) whether you have ever told me of the drive from Sorrento to this place. Anyhow, I wish that you could have taken it with me this day. "Thank God for this day!" We came to Sorrento by steamer, and at 10:30 got away in a carriage, lunching at the half-way village of Positano; and proceeding through Amalfi to Ravello, high up on the mountain side, whence back here in time for a 7:15 o'clock dinner. Practically six hours driving through a scenery of which I had never realized the beauty, or rather the interest, from previous descriptions. The lime-stone mountains are as *strong* as anything in Switzerland, though of course much smaller. The road, a *Cornice* affair cut for the most part on the face of cliffs, and crossing little ravines (with beaches) on the side of which nestle hamlets, is positively ferocious in its grandeur, and on the side of it the azure sea, dreaming and blooming like a bed of violets. I did n't look for such Swiss strength, having heard of naught but beauty. It seems as if this were a race such that, when anyone wished to express an emotion of any kind, he went and built a bit of stone-wall and limed it onto the rock, so that now, when they have accumulated, the works of God and man are inextricably mixed, and it is as if mankind had been a kind of immemorial coral insect. Every possible square yard is terraced up, reclaimed and planted, and the human dwellings are the fiercest examples of cliff-building, cave-habitation, staircase and footpath you can imagine. How I do wish that you could have been along today. . . .

Mar. 31, 1905.

From half-past four to half-past six I walked alone through the *old* Naples, hilly streets, paved from house to house and swarming with the very poor, vocal with them too (their voices carry so that every child seems to be calling to the whole street, goats, donkeys, chickens, and an occasional cow mixed in), and no light of heaven getting indoors. The street floor composed of cave-like shops, the people doing their work on chairs in the street for the sake of light, and in the black inside, beds and a stove visible among the implements of trade. Such light and shade, and grease and grime, and swarm, and apparent amiability would be hard to match. I have come here too late in life, when the picturesque has lost its serious reality. Time was when hunger for it haunted me like a passion, and such sights would have then been the solidest of mental food. I put up then with such inferior substitutional suggestions as Geneva and Paris afforded — but these black old Naples streets are not suggestions, they are the reality itself — full orchestra. I have got such an impression of the essential sociability of this race, especially in the country. A smile will go so far with them — even without the accompanying copper. And the children are so sweet. Tell Aleck to drop his other studies, learn *Italian* (real Italian, not the awful gibberish I try to speak), cultivate his beautiful smile, learn a sentimental song or two, bring a tambourine or banjo, and come down here and fraternize with the common people along the coast — he can go far, and make friends, and be a social success, even if he should go back to a clean hotel of some sort for sleep every night. . . .

To his Daughter.

On board S. S. Orénogne, approaching
PIRÆUS, GREECE, *Apr.* 3, 1905.

DARLING PEG,— Your loving Dad is surely in luck sailing over this almost oily sea, under the awning on deck, past the coast of Greece (whose snow-capped mountains can be seen on the horizon), towards the Piræus, where we are due to arrive at about two. I had some misgivings about the steamer from Marseilles, but she has turned out splendid, and the voyage perfect. A 4000-ton boat, bran new as to all her surface equipment, stateroom all to myself, by a happy stroke of luck (the boat being full), clean absolutely, large open window, sea like Lake Champlain, with the color of Lake Leman, about a hundred and twenty first-class passengers of the most interesting description, one sixth English archeologists, one sixth English tourists, one third French archeologists, etc.,— an international archeological congress opens at Athens this week,— the rest Dagoes *quelconques*, many distinguished men, almost all educated and pronounced individualities, and so much acquaintance and sociability, that the somewhat small upper deck on which I write resounds with conversation like an afternoon tea. The meals are tip-top, and the whole thing almost absurdly ideal in its kind. I only wish your mother could be wafted here for one hour, to sit by my side and enjoy the scene. The best feature of the boat is little Miss Boyd, the Cretan excavatress, from Smith College, a perfect little trump of a thing, who has been through the Greco-Turkish war as nurse (as well as being nurse at Tampa during our Cuban war), and is the simplest, most generally intelligent little thing, who knows Greece by heart and can smooth one's path beautifully. Waldstein of Cambridge is on board, also M. Sylvain of the Théâtre Français, and his daughter — going to recite prologues or something at the representation of Sophocles's "Antigone," which is to take place — he looking just like your uncle Henry — both eminent comedians — I mean the two Sylvains. On the bench opposite me is the most beautiful woman on board, a sort of Mary Salter translated into French, though she is with rather common men. Well, now I will stop, and use my Zeiss glass on the land, which is getting nearer. My heart wells over with love and gratitude at having such a family — meaning Alice, you, Harry, Bill, Aleck, and Mother-in-law — and resolutions to live so as to be more worthy of them. I will finish this on land.

Well, dear family,— We got in duly in an indescribable *embrouillement* of small boats (our boatman, by the way, when Miss Boyd asked him his name, replied "Dionysos"; our wine-bottle was labelled "John Solon and Co."), sailing past the Island of Ægina and the Bay of Salamis, with the Parthenon visible ahead — a worthy termination to a delightful voyage. We drove the three miles from the Piræus in a carriage, common and very dusty country road, also close by the Parthenon, through the cheap little town to this hotel, after which George Putnam and I, washing our hands, strolled forth to see what we could, the first thing being Mrs. Sam Hoar at the theatre of Bacchus. Then the rest of the Acropolis, which is all and more than all the talk. There is a mystery of *rightness* about that Parthenon that I cannot understand. It sets a standard for other human things, showing that absolute rightness is not out of reach. But I am not in descriptive mood, so I spare you. Suffice it that I could n't keep the tears from welling into my eyes. "J'ai vu la beauté parfaite." Santayana is in a neighboring hotel, but we have missed each other thrice. The Forbeses are on the Peloponnesus, but expected back tomorrow. Well, dear ones all, good-night! Thus far, and no farther! Hence I turn westward again. The Greek lower orders seem far less avid and rapacious than the Southern Italians. God bless you all. I must get to another hotel, and be more to myself. Good and dear as the Putnams are and extremely helpful as they 've been, it keeps me too much in company. Good-night again.

Your loving father, *respective* husband,

W. J.

To Mrs. James.

ROME, *Apr.* 25, 1905.

. . . Strong telegraphed me yesterday from Lausanne that he . . . expected to be at Cannes on the 4th of May. I was glad of this, for I had been feeling more and more as if I ought to stay here, and it makes everything square out well. This morning I went to the meeting-place of the Congress to inscribe myself definitely, and when I gave my name, the lady who was taking them almost fainted, saying that all Italy loved me, or words to that effect, and called in poor Professor de Sanctis, the Vice President or Secretary or whatever, who treated me in the same manner, and finally got me to consent to make an address at one of the general meetings, of which there are four, in place of Sully, Flournoy, Richet, Lipps, and Brentano, who were announced but are not to come. I fancy they have been pretty unscrupulous with their program here, printing conditional futures as categorical ones. So I 'm in for it again, having no power to resist flattery. I shall try to express my "Does Consciousness Exist?" in twenty minutes — and possibly in the French tongue! Strange after the deep sense of nothingness that has been besetting me the last two weeks (mere fatigue symptom) to be told that *my* name was attracting many of the young professors to the Congress!

Then I went to the Museum in the baths of Diocletian or whatever it is, off there by the R. R., then to the Capitol, and then to lunch off the Corso, at a restaurant, after buying a French book whose author says in his preface that Sully, W. J., and Bergson are his masters. And I am absolute O in my own home! . . .

Apr. 30, 1905. 7 P.M.

. . . If you never had a tired husband, at least you 've got one now! The *ideer* of being in such delightful conditions and interesting surroundings, and being conscious of nothing but one's preposterous physical distress, is too ridiculous! I have just said good-bye to my circle of admirers, relatively youthful, at the hotel door, under the pretext (a truth until this morning) that I had to get ready to go to Lausanne tonight, and I taper off my activity by subsiding upon you. Yesterday till three, and the day before till five, I was writing my address, which this morning I gave — in French. I wrote it carefully and surprised myself by the ease with which I slung the Gallic accent and intonation, being excited by the occasion.[1] Janet expressed himself as *stupéfait*, from the linguistic point of view. The thing lasted 40 minutes, and was followed by a discussion which showed that the critics with one exception had wholly failed to catch the point of view; but that was quite *en régle*, so I don't care; and I have given the thing to Clapa-

---

[1] This address, "La Notion de Conscience," was printed first in the *Archives de Psychologie*, 1905, vol. v, p. 1. It will also be found in the *Essays in Radical Empiricism*.

rède to print in Flournoy's "Archives." The Congress was far too vast, but filled with strange and interesting creatures of all sorts, and socially *very* nutritious to anyone who can stand sociability without distress. A fête of some sort every day — this P.M. I have just returned from a great afternoon tea given us by some "Minister" at the Borghese Palace — in the Museum. (The King, you know, has bought the splendid Borghese park and given it to the City of Rome as a democratic possession *in perpetuo*. A splendid gift.) The pictures too! Tonight there is a great banquet with speeches, to which of course I can't go. I lunched at the da Vitis,— a big table full, she very simple and nice,— and I have been having this afternoon a very good and rather intimate talk with the little band of "pragmatists," Papini, Vailati, Calderoni, Amendola, etc., most of whom inhabit Florence, publish the monthly journal "Leonardo" at their own expense, and carry on a very serious philosophic movement, apparently *really* inspired by Schiller and myself (I never could believe it before, although Ferrari had assured me), and show an enthusiasm, and also a literary swing and activity that I know nothing of in our own land, and that probably our damned academic technics and Ph.D.-machinery and university organization prevents from ever coming to a birth. These men, of whom Ferrari is one, are none of them *Fach-philosophers*, and few of them teachers at all. It has given me a certain new idea of the way in which truth ought to find its way into the world.

I have seen such a lot of *important*-looking faces,— probably everything in the stock in the shop-window,— and witnessed such charmingly gracious manners, that it is a lesson. The woodenness of our Anglo-Saxon social ways! I had a really splendid audience for quality this A.M. (about 200), even though they did n't understand. . . .

To George Santayana.

ORVIETO, *May* 2, 1905.

DEAR SANTAYANA,— I came here yesterday from Rome and have been enjoying the solitude. I stayed at the exquisite Albergo de Russie, and did n't shirk the Congress — in fact they stuck me for a "general" address, to fill the vacuum left by Flournoy and Sully, who had been announced and came not (I spoke *agin* "consciousness," but nobody understood) and I got *fearfully tired.* On the whole it was an agreeable nightmare — agreeable on account of the perfectly charming *gentillezza* of the bloody Dagoes, the way they caress and flatter you — "il piu grand psicologo del mondo," etc., and of the elaborate provisions for general entertainment — nightmare, because of my absurd bodily fatigue. However, these things are "neither here nor there." What I really write to you for is to tell you to send (if not sent already) your "Life of Reason" to the "Revue de Philosophie," or rather to its editor, M. Peillaube, Rue des Revues 160, and to the editor of "Leonardo" (the great little Florentine philosophical journal), Sig. Giovanni Papini, 14 Borgo Albizi, Florence. The most interesting, and in fact genuinely edifying, part of my trip has been meeting this little *cénacle*, who have taken my own writings, *entre autres, au grand sérieux,* but who are carrying on their philosophical mission in anything but a technically serious way, inasmuch as "Leonardo" (of which I have hitherto only known a few odd numbers) is devoted to good and lively literary form. The sight of their belligerent young enthusiasm has given me a queer sense of the gray-plaster temperament of our bald-headed young Ph.D.'s, boring each other at seminaries, writing those direful reports of literature in the "Philosophical Review" and elsewhere, fed on "books of reference," and never confounding "Æsthetik" with "Erkentnisstheorie." Faugh! I shall never deal with them again — on *those* terms! Can't you and I, who in spite of such divergence have yet so much in common in our *Weltanschauung*, start a systematic movement at Harvard against the desiccating and pedantifying process? I have been cracking you up greatly to both Peillaube and Papini, and quoted you twice in my speech, which was in French and will be published in Flournoy's "Archives de Psychologie." I hope you're enjoying the Eastern Empire to the full, and that you had some Grecian "country life." Münsterberg has been called to Koenigsberg and has refused. Better be America's ancestor than Kant's successor! Ostwald, to my great delight, is coming to us next year, not as your replacer, but in exchange with Germany for F. G. Peabody. I go now to Cannes, to meet Strong, back from his operation. Ever truly yours,

WM. JAMES.

To Mrs. James.

CANNES, *May* 13, 1905.

. . . I came Sunday night, and this is Saturday. The six days have been busy ones in one sense, but have rested me very much in another. No sight-seeing fatigues, but more usual, and therefore more normal occupations. . . . I have written some 25 letters, long and short, to European correspondents since being here, have walked and driven with Strong, and have had philosophy hot and heavy with him almost all the time. I never knew such an unremitting, untiring, monotonous addiction as that of his mind to truth. He goes by points, pinning each one definitely, and has, I think, the very clearest mind I ever knew. Add to it his absolute sincerity and candor and it is no wonder that he is a "growing" man. I suspect that he will outgrow us all, for his rate accelerates, and he never stands still. He is an admirable philosophic figure, and I am glad to say that in most things he and I are fully in accord. He gains a great deal from such talks, noting every point down afterwards, and I gain great stimulation, though in a vaguer way. I shall be glad, however, on Monday afternoon, to relax. . . .

To Mrs. James.

[Post-card]

GENEVA, *May* 17, 1905.

So far, thank Heaven, on my way towards home! A rather useful time with the superior, but sticky X——, at Marseilles, and as far as Lyons in the train, into which an hour beyond Lyons there came (till then I was alone in my compartment) a Spanish bishop, canon and "familar," an aged holy woman, sister of the bishop, a lay-brother and sister, a dog, and more baggage than I ever saw before, including a feather-bed. They spoke no French — the bishop about as much Italian as I, and the lay-sister as much of English as I of Spanish. They took out their rosaries and began mumbling their litanies forthwith, whereon I took off my hat, which seemed to touch them so, when they discovered I was a Protestant, that we all grew very affectionate and I soon felt ashamed of the way in which I had at first regarded their black and superstitious invasion of my privacy. Good, saintly people on their way to Rome. I go now to our old haunts and to the Flournoys'. . . .

W.

To H. G. Wells.

S. S. CEDRIC, *June* 6, 1905.

MY DEAR MR. WELLS,— I have just read your "Utopia" (given me by F. C. S. Schiller on the one day that I spent in Oxford on my way back to Cambridge, Mass., after a few weeks on the Continent), and "Anticipations," and "Mankind in the Making" having duly preceded, together with numerous other lighter volumes of yours, the "summation of stimuli" reaches the threshold of discharge and I can't help overflowing in a note of gratitude. You "have your faults, as who has not?" but your virtues are unparalleled and transcendent, and I believe that you will prove to have given a shove to the practical thought of the next generation that will be amongst the greatest of its influences for good. All in the line of the English genius too, no wire-drawn French doctrines, and no German shop technicalities inflicted in an *unerbittlich consequent* manner, but everywhere the sense of the full concrete, and the air of freedom playing through all the joints of your argument. You have a tri-dimensional human heart, and to use your own metaphor, don't see different levels projected on one plane. In this last book you beautifully soften cocksureness by the penumbra of the outlines — in fact you 're a trump and a jewel, and for human perception you beat Kipling, and for hitting off a thing with the right word, you are unique. Heaven bless and preserve you! — You are now an eccentric; perhaps 50 years hence you will figure as a classic! Your Samurai chapter is magnificent, though I find myself wondering what developments in the way of partisan politics those same Samurai would develop, when it came to questions of appointment and running this or that man in. *That* I believe to be human nature's ruling passion. Live long! and keep writing; and believe me, yours admiringly and sincerely,

WM. JAMES.

To Henry L. Higginson.

CAMBRIDGE, *July* 18 [1905].

DEAR H.,— You asked me how rich I was getting by my own (as distinguished from *your*) exertions. . . .

I find on reaching home today a letter from Longmans, Green & Co. with a check . . . which I have mailed to your house in State Street. . . .

This ought to please you slightly; but don't reply! Instead, think of the virtues of Roosevelt, either as permanent sovereign of this great country, or as President of Harvard University. I've been having a discussion with Fanny Morse about him, which has resulted in making me his faithful henchman for life, Fanny was so violent. Think of the mighty good-will of him, of his enjoyment of his post, of his power as a preacher, of the number of things to which he gives his attention, of the safety of his second thoughts, of the increased courage he is showing, and above all of the fact that he is an open, instead of an underground leader, whom the voters can control once in four years, when he runs away, whose heart is in the right place, who is an enemy of red tape and quibbling and everything that in general the word "politician" stands for. That significance of him in the popular mind is a great national asset, and it would be a shame to let it run to waste until it has done a lot more work for us. His ambitions are not selfish — he wants to do good only! Bless him — and damn all his detractors like you and F. M.! [1]

Don't reply, but vote! Your affectionately

WM. JAMES.

To T. S. Perry.

CAMBRIDGE, *Aug.* 24, 1905.

DEAR THOS! — You're a *philosophe sans le savoir* and, when you write your treatise against philosophy, you will be classed as the arch-metaphysician. Every philosopher

[1] "My own desire to see Roosevelt president here for a limited term of years was quenched by a speech he made at the Harvard Union a couple of years ago." (To D. S. Miller, Jan. 2, 1908.)

(W. J., *e.g.*) pretends that all the others are metaphysicians against whom he is simply defending the rights of common sense. As for Nietzsche, the worst break of his I recall was in a posthumous article in one of the French reviews a few months back. In his high and mighty way he was laying down the law about all the European countries. Russia, he said, is "the only one that has any possible future — and that she owes to the strength of the principle of autocracy to which she alone remains faithful." Unfortunately one can't appeal to the principle of democracy to explain Japan's recent successes.

I am very glad you 've done something about poor dear old John Fiske, and I should think that you would have no difficulty in swelling it up to the full "Beacon Biography" size. If you want an extra anecdote, you might tell how, when Chauncey Wright, Chas. Peirce, St. John Green, Warner and I appointed an evening to discuss the "Cosmic Philosophy," just out, J. F. went to sleep under our noses.

I hope that life as a farmer agrees with you, and that your "womenkind" wish nothing better than to be farmers' wives, daughters or other relatives. Unluckily we let our farm this summer; so I am here in Cambridge with Alice, both of us a prey to as bad an attack of grippe as the winter solstice ever brought forth. Today, the 10th day, I am weaker than any kitten. Don't ever let *your* farm! Affectionately,

W. J.

To Dickinson S. Miller.

CAMBRIDGE, *Nov.* 10, 1905.

DEAR MILLER,— W. R. Warren has just been here and says he has just seen you; the which precipitates me into a letter to you which has long hung fire. I hope that all goes

well. You must be in a rather cheerful quarter of the City.
Do you go home Sundays, or not? I hope that the work is
congenial. How do you like your students as compared
with those here? I reckon you get more out of your colleagues than you did here — barring of course *der Einzige*.
We are all such old stories to each other that we say nothing.
Santayana is the only [one] about whom we had any curiosity, and he has now quenched that. Perry and Holt
have some ideas in reserve. . . . The fact is that the class-
room exhausts our powers of speech. Royce has never
made a syllable of reference to all the stuff I wrote last
year — to me, I mean. He may have spoken of it to others,
if he has read. it, which I doubt. So we live in parallel
trenches and hardly show our heads.

Santayana's book [1] is a great one, if the inclusion of op-
posites is a measure of greatness. I think it will probably
be reckoned great by posterity. It has no *rational* foundation, being merely one man's way of viewing things: so much
of experience admitted and no more, so much criticism and
questioning admitted and no more. He is a paragon of
Emersonianism — declare your intuitions, though no other
man share them; and the integrity with which he does it
is as fine as it is rare. And his naturalism, materialism,
Platonism, and atheism form a combination of which the
centre of gravity is, I think, very deep. But there is something profoundly alienating in his unsympathetic tone, his
"preciousness" and superciliousness. The book is Emerson's first rival and successor, but how different the reader's
feeling! The same things in Emerson's mouth would sound
entirely different. E. receptive, expansive, as if handling
life through a wide funnel with a great indraught; S. as if
through a pin-point orifice that emits his cooling spray out-

---

[1] *The Life of Reason.* New York, 1905.

ward over the universe like a nose-disinfectant from an "atomizer." . . . I fear that the real originality of the book will be lost on nineteen-twentieths of the members of the Philosophical and Psychological Association!! The enemies of Harvard will find lots of blasphemous texts in him to injure us withal. But it is a great feather in our cap to harbor such an absolutely free expresser of individual convictions. But enough!

"Phil. 9" is going well. I think I *lecture* better than I ever did; in fact I know I do. But this professional evolution goes with an involution of all miscellaneous faculty. I am well, and efficient enough, but purposely going slow so as to keep efficient into the Palo Alto summer, which means that I have written nothing. I am pestered by doubts as to whether to put my resignation through this year, in spite of opposition, or to drag along another year or two. I think it is inertia against energy, energy in my case meaning being my own man absolutely. American philosophers, young and old, seem scratching where the wool is short. Important things are being published; but all of them too technical. The thing will never clear up satisfactorily till someone writes out its resultant in decent English. . . .

The reader will have understood "the Palo Alto summer" to refer to the lectures to be delivered at Stanford University during the coming spring. The Stanford engagement was again in James's mind when he spoke, in the next letter, of "dreading the prospect of lecturing till mid-May."

To Dickinson S. Miller.

CAMBRIDGE, *Dec.* 6, 1905.

DEAR MILLER,— . . . You seem to take radical empiricism more simply than I can. What I mean by it is the thesis that there is no fact "not actually experienced to be such." In other words, the concept of "being" or "fact" is not wider than or prior to the concept "content of experience"; and you can't talk of *experiences being* this or that, but only of *things experienced as being* this or that. But such a thesis would, it seems to me, if literally taken, force one to drop the notion that in point of fact one experience is *ex* another, so long as the *ex*-ness is not itself a "content" of experience. In the matter of two minds not having the same content, it seems to me that your view commits you to an assertion *about their experiences;* and such an assertion assumes a realm in which the experiences lie, which overlaps and surrounds the "content" of them. This, it seems to me, breaks down radical empiricism, which I hate to do; and I can't yet clearly see my way out of the quandary. I am much boggled and muddled; and the total upshot with me is to see that all the hoary errors and prejudices of man in matters philosophical are based on something pretty inevitable in the structure of our thinking, and to distrust summary executions by conviction of contradiction. I suspect your execution of being too summary; but I have copied the last paragraph of the sheets (which I return with heartiest thanks) for the extraordinarily neat statement. . . .

I dread the prospect of lecturing till mid-May, but the wine being ordered, I must drink it. I dislike lecturing more and more. Have just definitely withdrawn my candidacy for the Sorbonne job, with great internal relief, and wish I could withdraw from the whole business, and get at writing.[1] Not a line of writing possible this year — except of course occasional note-making. All the things that one is

[1] He had been "sounded" regarding an appointment as Harvard Exchange Lecturer at the Sorbonne, and had at first been inclined to accept.

really concerned with are too nice and fine to use in lectures. You remember the definition of T. H. Greene's student: "The universe is a thick complexus of intelligible relations." Yesterday I got *my* system similarly defined in an examination-book, by a student whom I appear to have converted to the view that "the Universe is a vague pulsating mass of next-to-next movement, always feeling its way along to a good purpose, or trying to." That is about as far as lectures can carry them. I particularly like the "trying to."

I wish I could have been at your recent discussion. I am getting impatient with the awful abstract rigmarole in which our American philosophers obscure the truth. It will be fatal. It revives the palmy days of Hegelianism. It means utter relaxation of intellectual duty, and God will smite it. If there's anything he hates, it is that kind of oozy writing.

I have just read Busse's book, in which I find a lot of reality by the way, but a pathetic waste of work on side issues — for against the Strong–Heymans view of things, it seems to me that he brings no solid objection whatever. Heymans's book is a wonder.[1]   Good-bye, dear Miller. *Come to us*, if you can, as soon as your lectures are over.

Your affectionate

W. J.

To Dickinson S. Miller.

[Post-card]

CAMBRIDGE, *Dec.* 9. 1905.

"My idea of Algebra," says a non-mathematically-minded student, "is that it is a sort of form of low cunning."

W. J.

---

[1] Busse, *Leib und Seele, Geist und Körper*; Heymans, *Einführung in die Metaphysik.*

To Daniel Merriman.

CAMBRIDGE, *Dec.* 9, 1905.

No, dear Merriman, not "e'en for thy sake." After an unblemished record of declining to give addresses, successfully maintained for four years (I have certainly declined 100 in the past twelve-month), I am not going to break down now, for Abbot Academy, and go dishonored to my grave. It is better, as the "Bhagavat-Gita" says, to lead your own life, however bad, than to lead another's, however good. Emerson teaches the same doctrine, and I live by it as bad and congenial a life as I can. If there is anything that God despises more than a man who is constantly making speeches, it is another man who is constantly accepting invitations. What must he think, when they are both rolled into one? Get thee behind me, Merriman,— I'm sure that your saintly partner would never have sent me such a request,— and believe me, as ever, fondly yours,

WM. JAMES.

To Miss Pauline Goldmark.

EL TOVAR,

GRAND CANYON, ARIZONA, *Jan.* 3, 1906.

DEAR PAOLINA,— I am breaking my journey by a day here, and it seems a good place from which to date my New Year's greeting to you. But we correspond so rarely that when it comes to the point of tracing actual words with the pen, the last impressions of one's day and the more permanent interest of one's life block the way for each other. I think, however, that a word about the Canyon may fitly take precedence. It certainly is equal to the brag; and, like so many of the more stupendous freaks of nature, seems at first-sight smaller and more manageable than one had supposed. But it grows in immensity as the eye penetrates it more intimately. It is so entirely alone in character, that one has no habits of association with "the likes" of it, and at first it seems a foreign curiosity; but already in this one day I am feeling myself grow nearer, and can well imagine that, with greater intimacy, it might become the passion of one's life — so far as "Nature" goes. The conditions have been unfavorable for intimate communion. Three degrees above zero, and a spring overcoat, prevent that forgetting of "self" which is said to be indispensable to absorption in Beauty. Moreover, I have kept upon the "rim," seeing the Canyon from several points some miles apart. I meant to go down, having but this day; but they could n't send me or any one today; and I confess that, with my precipice-disliking soul, I was relieved, though it very likely would have proved less uncomfortable than I have been told. (I resolved to go, in order to be worthy of being your correspondent.) As Chas. Lamb says, there is nothing so nice as doing good by stealth and being found out by accident, so I now say it is even nicer to make heroic decisions and to be prevented by "circumstances beyond your control" from even trying to execute them. But if ever I get here in summer, I shall go straight down and live there. I 'm sure that it is indispensable. But it is vain to waste descriptive words on the wondrous apparition, with its symphonies of architecture and of color. I have just been watching its peaks blush in the setting sun, and slowly lose their fire. Night nestling in the depths. Solemn, solemn! And a unity of design that makes it seem like an individual, an animated being. Good-night, old chasm! . . .

To Henry James.

STANFORD UNIVERSITY, *Feb.* 1, 1906.

BELOVED H.,— Verily 't is long since I have written to thee, but I have had many and mighty things to do, and lately many business letters to write, so I came not at it. Your last was your delightful reply to my remarks about your "third manner," wherein you said that you would consider your bald head dishonored if you ever came to pleasing *me* by what you wrote, so shocking was my taste.[1] Well! only write *for* me, and leave the question of pleasing open! I have to admit that in "The Golden Bowl" and "The Wings of the Dove," you have succeeded *in getting there* after a fashion, in spite of the perversity of the method and its *longness*, which I am not the only one to deplore.

But enough! let me tell you of my own fortunes!

I got here (after five pestilentially close-aired days in the train, and one entrancing one off at the Grand Canyon of the Colorado) on the 8th, and have now given nine lectures, to 300 enrolled students and about 150 visitors, partly colleagues. I take great pains, prepare a printed syllabus, very fully; and really feel for the first time in my life, as if I were lecturing *well*. High time, after 30 years of practice! It earns me $5000, if I can keep it up till May 27th; but apart from that, I think it is a bad way of expending energy. I ought to be writing my everlastingly postponed book, which this job again absolutely adjourns. I can't write a line of it while doing this other thing. (A propos to which, I got a telegram from Eliot this A.M., asking if I would be Harvard Professor for the first half of next year at the University of Berlin. I had no difficulty in declining that, but I probably shall not decline *Paris*, if they offer it to me year after next.) I am expecting Alice to arrive in a fortnight. I have got a very decent little second story, just enough for the two of us, or rather amply enough, sunny, good fire-place, bathroom, little kitchen, etc., on one of the three residential streets of the University land, and with a

[1] *Vide Letters of Henry James*, vol. II, p. 43.

boarding-house for meals just opposite, we shall have a sort of honeymoon picnic time. And, sooth to say, Alice must need the simplification. . . .

You 've seen this wonderful spot, so I needn't describe it. It is really a miracle; and so simple the life and so benign the elements, that for a young ambitious professor who wishes to leave his mark on Pacific civilization while it is most plastic, or for *any one* who wants to teach and work under the most perfect conditions for eight or nine months, and *who is able to get to the East, or Europe, for the remaining three*, I can't imagine anything finer. It is Utopian. Perfection of weather. Cold nights, though above freezing. Fire pleasant until 10 o'clock A.M., then unpleasant. In short, the "simple life" with all the essential higher elements thrown in as communal possessions. The drawback is, of course, the great surrounding human vacuum — the historic silence fairly rings in your ears when you listen — and the social insipidity. I 'm glad I came, and with God's blessing I may pull through. One calendar month is over, anyway. Do you know aught of G. K. Chesterton? I 've just read his "Heretics." A tremendously strong writer and true thinker, despite his mannerism of paradox. Wells's "Kipps" is good. Good-bye. Of course you 're breathing the fog of London while I am bathed in warmest lucency. Keep well. Your loving,

W. J.

To Theodore Flournoy.

STANFORD UNIVERSITY, *Feb.* 9, 1906.

DEAR FLOURNOY.— Your post-card of Jan. 22nd arrives and reminds me how little I have communicated with you during the past twelve months. . . .

Let me begin by congratulating Mlle. Alice, but more

particularly Mr. Werner, on the engagement which you announce. Surely she is a splendid prize for anyone to capture. I hope that it has been a romantic love-affair, and will remain so to the end. May her paternal and maternal example be the model which their married life will follow! They could find no better model. You do not tell the day of the wedding — probably it is not yet appointed.

Yes! [Richard] Hodgson's death was ultra-sudden. He fell dead while playing a violent game of "hand-ball." He was tremendously athletic and had said to a friend only a week before that he thought he could reasonably count on twenty-five years more of life. None of his work was finished, vast materials amassed, which no one can ever get acquainted with as he had gradually got acquainted; so now good-bye forever to at least two unusually solid and instructive books which he would have soon begun to write on "psychic" subjects. As a *man*, Hodgson was splendid, a real man; as an investigator, it is my private impression that he lately got into a sort of obsession about Mrs. Piper, cared too little for other clues, and continued working with her when all the sides of her mediumship were amply exhibited. I suspect that our American Branch of the S. P. R. will have to dissolve this year, for lack of a competent secretary. Hodgson was our only worker, except Hyslop, and *he* is engaged in founding an "Institute" of his own, which will employ more popular methods. To tell the truth, I'm rather glad of the prospect of the Branch ending, for the Piper-investigation — and nothing else — had begun to bore me to extinction. . . .

To change the subject — you ought to see this extraordinary little University. It was founded only fourteen years ago in the absolute wilderness, by a pair of rich Californians named Stanford, as a memorial to their only child, a son who died at 16. Endowed with I know not how many square miles of land, which some day will come into the market and yield a big income, it has already funds that yield $750,000 yearly, and buildings, of really *beautiful* architecture, that have been paid for out of income, and have cost over $5,000,000. (I mention the cost to let you see that they must be solid.) There are now 1500 students of both sexes, who pay nothing for tuition, and a town of 15,000 inhabitants has grown up a mile away, beyond the gates. The landscape is exquisite and classical, San Francisco only an hour and a quarter away by train; the climate is one of the most perfect in the world, life is absolutely simple, no one being rich, servants almost unattainable (most of the house-work being done by students who come in at odd hours), many of them Japanese, and the professors' wives, I fear, having in great measure to do their own cooking. No social excesses or complications therefore. In fact, nothing but essentials, and *all* the essentials. Fine music, for example, every afternoon, in the Church of the University. There could n't be imagined a better environment for an intellectual man to teach and work in, for eight or nine months in the year, if he were then free to spend three or four months in the crowded centres of civilization — for the social insipidity is great here, and the historic vacuum and silence appalling, and one ought to be free to change.

Unfortunately the authorities of the University seem not to be gifted with imagination enough to see its proper rôle. Its geographical environment and material basis being unique, they ought to aim at unique quality all through, and get *sommités* to come here to work and teach, by offering large stipends. They might, I think, thus easily build up something very distinguished. Instead of which, they pay small sums to young men who chafe at not being able to travel, and whose wives get worn out with domestic drudgery. The whole thing *might* be Utopian; it *is* only half-Utopian. A characteristic American affair! But the half-success is great enough to make one see the great advantages that come to this country from encouraging public-spirited millionaires to indulge their freaks, however eccentric. In what the Stanfords have already done, there is an assured potentiality of great things of *some* sort for all future time. My coming here is an exception. They have had psychology well represented from the first by Frank Angell and Miss Martin; but no philosophy except for a year at a time. I start a new régime — next year they will have two good professors.

I lecture three times a week to 400 listeners, printing a syllabus daily, and making them read Paulsen's textbook for examinations. I find it hard work,[1] and only pray that I may have strength to run till June without collapsing. The students, though rustic, are very earnest and wholesome.

I am pleased, but also amused, by what you say of Woodbridge's Journal: "la palme est maintenant à l'Amérique." It is true that a lot of youngsters in that Journal are doing some real thinking, but of all the *bad writing* that the world has seen, I think that our American writing is getting to be the worst. X——'s ideas have unchained formlessness of expression that beats the bad writing of the Hegelian epoch in Germany. I can hardly believe you sincere when you praise that journal as you do. I am so busy teaching

---

[1] "Also outside 'addresses,' impossible to refuse. Damn them! Four in this Hotel [in San Francisco] where I was one of four orators who spoke for two hours on 'Reason and Faith,' before a Unitarian Association of Pacific Coasters. Consequence: *gout* on waking this morning! *Unitarian gout* — was such a thing ever heard of?" (To T. S. Perry, Feb. 6, 1906.)

that I do no writing and but little reading this year. I have declined to go to Paris next year, and also declined an invitation to Berlin, as "International Exchange" [Professor]. The year after, if asked, I *may* go to Paris — but never to Berlin. We have had Ostwald, a most delightful human *Erscheinung*, as international exchange at Harvard this year. But I don't believe in the system. . . .

To F. C. S. Schiller.

HOTEL DEL MONTE,
MONTEREY, CAL., *Apr.* 7, 1906.

. . . What I really want to write about is Papini, the concluding chapter of his "Crepuscolo dei Filosofi," and the February number of the "Leonardo." Likewise Dewey's "Beliefs and Realities," in the "Philosophical Review" for March. I must be very damp powder, slow to burn, and I must be terribly respectful of other people, for I confess that it is only after reading these things (in spite of all you have written to the same effect, and in spite of your tone of announcing judgment to a sinful world), that I seem to have grasped the full import for life and regeneration, the *great* perspective of the programme, and the renovating character for *all things*, of Humanism; and the outwornness as of a scarecrow's garments, simulating life by flapping in the wind of nightfall, of all intellectualism, and the blindness and deadness of all who worship intellectualist idols, the Royces and Taylors, and, worse than all, their followers, who, with no inward excuse of nature (being too unoriginal really to *prefer* anything), just blunder on to the wrong scent, when it is so easy to catch the right one, and then stick to it with the fidelity of inorganic matter. Ha! ha! would that I were young again with this inspiration! Papini is a jewel! To think of that little Dago putting himself ahead of every one of us (even of you, with his *Uomo-Dio*) at a single stride. And what a writer! and what fecundity! and what courage (careless of nicknames, for it is so easy to call him now the Cyrano de Bergerac of Philosophy)! and what humor and what truth! Dewey's powerful stuff seems also to ring the death-knell of a sentenced world. Yet none of *them* will see it — Taylor will still write his refutations, etc., etc., when the living world will all be drifting after *us*. It is queer to be assisting at the *éclosion* of a great new mental epoch, life, religion, and philosophy in one — I wish I did n't have to lecture, so that I might bear some part of the burden of writing it all out, as we must do, pushing it into all sort of details. But I must for one year longer. We don't get back till June, but pray tell Wells (whose address *fehlt mir*) to make our house his head-quarters if he gets to Boston and finds it the least convenient to do so. Our boys will hug him to their bosoms. Ever thine,

W. J.

The San Francisco earthquake occurred at about five o'clock in the morning on April 18. Rumors of the destruction wrought in the city reached Stanford within a couple of hours and were easily credited, for buildings had been shaken down at Stanford. Miss L. J. Martin, a member of the philosophical department, was thrown into great anxiety about relatives of hers who were in the city, and James offered to accompany her in a search for them, and left Stanford with her by an early morning train. He also promised Mrs. Wm. F. Snow to try to get her news of her husband. Miss Martin found her relatives, and James met Dr. Snow early in the afternoon, and then spent several hours in wandering about the stricken city. He subsequently wrote an account of the disaster, which may be found in "Memories and Studies."[1]

To Miss Frances R. Morse.

STANFORD UNIVERSITY, *Apr.* 22, 1906.

DEAREST FANNY,— Three letters from you and nary one from us in all these weeks! Well, I have been heavily burdened, and although disposed to write, have kept postponing; and with Alice — cooking, washing dishes and doing housework, as well as keeping up a large social life — it has been very much the same. All is now over, since the earthquake; I mean that lectures and syllabuses are called

---

[1] Dr. Snow kindly wrote an account of the afternoon that he spent in James's company in the city and it may here be given in part.

"When I met Professor James in San Francisco early in the afternoon of the day of the earthquake, he was full of questions about my personal feelings and reactions and my observations concerning the conduct and evidences of self-control and fear or other emotions of individuals with whom I had been closely thrown, not only in the medical work which I did, but in the experiences I had on the fire-lines in dragging hose and clearing buildings in advance of the dynamiting squads.

"I described to him an incident concerning a great crowd of people who desired to make a short cut to the open space of a park at a time when there was danger of all of them not getting across before certain buildings were dynamited. Several of the city's police had stretched a rope across this street and were volubly and vigorously combating the onrush of the crowd, using their clubs rather freely. Some one cut the rope. At that instant, a lieutenant of the regular army with three privates appeared to take up guard duty. The lieutenant placed his guard and passed on. The three soldiers immediately began their beat, dividing the width of the street among themselves. The crowd waited, breathless, to see what the leaders of the charge upon the police would now do. One man started to run across the street and was knocked down cleverly by the sentry, with the butt of his gun. This sentry coolly continued his patrol and the man sat up, apparently thinking himself wounded, then scuttled back into the crowd, drawing from every one a laugh which was evidently with the soldiers. Immediately, the crowd began to melt away and proceed up a side street in the direction laid out for them.

"In connection with this story Professor James casually mentioned that not long before, where there were no soldiers or police, he had run on to a crowd stringing a man to a lamp-post because of his endeavor to rob the body of a woman of some rings. At the time, I did not learn other details of this particular incident, as Professor James was so full of the many scenes he had witnessed and was particularly intent on gathering from me impressions of what I had seen. I suppose he had similarly been gathering observations from others whom he met.

"An incident which struck me as humorous at the time was that he should have

off, and no more exams. to be held ("ill-wind," etc.), so one can write. We shall get East again as soon as we can manage it, and tell you face to face. We can now pose as experts on Earthquakes — pardon the egotistic form of talking about the latter, but it makes it more real. The last thing Bakewell said to me, while I was leaving Cambridge, was: "I hope they 'll treat you to a little bit of an earthquake while you 're there. It 's a pity you should n't have that local experience." Well, when I lay in bed at about half-past five that morning, wide-awake, and the room began to sway, my first thought was, "Here 's Bakewell's earthquake, after all"; and when it went crescendo and reached fortissimo in less than half a minute, and the room was shaken like a rat by a terrier, with the most vicious expression you can possibly imagine, it was to my mind absolutely an *entity* that had been waiting all this time holding back its activity, but at last saying, "Now, *go* it!" and it was impossible not to conceive it as animated by a will, so vicious was the temper displayed — everything *down*, in the room, that could go down, bureaus, etc., etc., and the shaking so rapid and vehement. All the while no fear, only admiration for the way a wooden house could prove its elasticity, and glee over the vividness of the manner in which such an "abstract idea" as "earthquake" could verify itself into sensible reality. In a couple of minutes everybody was in the street, and then we saw, what I had n't suspected in my room,

gathered up a box of "Zu-zu gingersnaps," and, as I recall it, some small pieces of cheese. I do not now recall his comment on where he had obtained these, but there was some humorous incident connected with the transaction, and he was quite happy and of opinion that he was enjoying a nourishing meal.

"Professor James told me vividly and in a few words the circumstances of the damage done by the earthquake at Stanford University, and I left him to make arrangements for going down to the University that night to provide for my family. As it turned out, Professor James returned to the campus before I did, and true to his promise thoughtfully hunted up Mrs. Snow and told her that he had seen me and that I was alive and well."

the extent of the damage.　Wooden houses almost all intact, but every chimney down but one or two, and the higher University buildings largely piles of ruins.　Gabble and babble, till at last automobiles brought the dreadful news from San Francisco.

I boarded the only train that went to the City, and got out in the evening on the only train that left.　I should n't have done it, but that our co-habitant here, Miss Martin, became obsessed by the idea that she *must* see what had become of her sister, and I had to stand by her.　Was very glad I did; for the spectacle was memorable, of a whole population in the streets with what baggage they could rescue from their houses about to burn, while the flames and the explosions were steadily advancing and making everyone move farther.　The fires most beautiful in the effulgent sunshine.　Every vacant space was occupied by trunks and furniture and people, and thousands have been sitting by them now for four nights and will have to longer. The fire seems now controlled, but the city is practically wiped out (thank Heaven, as to much of its architecture!). The order has been wonderful, even the criminals struck solemn by the disaster, and the military has done great service.

But you will know all these details by the papers better than I know them now, before this reaches you, and in three weeks we shall be back.

I am very glad that Jim's [Putnam] lectures went off so well.　He wrote me himself a good letter — won't you, by the way, send him this one as a partial answer? — and his syllabus was first-rate and the stuff must have been helpful.　It is jolly to think of both him and Marian really getting off together to enjoy themselves!　But between Vesuvius and San Francisco enjoyment has small elbow-room. Love to your mother, dearest Fanny, to Mary and the men folks, from us both. Your ever affectionate,

W. J.

A few days after the eathquake, train-service from Stanford to the East was reëstablished and James and his wife returned to Cambridge. The reader will infer correctly from the next letter that Henry James (and William James, Jr., who was staying with him in Rye) had been in great anxiety and had been by no means reassured by the brief cablegram which was the only personal communication that it was possible to send them during the days immediately following the disaster.

To Henry James and William James, Jr.

CAMBRIDGE, *May* 9, 1906.

DEAREST BROTHER AND SON,— Your cablegram of response was duly received, and we have been also "joyous" in the thought of your being together. I knew, of course, Henry, that you would be solicitous about us in the earthquake, but did n't reckon at all on the extremity of your anguish as evinced by your frequent cablegrams home, and finally by the letter to Harry which arrived a couple of days ago and told how you were unable to settle down to any other occupation, the thought of our mangled forms, hollow eyes, starving bodies, minds insane with fear, haunting you so. We never reckoned on this extremity of anxiety on your part, I say, and so never thought of cabling you direct, as we might well have done from Oakland on the day we left, namely April 27th. I much regret this callousness on our part. For *all* the anguish was yours; and in general this experience only rubs in what I have always known, that in battles, sieges and other great calamities, the pathos and agony is in general solely felt by those at a distance; and although physical pain is suffered most by its immediate victims, those at the *scene of action* have no *sentimental* suffering whatever. Everyone at San Francisco seemed in a good hearty frame of mind; there was work for every moment of the day and a kind of uplift in the sense of a "common lot" that took away the sense of loneliness that (I imagine) gives the sharpest edge to the more usual kind of misfortune that may befall a man. But it was a queer sight, on our journey through the City on the 26th (eight days after the disaster), to see the inmates of the houses of the quarter left standing, all cooking their dinners at little brick camp-fires in the middle of the streets, the chimneys being condemned. If such a disaster had to happen, somehow it could n't have chosen a better place than San Francisco (where everyone knew about camping, and was familiar with the creation of civilizations out of the bare ground), and at five-thirty in the morning, when few fires were lighted and everyone, after a good sleep, was in bed. Later, there would have been great loss of life in the streets, and the more numerous foci of conflagration would have burned the city in one day instead of four, and made things vastly worse.

In general you may be sure that when any disaster befalls our country it will be *you* only who are wringing of hands, and we who are smiling with "interest or laughing with gleeful excitement." I did n't hear one pathetic word uttered at the scene of disaster, though of course the crop of "nervous wrecks" is very likely to come in a month or so.

Although we have been home six days, such has been the stream of broken occupations, people to see, and small urgent jobs to attend to, that I have written no letter till now. Today, one sees more clearly and begins to rest. "Home" looks extraordinarily pleasant, and though damp and chilly, it is the divine budding moment of the year. Not, however, the lustrous light and sky of Stanford University. . . .

I have just read your paper on Boston in the "North American Review." I am glad you threw away the scabbard and made your critical remarks so straight. What you say about "pay" here being the easily won "salve" for privations, in view of which we cease to "mind" them, is as true as it is strikingly pat. *Les intellectuels,* wedged between the millionaires and the handworkers, are the really pinched class here. They feel the frustrations and they can't get the salve. *My* attainment of so much pay in the past few years brings home to me what an all-benumbing salve it is. That whole article is of your best. We long to hear from W., Jr. No word yet. Your ever loving,

W. J.

In "The Energies of Men" there is a long quotation from an unnamed European correspondent who had been subjecting himself to Yoga disciplinary exercise. What follows is a comment written upon the first receipt of the report quoted in the "Energies."

To W. Lutoslawski.

CAMBRIDGE, *May* 6, 1906.

. . . Your long and beautiful letter about Yoga, etc., greets me on my return from California. It is a most precious human document, and some day, along with that sketch of your religious evolution and other shorter letters of yours, it must see the light of day. What strikes me first in it is the evidence of improved moral "tone" — a calm, firm, sustained joyousness, hard to describe, and striking a new note in your epistles — which is already a convincing argument of the genuineness of the improvement wrought in you by Yoga practices. . . .

You are mistaken about my having tried Yoga discipline — I never meant to suggest that. I have read several books (A. B., by the way, used to be a student of mine, but in spite of many noble qualities, he always had an unbalanced mind — obsessed by certain morbid ideas, etc.), and in the slightest possible way tried breathing exercises. These go terribly against the grain with me, are extremely disagreeable, and, even when tried this winter (somewhat perseveringly), to put myself asleep, after lying awake at night, failed to have any soporific effect. What impresses me most in your narrative is the obstinate strength of will shown by yourself and your chela in your methodical abstentions and exercises. When could I hope for such will-power? I find, when my general energy is *in Anspruch genommen* by hard lecturing and other professional work, that then particularly what little *ascetic* energy I have has to be remitted, because the exertion of inhibitory and stimulative will required increases my general fatigue instead of "tonifying" me.

But your sober experience gives me new hopes. Your whole narrative suggests in me the wonder whether the Yoga discipline may not be, after all, in all its phases, simply a methodical way of *waking up deeper levels of will-power than are habitually used*, and thereby increasing the individual's vital tone and energy. I have no doubt whatever that most people live, whether physically, intellectually or morally, in a very restricted circle of their potential being. They *make use* of a very small portion of their possible consciousness, and of their soul's resources in general, much like a man who, out of his whole bodily organism, should get into a habit of using and moving only his little finger. Great emergencies and crises show us how much greater our vital resources are than we had supposed. Pierre Janet discussed lately some cases of pathological impulsion or obsession in what he has called the "psychasthenic" type of individual, bulimia, exaggerated walking, morbid love of feeling pain, and explains the phenomenon as based on the underlying *sentiment d'incomplétude*, as he calls it, or *sentiment de l'irréel* with which these patients are habitually afflicted, and which they find is abolished by the violent appeal to some exaggerated activity or other, discovered accidentally perhaps, and then used habitually. I was reminded of his article in reading your descriptions and prescriptions. May the Yoga practices not be, after all, methods of getting at our deeper functional levels? And thus only be substitutes for entirely different crises that may occur in other individuals, religious crises, indignation-crises, love-crises, etc.?

What you say of diet is in striking accordance with the views lately made popular by Horace Fletcher — I dare say you have heard of them. You see I am trying to generalize the Yoga idea, and redeem it from the pretension that, for example, there is something intrinsically holy in the various grotesque postures of Hatha Yoga. I have spoken with various Hindus, particularly with three last winter, one a Yogi and apostle of Vedanta; one a "Christian" of scientific training; one a Bramo-Somaj professor. The former made great claims of increase of "power," but admitted that those who had it could in no way demonstrate it *ad oculos*, to outsiders. The other two both said that Yoga was less and less frequently practised by the more intellectual, and that the old-fashioned *Guru* was becoming quite a rarity.

I believe with you, fully, that the so-called "normal man"

of commerce, so to speak, the healthy philistine, is a mere extract from the potentially realizable individual whom he represents, and that we all have reservoirs of life to draw upon, of which we do not dream. The practical problem is "how to get at them." And the answer varies with the individual. Most of us never can, or never do get at them. *You* have indubitably got at your own deeper levels by the Yoga methods. I hope that what you have gained will never again be lost to you. You must keep there! *My* deeper levels seem very hard to find — I am so rebellious at all formal and prescriptive methods — a dry and bony *individual*, repelling fusion, and avoiding voluntary exertion. No matter, art is long! and *qui vivra verra*. I shall try fasting and again try breathing — discovering perhaps some individual rhythm that is more tolerable. . . .

To John Jay Chapman.

CAMBRIDGE, *May* 18, 1906.

DEAR OLD JACK C.,— Having this minute come into the possession of a new type-writer, what can I do better than express my pride in the same by writing to you? [1]

I spent last night at George Dorr's and he read me several letters from you, telling me also of your visit, and of how well you seemed. For years past I have been on the point of writing to you to assure [you] of my continued love and to express my commiseration for your poor wife, who has had so long to bear the brunt of your temper — you see I have been there already and I know how one's irritability is exasperated by conditions of nervous prostration — but now I can write and congratulate you on having recovered, temper and all. (As I write, it bethinks me that

[1] James had not used a type-writer since the time when his eyes troubled him in the seventies. The machine now had the fascination of a strange toy again.

in a previous letter I have made identical jokes about your temper which, I fear, will give Mrs. Chapman a very low opinion of my humoristic resources, and in sooth they are small; but we are as God makes us and must not try to be anything else, so pray condone the silliness and let it pass.) The main thing is that you seem practically to have recovered, in spite of everything; and I am heartily glad.

I too am well enough for all practical purposes, but I have to go slow and not try to do too many things in a day. Simplification of life and consciousness I find to be the great thing, but a hard thing to compass when one lives in city conditions. How our dear Sarah Whitman lived in the sort of railroad station she made of her life — I confess it's a mystery to me. If I lived at a place called Barrytown, it would probably go better — don't you ever go back to New York to live!

Alice and I had a jovial time at sweet little Stanford University. It was the simple life in the best sense of the term. I am glad for once to have been part of the working machine of California, and a pretty deep part too, as it afterwards turned out. The earthquake also was a memorable bit of experience, and altogether we have found it mind-enlarging and are very glad we ben there. But the whole intermediate West is awful — a sort of penal doom to have to live there; and in general the result with me of having lived 65 years in America is to make me feel as if I had at least bought the right to a certain capriciousness, and were free now to live for the remainder of my days wherever I prefer and can make my wife and children consent — it is more likely to be in rural than in urban surroundings, and in the maturer than in the *rawrer* parts of the world. But the first thing is to get out of the treadmill of teaching, which I hate and shall resign from next year. After that,

I can use my small available store of energy in writing, which is not only a much more economical way of working it, but more satisfactory in point of quality, and more lucrative as well.

Now, J. C., when are you going to get at writing again? The world is hungry for your wares. No one touches certain deep notes of moral truth as you do, and your humor is *köstlich* and *impayable*. You ought to join the band of "pragmatistic" or "humanistic" philosophers. I almost fear that Barrytown may not yet have begun to be disturbed by the rumor of their achievements, the which are of the greatest, and seriously I du think that the world of thought is on the eve of a renovation no less important than that contributed by Locke. The leaders of the new movement are Dewey, Schiller of Oxford, in a sense Bergson of Paris, a young Florentine named Papini, and last and least worthy, W. J. H. G. Wells ought to be counted in, and if I mistake not G. K. Chesterton as well.[1] I hope you know and love the last-named writer, who seems to me a great teller of the truth. His systematic preference for contradictions and paradoxical forms of statement seems to me a mannerism somewhat to be regretted in so wealthy a mind; but that is a blemish from which some of our very greatest intellects are not altogether free — the philosopher of Barrytown himself being not wholly exempt. Join us, O Jack, and in the historic and perspective sense your fame will be secure. All future Histories of Philosophy will print your name.

But although my love for you is not exhausted, my typewriting energy is. It communicates stiffness and cramps, both to the body and the mind. Nevertheless I think I have been doing pretty well for a first attempt, don't you?

[1] He did mistake, as Mr. Chesterton's subsequent utterances showed.

If you return me a good long letter telling me more particularly about the process of your recovery, I will write again, even if I have to take a pen to do it, and in any case I will do it much better than this time.

Believe me, dear old J. C., with hearty affection and delight at your recovery — all these months I have been on the brink of writing to find out how you were — and with very best regards to your wife, whom some day I wish we may be permitted to know better. Yours very truly,

WM. JAMES.

Everyone dead! Hodgson, Shaler, James Peirce this winter — to go no further afield! *Resserrons les rangs!*

To Henry James.

CAMBRIDGE, *Sept.* 10, 1906.

DEAREST H.,—I got back from the Adirondacks, where I had spent a fortnight, the night before last, and in three or four hours Alice, Aleck and I will be spinning towards Chocorua, it being now five A.M. Elly [Temple] Hunter will join us, with Grenville, in a few days; but for the most part, thank Heaven, we shall be alone till the end of the month. I found two letters from you awaiting me, and two from Bill. They all breathed a spirit of happiness, and brought a waft of the beautiful European summer with them. It has been a beautiful summer here too; and now, sad to say, it is counting the last beads of its chaplet of hot days out — the hot days which are really the absolutely friendly ones to man — you wish they would get cooler when you have them, and when they are departed, you wish you could have their exquisite gentleness again. I have just been reading in the volume by Richard Jefferies called the "Life of the Fields" a wonderful rhapsody, "The Pageant of Summer." It needs to be read twice over and

very attentively, being nothing but an enumeration of all
the details visible in the corner of an old field with a hedge
and ditch. But rightly taken in, it is probably the highest
flight of human genius in the direction of nature-worship.
I don't see why it should not count as an immortal thing.
You missed it, when here, in not getting to Keene Valley,
where I have just been, and of which the sylvan beauty,
especially by moonlight, is probably unlike aught that
Europe has to show. Imperishable freshness! . . .

This is definitely my last year of lecturing, but I wish it
were my first of non-lecturing. Simplification of the field
of duties I find more and more to be the *summum bonum*
for me; and I live in apprehension lest the Avenger should
cut me off before I get my message out. Not that the
message is particularly needed by the human race, which
can live along perfectly well without any one philosopher;
but objectively I hate to leave the volumes I have already
published without their logical complement. It is an es-
thetic tragedy to have a bridge begun, and stopped in the
middle of an arch.

But I hear Alice stirring upstairs, so I must go up and
finish packing. I hope that you and W. J., Jr., will again
form a harmonious combination. I hope also that he will
stop painting for a time. He will do all the better, when he
gets home, for having had a fallow interval.

Good-bye! and my blessing upon both of you. Your
ever loving,

W. J.

To H. G. Wells.

CHOCORUA, *Sept.* 11, 1906.

DEAR MR. WELLS,— I've read your "Two Studies in
Disappointment" in "Harper's Weekly," and must thank

you from the bottom of my heart. *Rem acu tetegisti!* Exactly that callousness to abstract justice is *the* sinister feature and, to me as well as to you, the incomprehensible feature, of our U. S. civilization. How you hit upon it so neatly and singled it out so truly (and talked of it so tactfully!) God only knows: He evidently created you to do such things! I never heard of the MacQueen case before, but I've known of plenty of others. When the ordinary American hears of them, instead of the idealist within him beginning to "see red" with the higher indignation, instead of the spirit of English history growing alive in his breast, he begins to pooh-pooh and minimize and tone down the thing, and breed excuses from his general fund of optimism and respect for expediency. "It's probably right enough"; "Scoundrelly, as you say," but understandable, "from the point of view of parties interested"— but understandable in onlooking citizens only as a symptom of the moral flabbiness born of the exclusive worship of the bitch-goddess Success. That — with the squalid cash interpretation put on the word success — is our national disease. Hit it hard! Your book *must* have a great effect. Do you remember the glorious remarks about success in Chesterton's "Heretics"? You will undoubtedly have written *the* medicinal book about America. And what good humor! and what tact! Sincerely yours,

Wm. James.

To Miss Theodora Sedgwick.

Chocorua, *Sept.* 13, 1906.

Dear Theodora,— Here we are in this sweet delicate little place, after a pretty agitated summer, and the quiet seems very nice. Likewise the stillness. I have thought often of you, and *almost* written; but there never seemed exactly to be time or place for it, so I let the sally of the heart to-you-ward suffice. A week ago, I spent a night with H. L. Higginson, whom I found all alone at his house by the Lake, and he told me your improvement had been continuous and great, which I heartily hope has really been the case. I don't see why it should not have been the case, under such delightful conditions. What good things friends are! And what better thing than lend it, can one do with one's house? I was struck by Henry Higginson's high level of mental tension, so to call it, which made him talk incessantly and passionately about one subject after another, never running dry, and reminding me more of myself when I was twenty years old. It isn't so much a man's eminence of elementary faculties that pulls him through. They may be rare, and he do nothing. It is the steam pressure to the square inch behind that moves the machine. The amount of that is what makes the great difference between us. Henry has it high. Previous to seeing him I had spent ten days in beautiful Keene Valley, dividing them between the two ends. The St. Hubert's end is, I verily believe, one of the most beautiful things in this beautiful world — too dissimilar to anything in Europe to be compared therewith, and consequently able to stand on its merits all alone. But the great [forest] fire of four years ago came to the very edge of wiping it out! And any year it may go.

I also had a delightful week all alone on the Maine Coast, among the islands.

Back here, one is oppressed by sadness at the amount of work waiting to be done on the place and no one to be hired to do it. The entire meaning and essence of "land" is something to be worked over — even if it be only a woodlot, it must be kept trimmed and cleaned. And for one who *can* work and who *likes* work with his arms and hands, there is nothing so delightful as a piece of land to work over — it responds to every hour you give it, and smiles with the "improvement" year by year. I neither can work now, nor do I like it, so an irremediable bad conscience afflicts my ownership of this place. With Cambridge as headquarters for August, and a little lot of land there, I think I could almost be ready to give up this place, and trust to the luck of hotels, and other opportunities of rustication without responsibility. But perhaps we can get this place [taken care of?] some day!

I don't know how much you read. I've taken great pleasure this summer in Bielshowski's "Life of Goethe" (a wonderful piece of art) and in Birukoff's "Life of Tolstoy."

Alice is very well and happy in the stillness here. Elly Hunter is coming this evening, tomorrow the Merrimans for a day, and then Mrs. Hodder till the end of the month.

Faithful love from both of us, dear Theodora. Your affectionate

W. J.

To his Daughter.   CAMBRIDGE, *Jan.* 20, 1907, 6.15 P.M.

SWEET PEGLEIN,— Just before tea! and your Grandam, Mar, and I going to hear the Revd. Percy Grant in the College chapel just after. We are getting to be great church-goers. 'T will have to be Crothers next. He, sweet man, is staying with the Brookses. After him, the Christian Science Church, and after that the deluge!

I have spent all day preparing next Tuesday's lecture, which is my last before a class in Harvard University, so help me God amen! I am almost *afraid* at so much freedom. Three quarters of an hour ago Aleck and I went for a walk in Somerville; warm, young moon, bare trees, clearing in the west, stars out, old-fashioned streets, not sordid

— a beautiful walk. Last night to Bernard Shaw's ex-*quis*-ite play of "Cæsar and Cleopatra" — exquisitely acted too, by F. Robertson and Maxine Elliot's sister Gert. Your Mar will have told you that, after these weeks of persistent labor, culminating in New York, I am going to take sanctuary on Saturday the 2nd of Feb. in your arms at Bryn Mawr. I do not want, wish, or desire to "talk" to the crowd, but your mother pushing so, if you and the philosophy club also pull, I mean pull *hard*, Jimmy [1] will try to articulate something not too technical. But it will have to be, if ever, on that Saturday night. It will also have to be very short; and the less of a "reception," the better, after it.

Your two last letters were tiptop. I never seen such *growth!*

I go to N. Y., to be at the Harvard Club, on Monday the 28th. Kühnemann left yesterday. A most dear man. Your loving

DAD.

To Henry James and William James, Jr.

CAMBRIDGE, *Feb.* 14, 1907.

DEAR BROTHER AND SON,—I dare say that you will be together in Paris when you get this, but I address it to Lamb House all the same. You twain are more "blessed" than I, in the way of correspondence this winter, for you give more than you receive, Bill's letters being as remarkable for wit and humor as Henry's are for copiousness, considering that the market value of what he either writes or types is so many shillings a word. When *I* write other things, I find it almost impossible to write letters. I've been at it *stiddy*, however, for three days, since my return

[1] As to "Jimmy," *vide* vol. I, p. 301 *supra.*

from New York, finding, as I did, a great stack of correspondence to attend to.   The first impression of New York, if you stay there not more than 36 hours, which has been my limit for twenty years past, is one of repulsion at the clangor, disorder, and permanent earthquake conditions. But this time, installed as I was at the Harvard Club (44th St.) in the centre of the cyclone, I caught the pulse of the machine, took up the rhythm, and vibrated *mit*, and found it simply magnificent.   I'm surprised at you, Henry, not having been more enthusiastic, but perhaps that superbly powerful and beautiful subway was not opened when you were there.   It is an *entirely* new New York, in soul as well as in body, from the old one, which looks like a village in retrospect.   The courage, the heaven-scaling audacity of it all, and the *lightness* withal, as if there was nothing that was not easy, and the great pulses and bounds of progress, so many in directions all simultaneous that the coördination is indefinitely future, give a kind of *drumming background* of life that I never felt before.   I'm sure that once *in* that movement, and at home, all other places would seem insipid.   I observe that your book,—"The American Scene,"— dear H., is just out.   I must get it and devour again the chapters relative to New York.   On my last night, I dined with Norman Hapgood, along with men who were successfully and happily in the vibration.   H. and his most winning-faced young partner, Collier, Jerome, Peter Dunne, F. M. Colby, and Mark Twain.   (The latter, poor man, is only good for monologue, in his old age, or for dialogue at best, but he's a dear little genius all the same.)   I got such an impression of easy efficiency in the midst of their bewildering conditions of speed and complexity of adjustment.   Jerome, particularly, with the world's eyes on his court-room, in the very crux of the Thaw trial, as if he had nothing serious to do.   Balzac ought to come to life again. His Rastignac imagination sketched the possibility of it long ago.   I lunched, dined, and sometimes breakfasted, out, every day of my stay, vibrated between 44th St., seldom going lower, and 149th, with Columbia University at 116th as my chief relay station, the magnificent space-devouring Subway roaring me back and forth, lecturing to a thousand daily,[1] and having four separate dinners at the Columbia Faculty Club, where colleagues severally compassed me about, many of them being old students of mine, wagged their tongues at me and made me explain.[2]   It was certainly the high tide of my existence, so far as *energizing* and being "recognized" were concerned, but I took it all very "easy" and am hardly a bit tired.   Total abstinence from every stimulant whatever is the one condition of living at a rapid pace.   I am now going whack at the writing of the rest of the lectures, which will be more original and (I believe) important than my previous works. . . .

To Moorfield Storey.

CAMBRIDGE, *Feb.* 21, 1907.

DEAR MOORFIELD,— Your letter of three weeks ago has inadvertently lain unnoticed — not because it did n't do

---

[1] *Cf.* pp. 16, 17, and 220 *supra*.

[2] Dr. Miller writes: "These four evenings at the Faculty Club were singularly interesting occasions.   One was a meeting of the Philosophical Club of New York, whose members, about a dozen in number, were of different institutions.   The others were impromptu meetings arranged either by members of the Department of Philosophy at Columbia or a wider group.   At one of them Mr. James sat in a literal circle of chairs, with professors of Biology, Mathematics, etc., as well as Philosophy, and answered in a particularly friendly and charming way the frank objections of a group that were by no means all opponents.   At the close, when he was thanked for his patience, he remarked in his humorously disclaiming manner that he was not accustomed to be taken so seriously.   Privately he remarked how pleasantly such an unaffected, easy meeting contrasted with a certain formal and august dinner club, the exaggerated amusement of the diners at each other's jokes, etc."

me good, but because I went to New York for a fortnight, and since coming home have been too druv to pay any tributes to friendship. I have n't got many letters either of condolence or congratulation on my retirement,— which, by the way, does n't take place till the end of the year,— the papers have railroaded me out too soon.[1] But I confess that the thought is sweet to me of being able to hear the College bell ring without any tendency to "move" in consequence, and of seeing the last Thursday in September go by, and remaining in the country careless of what becomes of its youth. It's the *harness* and the *hours* that are so galling! I expect to shed truths in dazzling profusion on the world for many years.

As for you, retire too! Let you, Eliot, Roosevelt and me, first relax; then take to landscape painting, which has a very soothing effect; then write out all the truths which a long life of intimacy with mankind has recommended to each of us as most useful. I think we can use the ebb tide of our energies best in that way. I'm sure that *your* contributions would be the most useful of all. Affectionately yours,

WM. JAMES.

To Theodore Flournoy.

CAMBRIDGE, *Mar.* 26, 1907.

DEAR FLOURNOY,— Your dilectissime letter of the 16th arrived this morning and I must scribble a word of reply. That's the way to write to a man! Caress him! flatter him! tell him that all Switzerland is hanging on his lips! You have made me really *happy* for at least twenty-four hours!

---

[1] His resignation did not take effect until the end of the Academic year, although his last meeting with the class to which he was giving a "half-course," occurred at the mid-year.

My dry and businesslike compatriots never write letters
like that. They write about themselves — you write about
me. You know the definition of an egotist: "a person
who insists on talking about *himself*, when you want to
talk about *yourself*." Reverdin has told me of the success
of your lectures on pragmatism, and if you have been com-
muning in spirit with me this winter, so have I with you.
I have grown more and more deeply into pragmatism, and
I rejoice immensely to hear you say, "je m'y sens tout
gagné." It is absolutely the only philosophy with *no* humbug in it, and I am certain that it is *your* philosophy. Have
you read Papini's article in the February "Leonardo"?
That seems to me really splendid. You say that my ideas
have formed the real *centre de ralliment* of the pragmatist
tendencies. To me it is the youthful and *empanaché* Papini
who has best put himself at the centre of equilibrium whence
all the motor tendencies start. He (and Schiller) has given
me great confidence and courage. I shall dedicate my book,
however, to the memory of J. S. Mill.

I hope that you are careful to distinguish in my own work
between the pragmatism and the "radical empiricism"
(Conception de Conscience,[1] etc.) which to my own mind
have no necessary connexion with each other. My first
proofs came in this morning, along with your letter, and
the little book ought to be out by the first of June. You
shall have a very early copy. It is exceedingly untech-
nical, and I can't help suspecting that it will make a real impression. Münsterberg, who hitherto has been rather pooh-
poohing my thought, now, after reading the lecture on truth
which I sent you a while ago, says I seem to be ignorant that Kant ever wrote, Kant having already said all

---

[1] "La Notion de Conscience," *Archives de Psychologie*, vol. v, No. 17, June,
1905. Later included in *Essays in Radical Empiricism*.

that I say. I regard this as a very good symptom. The third stage of opinion about a new idea, already arrived: *1st:* absurd! *2nd:* trivial! *3rd: we* discovered it! I don't suppose you mean to print these lectures of yours, but I wish you would. If you would translate my lectures, what could make me happier? But, as I said apropos of the "Varieties," I hate to think of you doing that drudgery when you might be formulating your own ideas. But, in one way or the other, I hope you will join in the great strategic combination against the forces of rationalism and bad abstractionism! A good *coup de collier* all round, and I verily believe that a new philosophic movement will begin. . . .

I thank you for your congratulations on my retirement. It makes me very happy. A professor has two functions: (1) to be learned and distribute bibliographical information; (2) to communicate truth. The *1st* function is the essential one, officially considered. The *2nd* is the only one I care for. Hitherto I have always felt like a humbug as a professor, for I am weak in the first requirement. Now I can live for the second with a free conscience. I envy you now at the Italian Lakes! But good-bye! I have already written you a long letter, though I only *meant* to write a line! Love to you all from

W. J.

To Charles A. Strong.

CAMBRIDGE, *Apr.* 9, 1907.

DEAR STRONG,— Your tightly woven little letter reached me this A.M., just as I was about writing to you to find out how you are. Your long silence had made me apprehensive about your condition, and this news cheers me up very much. Rome is great; and I like to think of you there; if I spend another winter in Europe, it shall be mainly in

Rome. You don't say where you 're staying, however, so my imagination is at fault. I hope it may be at the *Russie*, that most delightful of hotels. I am overwhelmed with duties, so I must be very brief *in re religionis*. Your warnings against my superstitious tendencies, for such I suppose they are,— this is the second heavy one I remember,— touch me, but not in the prophetic way, for they don't weaken my trust in the healthiness of my own attitude, which in part (I fancy) is less remote from your own than you suppose. For instance, my "God of things as they are," being part of a pluralistic system, is responsible for only such of them as he knows enough and has enough power to have accomplished. For the rest he is identical with your "ideal" God. The "omniscient" and "omnipotent" God of theology I regard as a disease of the philosophy-shop. But, having thrown away so much of the philosophy-shop, you may ask me why I don't throw away the whole? That would mean too strong a negative will-to-believe for me. It would mean a dogmatic disbelief in any extant consciousness higher than that of the "normal" human mind; and this in the teeth of the extraordinary vivacity of man's psychological commerce with something ideal that *feels as if it* were also actual (I have no such commerce — I wish I had, but I can't close my eyes to its vitality in others); and in the teeth of such analogies as Fechner uses to show that there may be other-consciousness than man's. If other, then why not higher and bigger? Why *may* we not be in the universe as our dogs and cats are in our drawing-rooms and libraries? It 's a will-to-believe on both sides: I am perfectly willing that others should disbelieve: why should you not be tolerantly interested in the spectacle of my belief? What harm does the little residuum or germ of actuality that I leave in God do? If ideal, why (except on epiphenomenist principles) may he not have got himself at least partly real by this time? I do not believe it to be healthy-minded to nurse the notion that ideals are self-sufficient and require no actualization to make us content. It is a quite unnecessarily heroic form of resignation and sour grapes. Ideals ought to aim at the *transformation of reality* — no less! When you defer to what you suppose a certain authority in scientists as confirming these negations, I am surprised. Of all insufficient authorities as to the total nature of reality, give me the "scientists," from Münsterberg up, or down. Their interests are most incomplete and their professional conceit and bigotry immense. I know no narrower sect or club, in spite of their excellent authority in the lines of fact they have explored, and their splendid achievement there. Their only authority *at large* is for *method* — and the pragmatic method completes and enlarges them there. When you shall have read my whole set of lectures (now with the printer, to be out by June 1st) I doubt whether you will find any great harm in the God I patronize — the poor thing is so largely an ideal possibility. Meanwhile I take delight, or *shall* take delight, in any efforts you may make to negate all superhuman consciousness, for only by these counter-attempts can a finally satisfactory modus vivendi be reached. I don't feel sure that I know just what you mean by "freedom," — but no matter. Have you read in Schiller's new Studies in Humanism what seem to me two excellent chapters, one on "Freedom," and the other on the "making of reality"? . . .

To F. C. S. Schiller.

CAMBRIDGE, *Apr.* 19, 1907.

DEAR SCHILLER, — Two letters and a card from you within ten days is pretty good. I have been in New York for a week, so have n't written as promptly as I should have done.

All right for the Gilbert Murrays! We shall be glad to see them.

Too late for "humanism" in my book — all in type! I dislike "pragmatism," but it seems to have the *international* right of way at present. Let 's both go ahead — God will know his own!

When your book first came I lent it to my student Kallen (who was writing a thesis on the subject), thereby losing it for three weeks. Then the grippe, and my own proofs followed, along with much other business, so that I 've only read about a quarter of it even now. The essays on Freedom and the Making of Reality seem to be written with my own heart's blood — it 's startling that two people should be found to think so exactly alike. A great argument for the truth of what they say, too! I find that my own chapter on Truth printed in the J. of P. already,[1] convinces no one as yet, not even my most *gleichgesinnten* cronies. It will have to be worked in by much future labor, for I *know* that I see all round the subject and they don't, and I think that the theory of truth is the key to all the rest of our positions.

You ask what I am going to "reply" to Bradley. But why need one reply to everything and everybody? B.'s article is constructive rather than polemic, is evidently sincere, softens much of his old outline, is difficult to read, and ought, I should think, to be left to its own destiny. How sweetly, by the way, he feels towards me as compared with you! All because you have been too bumptious. I confess I think that your *gaudium certaminis* injures your influence. *We* 've got a thing big enough to set forth now affirmatively, and I think that readers generally hate *minute* polemics and recriminations. All polemic of ours should,

---

[1] "Pragmatism's Conception of Truth." Included in *Selected Essays and Reviews*.

I believe, be either very broad statements of contrast, or fine points treated singly, and as far as possible impersonally. Inborn rationalists and inborn pragmatists will never convert each other. We shall always look on them as spectral and they on us as trashy — irredeemably both! As far as the rising generation goes, why not simply express ourselves positively, and trust that the truer view quietly will displace the other. Here again "God will know his own." False views don't need much direct refutation — they get superseded, and I feel absolutely certain of the supersessive power of pragmato-humanism, if persuasively enough set forth. . . . The world is wide enough to harbor various ways of thinking, and the present Bradley's units of mental operation are so diverse from ours that the labor of reckoning over from one set of terms to the other does n't bring reward enough to pay for it. Of course his way of treating "truth" as an entity trying all the while to identify herself with reality, while reality is equally trying to identify herself with the more ideal entity truth, is n't *false*. It's one way, very remote and allegorical, of stating the facts, and it "agrees" with a good deal of reality, but it has so little pragmatic value that its tottering form can be left for time to deal with. The good it does him is small, for it leaves him in this queer, surly, grumbling state about the best that can be done by it for philosophy. His great vice seems to me his perversity in logical activities, his bad reasonings. I vote to go on, from now on, not trying to keep account of the relations of his with our system. He can't be influencing disciples, being himself nowadays so difficult. And once for all, there *will* be minds who *cannot help* regarding our growing universe as *sheer trash*, metaphysically considered. Yours ever,

W. J.

The next letter is addressed to an active promoter of reform in the treatment of the insane, the author of "A Mind that Found Itself." The Connecticut Society for Mental Hygiene and the National Committee for Mental Hygiene have already performed so great a public service, that anyone may now see that in 1907 the time had come to employ such instrumentalities in improving the care of the insane. But when Mr. Beers, just out of an asylum himself, appeared with the manuscript of his own story in his hands, it was not so clear that these agencies were needed, nor yet evident to anyone that he was a person who could bring about their organization.

James's own opinion as to the treatment of the insane is not in the least overstated in the following letter. He recognized the genuineness of Mr. Beers's personal experience and its value for propaganda, and he immediately helped to get it published. From his first acquaintance with Mr. Beers, he gave time, counsel, and money to further the organization of the Mental Hygiene Committee; and he even departed, in its interest, from his fixed policy of "keeping out of Committees and Societies." He lived long enough to know that the movement had begun to gather momentum; and he drew great satisfaction from the knowledge.

To Clifford W. Beers.

CAMBRIDGE, *Apr.* 21, 1907.

DEAR MR. BEERS,— You ask for my opinion as to the advisability and feasibility of a National Society, such as you propose, for the improvement of conditions among the insane.

I have never ceased to believe that such improvement is one of the most "crying" needs of civilization; and the functions of such a Society seem to me to be well drawn up by you.   Your plea for its being founded before your book appears is well grounded, you being an author who naturally would like to cast seed upon a ground already prepared for it to germinate practically without delay.

I have to confess to being myself a very impractical man, with no experience whatever in the details, difficulties, etc., of philanthropic or charity organization, so my opinion as to the *feasibility* of your plan is worth nothing, and is undecided.   Of course the first consideration is to get your money, the second, your Secretary and Trustees.   All that *I* wish to bear witness to is the great need of a National Society such as you describe, or failing that, of a State Society somewhere that might serve as a model in other States.

Nowhere is there massed together as much suffering as in the asylums.   Nowhere is there so much sodden routine, and fatalistic insensibility in those who have to treat it. Nowhere is an ideal treatment more costly.   The officials in charge grow resigned to the conditions under which they have to labor.   They cannot plead their cause as an auxiliary organization can plead it for them.   Public opinion is too glad to remain ignorant.   As mediator between officials, patients, and the public conscience, a society such as you sketch is absolutely required, and the sooner it gets under way the better.[1]   Sincerely yours,

WILLIAM JAMES.

At the date of the next letter William James, Jr., was studying painting in Paris.

[1] The story of the Committee for Mental Hygiene is interestingly told in Part V of the 4th Edition of C. W. Beers's *A Mind that Found Itself*.   Several letters from James are incorporated in the story.   *Vide* pp. 339 and 340; also pp. 320, 352.

To his Son William.

CAMBRIDGE, *Apr.* 24, 1907.

DEAREST BILL,— I have n't written to you for ages, yet you keep showering the most masterly and charming epistles upon all of us in turn, including the fair Rosamund.[1] Be sure they are appreciated! Your Ma and I dined last night at Ellen and Loulie Hooper's to meet Rosalind Huide-koper and her swain. Loulie had heard from Bancel [La Farge] of your getting a "mention"— if for the model, I 'm not surprised; if for the composition, I 'm immensely pleased. Of course you 'll tell us of it! We 've had a very raw cold April, and today it 's blowing great guns from all quarters of the sky, preparatory to clearing from the N.W., I think. We are rooting up the entire lawn to a depth of 18 inches to try to regenerate it. Four diggers and two carts have been at it for a week, with your mother, bareheaded and cloaked, and ruddy-cheeked, sticking to them like a burr. She does n't handle pick or shovel, but she stands there all day long in a way it would do your heart good to see; and so democratic and hearty withal that I 'm sure they like it, though working under such a great task-master's eye deprives them of those intervals of stolen leisure so dear to "workers" of every description. She makes it up to them by inviting them to an afternoon tea daily, with piles of cake and doughnuts. I fancy they like her well.

We 've let Chocorua to the Goldmarks. Aleck took his April recess along with his schoolmate Henderson and Gerald Thayer, partly on the summit, partly around the base, of Monadnock. The weather was fiercely wintry, and your mother and I said "poor blind little Aleck — he 's got to learn thru experience." [She said "through"!]

[1] Mrs. James's niece, Rosamund Gregor, age 6.

He came back happier and more exultant than I 've ever seen him, and six months older morally and intellectually for the week with Gerald and Abbott Thayer. A great step forward. They burglarized the Thayer house, and were tracked and arrested by the posse, and had a paragraph in the Boston "Globe" about the robbery. As the thing involved an ascent of Monadnock after dark, with their packs, in deep snow, a day and a night there in snowstorm, a 16-mile walk and out of bed till 2 A.M. the night of the burglary, a "lying low" indoors all the next day at the Hendersons' empty house, three in a bed and the police waking them at dawn, I ventured to suggest a doubt as to whether the Thayer household were the greatest victims of the illustrious practical joke. "What," cries Aleck, starting to his feet, "nine men with revolvers and guns around your bed, and a revolver pointed close to your ear as you wake — don't you call that a success, I should like to know?" The Tom Sawyer phase of evolution is immortal! Gerald, who is staying with us now, is really a splendid fellow. I 'm so glad he 's taken to Aleck, who now is aflame with plans for being an artist. I wish he might — it would certainly suit his temperament better than "business."

There 's the lunch bell.

I have got my "Pragmatism" proofs all corrected. The most important thing I 've written yet, and bound, I am sure, to stir up a lot of attention. But I 'm dog-tired; and, in order to escape the social engagements that at this time of year grow more frequent than ever, I 'm going off on Friday (this is Wednesday) to the country somewhere for ten days. If only there might be warm weather! We 've just backed out from a dinner to William Leonard Darwin and his wife, and the Geo. Hodgeses, etc. W. T. Stead spent three hours here on Sunday and lectured in the Union on Monday — a splendid fellow whom I could get along with after a fashion. Let no one run him down to you. I 've been to New York to the Peace Congress. Interesting but tiresome.

Mary Salter is with us. Margaret and Rosamund just arrived at 107. No news else! Yours,

W. J.

To Henry James.

SALISBURY, CONN., *May* 4, 1907.

DEAREST H.— ... I've been so overwhelmed with work, and the mountain of the *Unread* has piled up so, that only in these days here have I really been able to settle down to your "American Scene," which in its peculiar way seems to me *supremely great*. You know how opposed your whole "third manner" of execution is to the literary ideals which animate my crude and Orson-like breast, mine being to say a thing in one sentence as straight and explicit as it can be made, and then to drop it forever; yours being to avoid naming it straight, but by dint of breathing and sighing all round and round it, to arouse in the reader who may have had a similar perception already (Heaven help him if he has n't!) the illusion of a solid object, made (like the "ghost" at the Polytechnic) wholly out of impalpable materials, air, and the prismatic interferences of light, ingeniously focused by mirrors upon empty space. But you *do* it, that 's the queerness! And the complication of innuendo and associative reference on the enormous scale to which you give way to it does so *build out* the matter for the reader that the result is to solidify, by the mere bulk of the process, the like perception from which *he* has to start. As air, by dint of its volume, will weigh like a corporeal body; so his own poor little initial perception, swathed in this gigantic envelopment of suggestive atmosphere, grows like a germ into something vastly bigger and more substantial. But it's the rummest method for one to employ systematically as you do nowadays; and you employ it at your peril. In this crowded and hurried reading age, pages that require such close attention remain unread and neglected. You can't skip a word if you are to get the effect, and 19 out of 20 worthy readers grow intolerant. The method seems perverse: "Say it *out*, for God's sake," they cry, "and have done with it." And so I say now, give us *one* thing in your older directer manner, just to show that, in spite of your paradoxical success in this unheard-of method, you *can* still write according to accepted canons. Give us that interlude; and then continue like the "curiosity of literature" which you have become. For gleams and innuendoes and felicitous verbal insinuations you are unapproachable, but the *core* of literature is solid. Give it to us *once* again! The bare perfume of things will not support existence, and the effect of solidity you reach is but perfume and simulacrum.

For God's sake don't *answer* these remarks, which (as Uncle Howard used to say of Father's writings) are but the peristaltic belchings of my own crabbed organism. For one thing, your account of America is largely one of its omissions, silences, vacancies. You work them up like solids, for those readers who already germinally perceive them (to others you are *totally* incomprehensible). I said to myself over and over in reading: "How much greater the triumph, if instead of dwelling thus only upon America's vacuities, he could make positive suggestion of what in 'Europe' or Asia may exist to fill them." That would be nutritious to so many American readers whose souls are only too ready to leap to suggestion, but who are now too inexperienced to know what is meant by the contrast-effect

from which alone your book is written. If you could supply
the background which is the foil, in terms more full and
positive! At present it is supplied only by the abstract
geographic term "Europe." But of course anything of
that kind is excessively difficult; and you will probably say
that you *are* supplying it all along by your novels. Well,
the verve and animal spirits with which you can keep your
method going, first on one place then on another, through
all those tightly printed pages is something marvelous; and
there are pages surely doomed to be immortal, those on the
"drummers," *e.g.*, at the beginning of "Florida." They are
in the best sense Rabelaisian.

But a truce, a truce! I had no idea, when I sat down,
of pouring such a bath of my own subjectivity over you.
Forgive! forgive! and don't reply, don't at any rate in the
sense of defending yourself, but only in that of attacking
me, if you feel so minded. I have just finished the proofs of
a little book called "Pragmatism" which even you *may*
enjoy reading. It is a very "sincere" and, from the point
of view of ordinary philosophy-professorial manners, a very
unconventional utterance, not particularly original at any
one point, yet, in the midst of the literature of the way of
thinking which it represents, with just that amount of
squeak or shrillness in the voice that enables one book to
tell, when others don't, to supersede its brethren, and be
treated later as "representative." I should n't be surprised if ten years hence it should be rated as "epoch-
making," for of the definitive triumph of that general way
of thinking I can entertain no doubt whatever — I believe
it to be something quite like the protestant reformation.

You can't tell how happy I am at having thrown off
the nightmare of my "professorship." As a "professor" I
always felt myself a sham, with its chief duties of being a

walking encyclopedia of erudition. I am now at liberty to be a *reality*, and the comfort is unspeakable — literally unspeakable, to be my own man, after 35 years of being owned by others. I can now live for truth pure and simple, instead of for truth accommodated to the most unheard-of requirements set by others. . . . Your affectionate

W. J.

This letter appears never to have been answered, although Henry James wrote on May 31, 1907: "You shall have, after a little more patience, a reply to your so rich and luminous reflections on my book — a reply almost as interesting as, and far more illuminating than, your letter itself."

To F. C. S. Schiller.

CAMBRIDGE, *May* 18, 1907.

. . . One word about the said proof [of your article]. It convinces me that you ought to be an academic personage, a "professor." For thirty-five years I have been suffering from the exigencies of being one, the pretension and the duty, namely, of meeting the mental needs and difficulties of other persons, needs that I could n't possibly imagine and difficulties that I could n't possibly understand; and now that I have shuffled off the professorial coil, the sense of freedom that comes to me is as surprising as it is exquisite. I wake up every morning with it. What! not to have to accommodate myself to this mass of alien and recalcitrant humanity, not to think under resistance, not to have to square myself with others at every step I make — hurrah! it is too good to be true. To be alone with truth and God! *Es ist nicht zu glauben!* What a future! What a vision of ease! But here you are loving it and courting it unnecessarily. You're fit to continue a professor in all your successive reincarnations, with never a release. It was so easy to let Bradley with his approximations and grumblings alone. So few people would find these last statements of his seductive enough to build them into their own thought. But you, for the pure pleasure of the operation, chase him up and down his windings, flog him into and out of his corners, stop him and cross-reference him and counter on him, as if required to do so by your office. It makes very difficult reading, it obliges one to re-read Bradley, and I don't believe there are three persons living who will take it in with the pains required to estimate its value. B. himself will very likely not read it with any care. It is subtle and clear, like everything you write, but it is too minute. And where a few broad comments would have sufficed, it is too complex, and too much like a criminal conviction in tone and temper. Leave him in his *dunklem Drange* — he is drifting in the right direction evidently, and when a certain amount of positive construction on our side has been added, he will say that that was what he had meant all along — and the world will be the better for containing so much difficult polemic reading the less.

I admit that your remarks are penetrating, and let air into the joints of the subject; but I respectfully submit that they are not *called for* in the interests of the final triumph of truth. That will come by the way of displacement of error, quite effortlessly. I can't help suspecting that you unduly magnify the influence of Bradleyan Absolutism on the undergraduate mind. Taylor is the only fruit so far — at least within my purview. One practical point: I don't quite like your first paragraph, and wonder if it be too late to have the references to me at least expunged. I can't recognize the truth of the ten-years' change of opinion about my "Will to Believe." I don't find anyone — not even my dearest friends, as Miller and Strong — one whit persuaded. Taylor's and Hobhouse's attacks are of recent date, etc. Moreover, the reference to Bradley's relation to me in this article is too ironical not to seem a little "nasty" to some readers; therefore out with it, if it be not too late.

See how different our methods are! All that Humanism needs now is to make applications of itself to special problems. Get a school of youngsters at work. Refutations of error should be left to the rationalists alone. They are a stock function of that school. . . .

I 'm fearfully *tired*, but expect the summer to get me right again. Affectionately thine,

W. J.

XVI

1907–1909

The Last Period (III) — Hibbert Lectures in Oxford — The Hodgson Report

THE story of the remaining years is written so fully in the letters themselves as to require little explanation.

Angina pectoris and such minor ailments as are only too likely to afflict a man of sixty-five years and impaired constitution interrupted the progress of reading and writing more and more. Physical exertion, particularly that involved in talking long to many people, now brought on pain and difficulty in breathing. But James still carried himself erect, still walked with a light step, and until a few weeks before his death wore the appearance of a much younger and stronger man than he really was. None but those near to him realized how often he was in discomfort or pain, or how constantly he was using himself to the limit of his endurance. He bore his ills without complaint and ordinarily without mention; although he finally made up his mind to try to discourage the appeals and requests of all sorts that still harassed him, by proclaiming the fact that he was an invalid. As his power of work became more and more reduced, frustrations became harder to bear, and the sense that they were unavoidable oppressed him. When an invitation to deliver a course of lectures on the Hibbert Foundation at Manchester College, Oxford, arrived, he was torn between an impulse to clutch at this engagement as a means of hastening the writing-out of certain material that was in his mind, and the fear, only too reasonable, that the obligation to have the lectures ready by a certain date would strain him to the snapping point. After some hesitation he agreed, however, and the lectures were, ultimately, prepared and delivered successfully.

In proportion as the number of hours a day that he could spend on literary work and professional reading decreased, James's general reading increased again. He began for the first time to browse in military biographies, and commenced to collect material for a study which he sometimes spoke of as a "Psychology of Jingoism," sometimes as a "Varieties of Military Experience." What such a work would have been, had he ever completed it, it is impossible to tell. It was never more than a rather vague project, turned to occasionally as a diversion. But it is safe to reckon that two remarkable papers — the "Energies of Men" (written in 1906) and the "Moral Equivalent of War" (written in 1909) — would have appeared to be related to this study. That it would not have been a utopian flight in the direction of pacifism need hardly be said. However he might have described it, James was not disposed to underestimate the "fighting instinct." He saw it as a persistent and highly irritable force, underlying the society of all the dominant races; and he advocated international courts, reduction of armaments, and any other measures that might prevent appeals to the war-waging passion as commendable devices for getting along without arousing it.

"The fatalistic view of the war-function is to me nonsense, for I know that war-making is due to definite motives and subject to prudential checks and reasonable criticisms, just like any other form of enterprise. . . . All these beliefs of mine put me squarely into the anti-militarist party. But I do not believe that peace either ought to be or will be permanent on this globe, unless the states pacifically organized preserve some of the old elements of army-discipline. . . . In the more or less socialistic future towards which mankind seems drifting, we must still subject ourselves collectively to those severities which answer to our real position upon this only partly hospitable globe. We must make new energies and hardihoods continue the manliness to which the military mind so faithfully clings. Martial virtues must be the enduring cement; intrepidity, contempt of softness, surrender of private interest, obedience to command, must still remain the rock upon which states are built — unless, indeed, we wish for dangerous reactions against common-wealths fit only for contempt, and liable to invite attack whenever a centre of crystallization for military-minded enterprise gets formed anywhere in their neighborhood." [1]

Any utterances about war, arbitration, and disarmament, are now likely to have their original meaning distorted by reason of what may justly be called the present fevered state of public opinion on such questions. It should be clear that the foregoing sentences were not directed to any particular question of domestic or foreign policy. They were part of a broad picture of the fighting instinct, and led up to a suggestion for diverting it into non-destructive channels. As to particular instances, circumstances were always to be reckoned with. James believed in organizing and strengthening the machinery of arbitration, but did not think that the day for universal arbitration had yet come. He saw a danger in military establishments, went so far — in the presence of the "jingoism" aroused by Cleveland's Venezuela message — as to urge opposition to any increase of the American army and navy, encouraged peace-societies, and was willing to challenge attention by calling himself a

[1] *Memories and Studies*, pp. 286 *et seq.*

pacifist.[1] "The first thing to learn in intercourse with others is non-interference with their own peculiar ways of being happy, provided those ways do not presume to interfere by violence with ours."[2]   Tolerance — social, religious, and political — was fundamental in his scheme of belief; but he took pains to make a proviso, and drew the line at tolerating interference or oppression. Where he recognized a military danger, there he would have had matters so governed as to meet it, not evade it. Writing of the British garrison in Halifax in 1897, he said: "By Jove, if England should ever be licked by a Continental army, it would only be Divine justice upon her for keeping up the Tommy Atkins recruiting system when the others have compulsory service."

In the case of one undertaking, which was much too troublesome to be reckoned as a diversion, he let himself be drawn away from his metaphysical work. He had taken no active part in the work of the Society for Psychical Research since 1896. In December, 1905, Richard Hodgson, the secretary of the American Branch, had died suddenly, and almost immediately thereafter Mrs. Piper, the medium whose trances Hodgson had spent years in studying, had purported to give communications from Hodgson's departed spirit. In 1909 James made a report to the S. P. R. on "Mrs. Piper's Hodgson control." The full report will be found in its Proceedings for 1909,[3] and the concluding pages, in which James stated, more analytically than elsewhere, the hypotheses which the phenomena suggested to him,

---

[1] The reader need hardly be reminded that new meanings and associations have attached themselves to this word in particular.

[2] *Talks to Teachers*, p. 265.

[3] Proceedings of (English) S. P. R., vol. XXIII, pp. 1–121. Also, Proc. American S. P. R., vol. III, p. 470.

have been reprinted in the volume of "Collected Essays and Reviews." At the same time he wrote out a more popular statement, in a paper which will be found in "Memories and Studies." As to his final opinion of the spirit-theory, the following letter, given somewhat out of its chronological place, states what was still James's opinion in 1910.

To Charles Lewis Slattery.

CAMBRIDGE, *Apr.* 21, 1907.

DEAR MR. SLATTERY,— My state of mind is this: Mrs. Piper has supernormal knowledge in her trances; but whether it comes from "tapping the minds" of living people, or from some common cosmic reservoir of memories, or from surviving "spirits" of the departed, is a question impossible for *me* to answer just now to my own satisfaction. The spirit-theory is undoubtedly not only the most natural, but the simplest, and I have great respect for Hodgson's and Hyslop's arguments when they adopt it. At the same time the electric current called *belief* has not yet closed in my mind.

Whatever the explanation be, trance-mediumship is an excessively complex phenomenon, in which many concurrent factors are engaged. That is why interpretation is so hard.

Make any use, public or private, that you like of this.

In great haste, yours,

WM. JAMES.

The next letter should be understood as referring to the abandonment of an excursion to Lake Champlain with Henry L. Higginson. The celebration alluded to in the last part of the letter had been arranged by the Cambridge Historical Society in honor of the hundredth anniversary of the birth of Louis Agassiz.

To Henry L. Higginson.

CHOCORUA, N. H., *circa, June* 1, 1907.

DEAR HENRY,— On getting your resignation by telephone, I came straight up here instead, without having time to write you my acceptance as I meant to; and now comes your note of the fourth, before I have done so.

I am exceedingly sorry, my dear old boy, that it is the doctor's advice that has made you fear to go. I hope the liability to relapse will soon fade out and leave you free again; for say what they will of *Alters Schwäche* and resignation to decay, and *entbehren sollst du, sollst entbehren,* it means only sour grapes, and the insides of one always want to be doing the free and active things. However, a river can still be lively in a shrunken bed, and we must not pay too much attention to the difference of level. If you should summon me again this summer, I can probably respond. I shall be here for a fortnight, then back to Cambridge again for a short time.

I thought the Agassiz celebration went off very nicely indeed, did n't you? — John Gray's part in it being of course the best. X —— was heavy, but respectable, and the heavy respectable *ought* to be one ingredient in anything of the kind. But how well Shaler would have done that part of the job had he been there! Love to both of you!

W. J.

To W. Cameron Forbes.

CHOCORUA, *June* 11, 1907.

DEAR CAMERON FORBES,— Your letter from Baguio of the 18th of April touches me by its genuine friendliness, and is a tremendous temptation. Why am I not ten years younger? Even now I hesitate to say no, and the only reason why I don't say yes, with a roar, is that certain rather serious drawbacks in the way of health of late seem to make me unfit for the various activities which such a visit ought to carry in its train. I am afraid my program from now onwards ought to be sedentary. I ought to be getting out a book next winter. Last winter I could hardly do any walking, owing to a trouble with my heart.

Does your invitation mean to include my wife? And have you a good crematory so that she might bring home my ashes in case of need?

I think if you had me on the spot you would find me a less impractical kind of an anti-imperialist than you have supposed me to be. I think that the manner in which the McKinley administration railroaded the country into its policy of conquest was abominable, and the way the country pucked up its ancient soul at the first touch of temptation, and followed, was sickening. But with the establishment of the civil commission McKinley did what he could to redeem things and now what the Islands want is CONTINUITY OF ADMINISTRATION to form new habits that may to some degree be hoped to last when we, as controllers, are gone. WHEN? that is the question. And much difference of opinion may be fair as to the answer. That we can't stay forever seems to follow from the fact that the educated Philippinos differ from all previous colonials in having been inoculated before our occupation with the ideas of the French Revolution; and that is a virus to which history shows as yet no anti-toxine. As I am at present influenced, I think that the U. S. ought to solemnly proclaim a date for our going (or at least for a plebiscitum as to whether we should go) and stand by all the risks. *Some* date, rather than indefinitely drift. And shape the whole interval towards securing things in view of the change. As to this, I may be wrong, and am always willing to be convinced. I wish

I could go, and see you all at work. Heaven knows I admire the spirit with which you are animated — a new thing in colonial work.

It must have been a great pleasure to you to see so many of the family at once. I have seen none of them since their return, but hope to do so ere the summer speeds. The only dark spot was poor F——'s death.

Believe me, with affectionate regards, yours truly,

WM. JAMES.

I am ordering a little book of mine, just out, to be sent to you. Some one of your circle may find entertainment in it.

To F. C. S. Schiller.

[Post-card]

CHOCORUA, *June* 13, 1907.

Yours of the 27th ult. received and highly appreciated. I'm glad you relish my book so well. You go on playing the Boreas and I shedding the sunbeams, and between us we'll get the cloak off the philosophic traveler! But *have* you read Bergson's new book?[1] It seems to me that nothing is important in comparison with that divine apparition. All *our* positions, real time, a growing world, asserted magisterially, and the beast intellectualism killed absolutely *dead!* The whole flowed round by a style incomparable as it seems to me. Read it, and digest it if you can. Much of it I can't yet assimilate.   [*No signature.*]

To Henri Bergson.

CHOCORUA, *June* 13, 1907.

O my Bergson, you are a magician, and your book is a marvel, a real wonder in the history of philosophy, making,

[1] *L'Évolution Créatrice.*

if I mistake not, an entirely new era in respect of matter, but unlike the works of genius of the "transcendentalist" movement (which are so obscurely and abominably and inaccessibly written), a pure classic in point of form. You may be amused at the comparison, but in finishing it I found the same after-taste remaining as after finishing "Madame Bovary," such a flavor of persistent *euphony*, as of a rich river that never foamed or ran thin, but steadily and firmly proceeded with its banks full to the brim. Then the aptness of your illustrations, that never scratch or stand out at right angles, but invariably simplify the thought and help to pour it along! Oh, indeed you are a magician! And if your next book proves to be as great an advance on this one as this is on its two predecessors, your name will surely go down as one of the great creative names in philosophy.

There! have I praised you enough? What every genuine philosopher (every genuine man, in fact) craves most is *praise* — although the philosophers generally call it "recognition"! If you want still more praise, let me know, and I will send it, for my features have been on a broad smile from the first page to the last, at the chain of felicities that never stopped. I feel rejuvenated.

As to the content of it, I am not in a mood at present to make any definite reaction. There is so much that is absolutely new that it will take a long time for your contemporaries to assimilate it, and I imagine that much of the development of detail will have to be performed by younger men whom your ideas will stimulate to coruscate in manners unexpected by yourself. To me at present the vital achievement of the book is that it inflicts an irrecoverable death-wound upon Intellectualism. It can never resuscitate! But it will die hard, for all the inertia of the past is in it, and the spirit of professionalism and pedantry as well as the æsthetic-intellectual delight of dealing with categories logically distinct yet logically connected, will rally for a desperate defense. The *élan vital*, all contentless and vague as you are obliged to leave it, will be an easy substitute to make fun of. But the beast *has* its death-wound now, and the manner in which you have inflicted it (interval *versus* temps d'arrêt, etc.) is masterly in the extreme. I don't know why this later *rédaction* of your critique of the mathematics of movement has seemed to me so much more telling than the early statement — I suppose it is because of the wider *use* made of the principle in the book. You will be receiving my own little "pragmatism" book simultaneously with this letter. How jejune and inconsiderable it seems in comparison with your great system! But it is so congruent with parts of your system, fits so well into interstices thereof, that you will easily understand why I am so enthusiastic. I feel that at bottom we are fighting the same fight, you a commander, I in the ranks. The position we are rescuing is "Tychism" and a really growing world. But whereas I have hitherto found no better way of defending Tychism than by affirming the spontaneous addition of *discrete* elements of being (or their subtraction), thereby playing the game with intellectualist weapons, you set things straight at a single stroke by your fundamental conception of the continuously creative nature of reality. I think that one of your happiest strokes is your reduction of "finality," as usually taken, to its status alongside of efficient causality, as the twin-daughters of intellectualism. But this vaguer and truer finality restored to its rights will be a difficult thing to give content to. Altogether your reality lurks so in the background, in this book, that I am wondering whether you *could n't* give it any more development *in concreto* here, or whether you perhaps were holding back developments, already in your possession, for a future volume. They are sure to come to you later anyhow, and to make a new volume; and altogether, the clash of these ideas of yours with the traditional ones will be sure to make sparks fly that will illuminate all sorts of dark places and bring innumerable new considerations into view. But the process may be slow, for the ideas are so revolutionary. Were it not for your style, your book might last 100 years unnoticed; but your way of writing is so absolutely commanding that your theories have to be attended to immediately. I feel very much in the dark still about the relations of the progressive to the regressive movement, and this great precipitate of nature subject to static categories. With a frank pluralism of *beings* endowed with vital impulses you can get oppositions and compromises easily enough, and a stagnant deposit; but after my one reading I don't exactly "catch on" to the way in which the continuum of reality resists itself so as to have to act, etc., etc.

The only part of the work which I felt like positively criticising was the discussion of the idea of nonentity, which seemed to me somewhat overelaborated, and yet did n't leave me with a sense that the last word had been said on the subject. But all these things must be very slowly digested by me. I can see that, when the tide turns in your favor, many previous tendencies in philosophy will start up, crying "This is nothing but what *we* have contended for all along." Schopenhauer's blind will, Hartmann's unconscious, Fichte's aboriginal freedom (reëdited at Harvard in the most "unreal" possible way by Münsterberg) will all be claimants for priority. But no matter — all the better if you are in some ancient lines of tendency. Mysticism also must make claims and doubtless just ones. I say nothing more now — this is just my first reaction; but I am so enthusiastic as to have said only two days ago, "I thank heaven that I have lived to this date — that I have witnessed the Russo-Japanese war, and seen Bergson's new book appear — the two great modern turning-points of history and of thought!" Best congratulations and cordialest regards!

WM. JAMES.

To T. S. Perry.

SILVER LAKE, N.H., June 24, 1907.

DEAR THOS.,— Yours of the 11th is at hand, true philosopher that you are. No one but one bawn & bred in the philosophic briar-patch could appreciate Bergson as you do, without in the least understanding him. I am in an identical predicament. This last of his is the *divinest* book that has appeared in *my* life-time, and (unless I am the falsest prophet) it is destined to rank with the greatest works of all time. The style of it is as wonderful as the matter. By all means send it to Chas. Peirce, but address him Prescott Hall, Cambridge. I am sending you my "Pragmatism," which Bergson's work makes seem like small potatoes enough.

Are you going to Russia to take Stolypin's place? or to head the Revolution? I would I were at Giverny to talk metaphysics with you, and enjoy a country where I am not responsible for the droughts and the garden. Have been here two weeks at Chocorua, getting our place ready for a tenant.

Affectionate regards to you all.

W. J.

To Dickinson S. Miller.

LINCOLN, MASS., *Aug. 5,* 1907.

DEAR MILLER,— I got your letter about "Pragmatism," etc., some time ago. I hear that you are booked to review it for the "Hibbert Journal." Lay on, Macduff! as hard as you can — I want to have the weak places pointed out. I sent you a week ago a "Journal of Philosophy"[1] with a word more about Truth in it, written *at* you mainly; but I hardly dare hope that I have cleared up my position. A letter from Strong, two days ago, written after receiving a proof of that paper, still thinks that I deny the existence of realities outside of the thinker; and [R. B.] Perry, who seems to me to have written far and away the most important critical remarks on Pragmatism (possibly the *only* important ones), accused Pragmatists (though he does n't name *me*) of ignoring or denying that the real object plays any part in deciding what ideas are true. I confess that such misunderstandings seem to me hardly credible, and cast a "lurid light" on the mutual understandings of philosophers generally. Apparently it all comes from the *word* Pragmatism — and a most unlucky word it may prove to have been. I am a natural realist. The world *per se* may be likened to a cast of beans on a table. By themselves they spell nothing. An onlooker may group them as he likes. He may simply count them all and map them. He may select groups and name these capriciously, or name them to suit certain extrinsic purposes of his. Whatever he does, so long as he *takes account* of them, his account is neither false nor irrelevant. If neither, why not call it true? It *fits* the beans-*minus*-him, and *expresses* the *total* fact, of beans-*plus*-him. Truth in this total sense is partially ambiguous, then. If

---

[1] "A Word More about Truth," reprinted in *Collected Essays and Reviews.*

he simply counts or maps, he obeys a subjective interest as much as if he traces figures. Let that stand for pure "intellectual" treatment of the beans, while grouping them variously stands for non-intellectual interests. All that Schiller and I contend for is that there is *no* "truth" without *some* interest, and that non-intellectual interests play a part as well as intellectual ones. Whereupon we are accused of denying the beans, or denying being in anyway constrained by them! It's too silly! . . .

To Miss Pauline Goldmark.

PUTNAM SHANTY,
KEENE VALLEY, *Sept.* 14, 1907.

DEAR PAULINE,— . . . No "camping" for me this side the grave! A party of fourteen left here yesterday for Panther Gorge, meaning to return by the Range, as they call your "summit trail." Apparently it is easier than when on that to me memorable day we took it, for Charley Putnam swears he has done it in five and a half hours. I don't well understand the difference, except that they don't reach Haystack over Marcy as we did, and there is now a good trail. Past and future play such a part in the way one feels the present. To these youngsters, as to me long ago, and to you today, the rapture of the connexion with these hills is partly made of the sense of future power over them and their like. That being removed from me, I can only mix memories of past power over them with the present. But I have always observed a curious *fading* in what Tennyson calls the "passion" of the past. Memories awaken little or no sentiment when they are too old; and I have taken everything here so prosily this summer that I find myself wondering whether the time-limit has been exceeded, and whether for emotional purpose I am a new self. We know not what we shall become; and that is what makes life so interesting. Always a turn of the kaleidoscope; and when one is utterly maimed for action, then the glorious time for *reading* other men's lives! I fairly revel in that prospect, which in its full richness has to be postponed, for I'm not sufficiently maimed-for-action yet. By going slowly and alone, I find I can compass such things as the Giant's Washbowl, Beaver Meadow Falls, etc., and they make me feel very good. I have even been dallying with the temptation to visit Cameron Forbes at Manila; but I have put it behind me for this year at least. I think I shall probably give some more lectures (of a much less "popular" sort) at Columbia next winter — so you see there's life in the old dog yet. Nevertheless, how different from the life that courses through *your* arteries and capillaries! Today is the first honestly fine day there has been since I arrived here on the 2nd. (They must have been heavily rained on at Panther Gorge yesterday evening.) After writing a couple more letters I will take a book and repair to "Mosso's Ledge" for the enjoyment of the prospect. . . .

To W. Jerusalem (Vienna).

St. Hubert's, N.Y. *Sept.* 15, 1907.

Dear Professor Jerusalem,— Your letter of the 1st of September, forwarded from Cambridge, reaches me here in the Adirondack Mountains today. I am glad the publisher is found, and that you are enjoying the drudgery of translating ["Pragmatism"]. Also that you find the book more and more in agreement with your own philosophy. I fear that its untechnicality of style — or rather its deliberate *anti*-technicality — will make the German *Gelehrtes Publikum*,[1] as well as the professors, consider it *oberfläch-*

[1] Learned public.

*liches Zeug*¹ — which it assuredly is not, although, being only a sketch, it ought to be followed by something *tighter* and abounding in discriminations. Pragmatism is an unlucky word in some respects, and the two meanings I give for it are somewhat heterogeneous. But it was already in vogue in France and Italy as well as in England and America, and it was *tactically* advantageous to use it. . . .

To Henry James.

STONEHURST, INTERVALE, N.H., *Oct.* 6, 1907.

DEAREST BROTHER,—I write this at the [James] Bryces', who have taken the Merrimans' house for the summer, and whither I came the day before yesterday, after closing our Chocorua house, and seeing Alice leave for home. We had been there a fortnight, trying to get some work done, and having to do most of it with our own hands, or rather with Alice's heroic hands, for mine are worth almost nothing in these degenerate days. It is enough to make your heart break to see the scarcity of "labor," and the whole country tells the same story. Our future at Chocorua is a somewhat problematic one, though I think we shall manage to pass next summer there and get it into better shape for good renting, thereafter, at any cost (not the renting but the shaping). After that what *I* want is a free foot, and the children are now not dependent on a family summer any longer. . . .

I spent the first three weeks of September — warm ones — in my beloved and exquisite Keene Valley, where I was able to do a good deal of uphill walking, with good rather than bad effects, much to my joy. Yesterday I took a three hours walk here, three quarters of an hour of it uphill. I have to go alone, and slowly; but it's none the worse for that and makes one feel like old times. I leave this P.M. for two more days at Chocorua — at the hotel. The fall is

<hr />

¹ Superficial stuff.

late, but the woods are beginning to redden beautifully. With the sun behind them, some maples look like stained-glass windows. But the penury of the human part of this region is depressing, and I begin to have an appetite for Europe again. Alice too! To be at Cambridge with no lecturing and no students to nurse along with their thesis-work is an almost incredibly delightful prospect. I am going to settle down to the composition of another small book, more original and ground-breaking than anything I have yet put forth (!), which I expect to print by the spring; after which I can lie back and write at leisure more routine things for the rest of my days.

The Bryces are wholly unchanged, excellent friends and hosts, and I like her as much as him. The trouble with him is that his insatiable love of information makes him try to pump *you* all the time instead of letting you pump *him*, and I have let my own tongue wag so, that, when gone, I shall feel like a fool, and remember all kinds of things that I have forgotten to ask him. I have just been reading to Mrs. B., with great gusto on her part and renewed gusto on mine, the first few pages of your chapter on Florida in "The American Scene." *Köstlich* stuff! I had just been reading to myself almost 50 pages of the New England part of the book, and fairly melting with delight over the Chocorua portion. Evidently that book will last, and bear reading over and over again — a few pages at a time, which is the right way for "literature" fitly so called. It all makes me wish that we had you here again, and you will doubtless soon come. I must n't forget to thank you for the gold pencil-case souvenir. I have had a plated silver one for a year past, now worn through, and experienced what a "comfort" they are. Good-bye, and Heaven bless you. Your loving

W. J.

To Theodore Flournoy.

CAMBRIDGE, *Jan.* 2, 1908.

... I am just back from the American Philosophical Association, which had a really delightful meeting at Cornell University in the State of New York. Mostly epistemological. We are getting to know each other and understand each other better, and shall do so year by year. Everyone cursed my doctrine and Schiller's about "truth." I think it largely is misunderstanding, but it is also due to our having expressed our meaning very ill. The general blanket-word pragmatism covers so many different opinions, that it naturally arouses irritation to see it flourished as a revolutionary flag. I am also partly to blame here; but it was *tactically* wise to use it as a title. Far more persons have had their attention attracted, and the result has been that everybody has been forced to think. Substantially I have nothing to alter in what I have said. . . .

I have just read the first half of Fechner's "Zend-Avesta," a wonderful book, by a wonderful genius. He had his vision and he knows how to discuss it, as no one's vision ever was discussed.

I may tell you in confidence (I don't talk of it here because my damned arteries may in the end make me give it up — for a year past I have a sort of angina when I make efforts) that I have accepted an invitation to give eight public lectures at Oxford next May. I was ashamed to refuse; but the work of preparing them will be hard (the title is "The Present Situation in Philosophy" [1]) and they doom me to relapse into the "popular lecture" form just as I thought I had done with it forever. (What I wished to write this winter was something ultra dry in form, impersonal and exact.) I find that my free and easy and personal way of writing, especially in "Pragmatism," has

---

[1] The lectures were published as *A Pluralistic Universe.*

made me an object of loathing to many respectable academic minds, and I am rather tired of awakening that feeling, which more popular lecturing on my part will probably destine me to increase.

. . . I have been with Strong, who goes to Rome this month. Good, truth-loving man! and a very penetrating mind. I think he will write a great book. We greatly enjoyed seeing your friend Schwarz, the teacher. A fine fellow who will, I hope, succeed.

A happy New Year to you now, dear Flournoy, and loving regards from us all to you all. Yours as ever

WM. JAMES.

To Norman Kemp Smith.
[Post-card]
CAMBRIDGE, *Jan.* 31, 1908.

I have only just "got round" to your singularly solid and compact study of Avenarius in "Mind." I find it clear and very clarifying, after the innumerable hours I have spent in trying to dishevel him. I have read the "Weltbegriff" three times, and have half expected to have to read both books over again to assimilate his immortal message to man, of which I have hitherto been able to make nothing. You set me free! I shall not re-read him! but leave him to his spiritual dryness and preposterous pedantry. His only really original idea seems to be that of the *Vitalreihe*, and that, so far as I can see, is quite false, certainly no improvement on the notion of adaptive reflex actions.

WM. JAMES.

To his Daughter.
CAMBRIDGE, *Apr.* 2, 1908.

DARLING PEG,— You must have wondered at my silence since your dear mother returned. I hoped to write to you each day, but the strict routine of my hours now crowded it out.   I write on my Oxford job till one, then lunch, then nap, then to my . . . doctor at four daily, and from then till dinner-time making calls, and keeping "out" as much as possible.   To bed as soon after 8 as possible — all my odd reading done between 3 and 5 A.M., an hour not favorable for letter-writing — so that my necessary business notes have to get in just before dinner (as now) or after dinner, which I hate and try to avoid.   I think I see my way clear to go [to Oxford] now, if I don't get more fatigued than at present.   Four and a quarter lectures are fully written, and the rest are down-hill work, much raw material being ready now. . . .

To Henry James.

CAMBRIDGE, *April* 15, 1908.

DEAREST HENRY,— Your good letter to Harry has brought news of your play, of which I had only seen an enigmatic paragraph in the papers.   I 'm right glad it is a success, and that such good artists as the Robertsons are in it.   I hope it will have a first-rate run in London.   Your apologies for not writing are the most uncalled-for things — your assiduity and the length of your letters to this family are a standing marvel — especially considering the market-value of your "copy"!   So waste no more in that direction.   'T is I who should be prostrating myself — silent as I 've been for months in spite of the fact that I 'm so soon to descend upon you.   The fact is I 've been trying to compose the accursed lectures in a state of abominable brain-fatigue — a race between myself and time.   I 've got six now done out of the eight, so I 'm safe, but sorry that the infernal nervous condition that with me always accompanies literary production must continue at Oxford and add itself to the other fatigues — a fixed habit of wakefulness, etc. I ought not to have accepted, but they 've panned out good, so far, and if I get through them successfully, I shall be very glad that the opportunity came. They will be a good thing to *have done*. Previously, in such states of fatigue, I have had a break and got away, but this time no day without its half dozen pages — but the thing hangs on so long! . . .

To Henry James.

R. M. S. Ivernia,
[Arriving at Liverpool], *Apr. 29*, 1908.

Dear H.,— Your letter of the 26th, unstamped or post-marked, has just been wafted into our lap — I suppose mailed under another cover to the agent's care.

I'm glad you're not hurrying from Paris — I feared you might be awaiting us in London, and wrote you a letter yesterday to the Reform Club, which you will doubtless get ere you get this, telling you of our prosperous though tedious voyage in good condition.

We cut out London and go straight to Oxford, *via* Chester. I have been sleeping like a top, and feel in good fighting trim again, eager for the scalp of the Absolute. My lectures will put his wretched clerical defenders fairly on the defensive. They begin on Monday. Since you 'll have the whole months of May and June, if you urge it, to see us, I pray you not to hasten back from "gay Paree" for the purpose. . . . Up since two A.M.

W. J.

To Miss Pauline Goldmark.

Patterdale, England, *July 2*, 1908.

Your letter, beloved Pauline, greeted me on my arrival here three hours ago. . . . How I *do wish* that I could be in

Italy alongside of you now, now or any time! You could do me so much good, and your ardor of enjoyment of the country, the towns and the folk would warm up my cold soul. I might even learn to speak Italian by conversing in that tongue with you. But I fear that you'd find me betraying the coldness of my soul by complaining of the heat of my body — a most unworthy attitude to strike. Dear Paolina, never, never think of whether your body is hot or cold; live in the *objective* world, above such miserable considerations. I have been up here eight days, Alice having gone down last Saturday, the 27th, to meet Peggy and Harry at London, after only two days of it. After all the social and other fever of the past six and a half weeks (save for the blessed nine days at Bibury), it looked like the beginning of a real vacation, and it would be such but for the extreme heat, and the accident of one of my recent malignant "colds" beginning. I have been riding about on stage-coaches for five days past, but the hills are so tree-less that one gets little shade, and the sun's glare is tre-mendous. It is a lovely country, however, for pedestrian-izing in cooler weather. Mountains and valleys compressed together as in the Adirondacks, great reaches of pink and green hillside and lovely lakes, the higher parts quite fully alpine in character but for the fact that no snow mountains form the distant background. A strong and noble region, well worthy of one's life-long devotion, if one were a Briton. And on the whole, what a magnificent land and race is this Britain! Every thing about them is of better quality than the corresponding thing in the U.S.—with but few excep-tions, I imagine. And the equilibrium is so well achieved, and the human tone so cheery, blithe and manly! and the manners so delightfully good. Not one *unwholesome*-looking man or woman does one meet here for 250 that one meets in America. Yet I believe (or suspect) that ours is eventually the bigger destiny, if we can only succeed in living up to it, and thou in 22nd St. and I in Irving St. must do our respective strokes, which after 1000 years will help to have made the glorious collective resultant. Meanwhile, as my brother Henry once wrote, thank God for a world that holds so rich an England, so rare an Italy! Alice is entirely *aufgegangen* in her idealization of it. And truly enough, the gardens, the manners, the manliness are an excuse.

But profound as is my own moral respect and admiration, for a *vacation* give me the Continent! The civilization here is too heavy, too *stodgy*, if one could use so unamiable a word. The very stability and good-nature of all things (of course we are leaving out the slum-life!) rest on the basis of the national stupidity, or rather unintellectuality, on which as on a safe foundation of non-explosible material, the magnificent minds of the élite of the race can coruscate as they will, safely. Not until those weeks at Oxford, and these days at Durham, have I had any sense of what a part the Church plays in the national life. So massive and all-pervasive, so authoritative, and on the whole so decent, in spite of the iniquity and farcicality of the whole thing. Never were incompatibles so happily yoked together. Talk about the genius of Romanism! It's nothing to the genius of Anglicanism, for Catholicism still contains some haggard elements, that ally it with the Palestinian desert, whereas Anglicanism remains obese and round and comfortable and decent with this world's decencies, without an *acute* note in its whole life or history, in spite of the shrill Jewish words on which its ears are fed, and the nitro-glycerine of the Gospels and Epistles which has been injected into its veins. Strange feat to have achieved! Yet the success is great — the whole Church-machine makes for all sorts of graces and decencies, and is not incompatible with a high type of Churchman, high, that is, on the side of moral and worldly virtue. . . .

How I wish you were beside me at this moment! A breeze has arisen on the Lake which is spread out before the "smoking-room" window at which I write, and is very grateful. The lake much resembles Lake George. Your ever grateful and loving

                                                    W. J.

To Charles Eliot Norton.
                    PATTERDALE, ENGLAND, *July* 6, 1908.

DEAR CHARLES,— Going to Coniston Lake the other day and seeing the moving little Ruskin Museum at Coniston (admission a penny) made me think rather vividly of you, and make a resolution to write to you on the earliest opportunity. It was truly moving to see such a collection of R.'s busy handiwork, exquisite and loving, in the way of drawing, sketching, engraving and note-taking, and also such a varied lot of photographs of him, especially in his old age. Glorious old Don Quixote that he was! At Durham, where Alice and I spent three and a half delightful days at the house of F. B. Jevons, Principal of one of the two colleges of which the University is composed, I had a good deal of talk with the very remarkable octogenarian Dean of the Cathedral and Lord of the University, a thorough liberal, or rather radical, in his mind, with a voice like a bell, and an alertness to match, who had been a college friend of Ruskin's and known him intimately all his life, and loved him. He knew not of his correspondence with you, of which I have been happy to be able to order Kent of Harvard Square to send him a copy. His name is Kitchin. The whole scene at Durham was tremendously impressive (though York Cathedral made the stronger impression on me). It was so unlike Oxford, so much more American in its personnel, in a way, yet nestling in the very bosom of those mediæval stage-properties and ecclesiastical-principality suggestions. Oxford is all spread out in length and breadth, Durham concentrated in depth and thickness. There is a great deal of flummery about Oxford, but I think if I were an Oxonian, in spite of my radicalism generally, I might vote against all change there. It is an absolutely unique fruit of human endeavor, and like the cathedrals, can never to the end of time be reproduced, when the conditions that once made it are changed. Let other places of learning go in for all the improvements! The world can afford to keep her one Oxford unreformed. I know that this is a superficial judgment in both ways, for Oxford does manage to keep pace with the utilitarian spirit, and at the same time preserve lots of her flummery unchanged. On the whole it is a thoroughly *democratic* place, so far as aristocracy in the strict sense goes. But I'm out of it, and doubt whether I want ever to put foot into it again. . . .

England has changed in many respects. The West End of London, which used at this season to be so impressive from its splendor, is now a mixed and mongrel horde of straw hats and cads of every description. Motor-buses of the most brutal sort have replaced the old carriages, Bond and Regent Streets are cheap-jack shows, everything is tumultuous and confused and has run down in quality. I have been "motoring" a good deal through this "Lake District," owing to the kindness of some excellent people in the hotel, dissenters who rejoice in the name of Squance and inhabit the neighborhood of Durham. It is wondrous fine, but especially adapted to trampers, which I no longer am. Altogether England seems to have got itself into a magnificently fine state of civilization, especially in regard to the cheery and wholesome tone of manners of the people, improved as it is getting to be by the greater infusion of the democratic temper. Everything here seems about twice as good as the corresponding thing with us. But I suspect we have the bigger eventual destiny after all; and give us a thousand years and we may catch up in many details. I think of you as still at Cambridge, and I do hope that physical ills are bearing on more gently. Lily, too, I hope is her well self again. You must n't think of answering this, which is only an ejaculation of friendship — I shall be home almost before you can get an answer over. Love to all your circle, including Theodora, whom I miss greatly. Affectionately yours,

WM. JAMES.

To Henri Bergson.

LAMB HOUSE, *July* 28, 1908.

DEAR BERGSON,— (can't we cease "Professor"-ing each other? — that title establishes a "disjunctive relation" between man and man, and our relation should be "endosmotic" socially as well as intellectually, I think),—

Jacta est alea, I am not to go to Switzerland! I find, after a week or more here, that the monotony and simplification is doing my nervous centres so much good, that my wife has decided to go off with our daughter to Geneva, and to leave me alone with my brother here, for repairs. It is a great disappointment in other ways than in not seeing you, but I know that it is best. Perhaps later in the season the *Zusammenkunft* may take place, for nothing is decided beyond the next three weeks.

Meanwhile let me say how rarely delighted your letter made me. There are many points in your philosophy which

I don't yet grasp, but I have seemed to myself to understand your anti-intellectualistic campaign very clearly, and that I have really done it so well in your opinion makes me proud. I am sending your letter to Strong, partly out of vanity, partly because of your reference to him. It does seem to me that philosophy is turning towards a new orientation. Are you a reader of Fechner? I wish that you would read his "Zend-Avesta," which in the second edition (1904, I think) is better printed and much easier to read than it looks at the first glance. He seems to me of the real race of prophets, and I cannot help thinking that *you*, in particular, if not already acquainted with this book, would find it very stimulating and suggestive. His day, I fancy, is yet to come. I will write no more now, but merely express my regret (and hope) and sign myself, yours most warmly and sincerely,

WM. JAMES.

The subject of the next letter was a volume of "Essays Philosophical and Psychological, in Honor of William James," [1] by nineteen contributors, which had been issued by Columbia University in the spring of 1908. A note at the beginning of the book said: "This volume is intended to mark in some degree its authors' sense of Professor James's memorable services in philosophy and psychology, the vitality he has added to those studies, and the encouragement that has flowed from him to colleagues without number. Early in 1907, at the invitation of Columbia University, he delivered a course of lectures there, and met the members of the Philosophical and Psychological Departments on several occasions for social discussion. They have an added motive for the present work in the recollections of this visit."

[1] New York: Longmans, Green & Co., 1908.

To John Dewey.

RYE, SUSSEX, *Aug.* 4, 1908.

DEAR DEWEY,— I don't know whether this will find you in the Adirondacks or elsewhere, but I hope 't will be on East Hill. My own copy of the Essays in my "honor," which took me by complete surprise on the eve of my departure, was too handsome to take along, so I have but just got round to reading the book, which I find at my brother Henry's, where I have recently come. It is a masterly set of essays of which we may all be proud, distinguished by good style, direct dealing with the facts, and hot running on the trail of truth, regardless of previous conventions and categories. I am sure it hitches the subject of epistemology a good day's journey ahead, and proud indeed am I that it should be dedicated to my memory.

Your own contribution is to my mind the most *weighty* — unless perhaps Strong's should prove to be so. I rejoice exceedingly that you should have got it out. No one yet has succeeded, it seems to me, in jumping into the centre of your vision. Once there, all the perspectives are clear and open; and when you or some one else of us shall have spoken the exact word that opens the centre to everyone, mediating between it and the old categories and prejudices, people will wonder that there ever could have been any other philosophy. That it is the philosophy of the future, I 'll bet my life. Admiringly and affectionately yours,

WM. JAMES.

To Theodore Flournoy.

LAMB HOUSE, RYE, *Aug.* 9, 1908.

DEAR FLOURNOY,— I can't make out from my wife's letters whether she has seen you face to face, or only heard accounts of you from Madame Flournoy. She reports you

very tired from the "Congress"— but I don't know what
Congress has been meeting at Geneva just now. I don't
suppose that you will go to the philosophical congress at
Heidelberg — I certainly shall not. I doubt whether philosophers will gain so much by talking with each other as
other classes of *Gelehrten* do. One needs to *frequenter* a
colleague daily for a month before one can begin to understand him. It seems to me that the collective life of philosophers is little more than an organization of misunderstandings. I gave eight lectures at Oxford, but besides
Schiller and one other tutor, only two persons ever *mentioned* them to me, and those were the two heads of Manchester College by whom I had been invited. Philosophical
work it seems to me must go on in silence and in print
exclusively.

You will have heard (either directly or indirectly) from
my wife of my reasons for not accompanying them to Geneva. I have been for more than three weeks now at my
brother's, and am much better for the simplification. I am
very sorry not to have met with you, but I think I took the
prudent course in staying away.

I have just read Miss Johnson's report in the last S. P. R.
"Proceedings," and a good bit of the proofs of Piddington's
on cross-correspondences between Mrs. Piper, Mrs. Verrall,
and Mrs. Holland, which is to appear in the next number.
You will be much interested, if you can gather the philosophical energy, to go through such an amount of tiresome
detail. It seems to me that these reports open a new chapter in the history of automatism; and Piddington's and
Johnson's ability is of the highest order. Evidently "automatism" is a word that covers an extraordinary variety of
fact. I suppose that you have on the whole been gratified
by the "vindication" of Eusapia [Paladino] at the hands of

Morselli *et al.* in Italy. Physical phenomena also seem to be entering upon a new phase in their history.

Well, I will stop, this is only a word of greeting and regret at not seeing you. I got your letter of many weeks ago when we were at Oxford. Don't take the trouble to *write* now— my wife will bring me all the news of you and your family, and will have given you all mine. Love to Madame F. and all the young ones, too, please. Your ever affectionate

W. J.

To Shadworth H. Hodgson.

PAIGNTON, S. DEVON, *Oct.* 3, 1908.

DEAR HODGSON,— I have been five months in England (you have doubtless heard of my lecturing at Oxford) yet never given you a sign of life. The reason is that I have sedulously kept away from London, which I admire, but at my present time of life abhor, and only touched it two or three times for thirty-six hours to help my wife do her "shopping" (strange use for an elderly philosopher to be put to). The last time I was in London, about a month ago, I called at your affectionately remembered No. 45, only to find you gone to Yorkshire, as I feared I should. I go back in an hour, en route for Liverpool, whence, with wife and daughter, I sail for Boston in the Saxonia. I am literally enchanted with rural England, yet I doubt whether I ever return. I never had a fair chance of getting acquainted with the country here, and if I were a stout pedestrian, which I no longer am, I think I should frequent this land every summer. But in my decrepitude I must make the best of the more effortless relations which I enjoy with nature in my own country. I have seen many philosophers, at Oxford, especially, and James Ward at Cambridge; but, apart from *very* few conversations, did n't get at close

will be a sort of turning-point in the history of philosophy. So many things converge towards an anti-rationalistic crystallization.

Qui vivra verra!

I am very glad indeed to go on board ship. For two months I have been more than ready to get back to my own habits, my own library and writing-table and bed. . . . I wish you, and all of you, a prosperous and healthy and resultful winter, and am, with old-time affection, your ever faithful friend,

WM. JAMES.

If the duty of writing weighs so heavily on you, why obey it? Why, for example, write any more reviews? I absolutely refuse to, and find that one great alleviation.

To Henri Bergson.

LONDON, *Oct.* 4, 1908.

DEAR BERGSON,—My brother was sorry that you could n't come. He wishes me to say that he is returning to Rye the day after tomorrow and is so engaged tomorrow that he will postpone the pleasure of meeting you to some future opportunity.

I need hardly repeat how much I enjoyed our talk today. You must take care of yourself and economize all your energies for your own creative work. I want very much to see what you will have to say on the *Substanzbegriff!* Why should life be so short? I wish that you and I and Strong and Flournoy and McDougall and Ward could live on some mountain-top for a month, together, and whenever we got tired of philosophizing, calm our minds by taking refuge in the scenery.

Always truly yours,

WM. JAMES.

To H. G. Wells.

CAMBRIDGE, *Nov.* 28, 1908.

DEAR WELLS,— "First and Last Things" is a great achievement. The first two "books" should be entitled "philosophy without humbug" and used as a textbook in all the colleges of the world. You have put your finger accurately on the true emphases, and — in the main — on what seem to me the true solutions (you are more monistic in your faith than I should be, but as long as you only call it "faith," that's your right and privilege), and the simplicity of your statements ought to make us "professionals" blush. I have been 35 years on the way to similar conclusions — simply because I started as a professional and had to *débrouiller* them from all the traditional school rubbish.

The other two books exhibit you in the character of the Tolstoy of the English world. A sunny and healthy-minded Tolstoy, as he is a pessimistic and morbid-minded Wells. Where the "higher synthesis" will be born, who shall combine the pair of you, Heaven only knows. But you are carrying on the same function, not only in that neither of your minds is boxed and boarded up like the mind of an ordinary human being, but all the contents down to the very bottom come out freely and unreservedly and simply, but in that you both have the power of contagious speech, and set the similar mood vibrating in the reader. Be happy in that such power has been put into your hands! This book is worth any 100 volumes on Metaphysics and any 200 of Ethics, of the ordinary sort.

Yours, with friendliest regards to Mrs. Wells, most sincerely,

WM. JAMES.

To Henry James.

CAMBRIDGE, *Dec.* 19, 1908.

DEAREST H.,— . . . I write this at 6.30 [A.M.], in the library, which the blessed hard-coal fire has kept warm all night. The night has been still, thermometer 20°, and the dawn is breaking in a pure red line behind Grace Norton's house, into a sky empty save for a big morning star and the crescent of the waning moon. Not a cloud — a true American winter effect. But somehow "le grand puits de l'aurore" does n't appeal to my sense of life, or challenge my spirits as formerly. It suggests no more enterprises to the decrepitude of age, which vegetates along, drawing interest merely on the investment of its earlier enterprises. The accursed "thoracic symptom" is a killer of enterprise with me, and I dare say that it is little better with you. But the less said of it the better — it does n't diminish!

My time has been consumed by interruptions almost totally, until a week ago, when I finally got down seriously to work upon my Hodgson report. It means much more labor than one would suppose, and very little result. I wish that I had never undertaken it. I am sending off a preliminary installment of it to be read at the S. P. R. meeting in January. That done, the rest will run off easily, and in a month I expect to actually begin the "Introduction to Philosophy," which has been postponed so long, and which I hope will add to income for a number of years to come. Your Volumes XIII and XIV arrived the other day — many thanks. We 're subscribing to two copies of the work, sending them as wedding presents. I hope it will sell. Very enticing-looking, but I can't settle down to the prefaces as yet, the only thing I have been able to read lately being Lowes Dickinson's last book, "Justice and Liberty," which seems to me a decidedly big achievement

from every point of view, and probably destined to have a
considerable influence in moulding the opinion of the educated. Stroke upon stroke, from pens of genius, the compet-
itive régime, so idolized 75 years ago, seems to be getting
wounded to death. What will follow will be something
better, but I never saw so clearly the slow effect of [the]
accumulation of the influence of successive individuals in
changing prevalent ideals. Wells and Dickinson will undoubtedly make the biggest steps of change. . . .

Well dear brother! a merry Christmas to you — to you
both, I trust, for I fancy Aleck will be with you when this
arrives — and a happy New Year at its tail! Your loving
                                                        W. J.

To T. S. Perry.

CAMBRIDGE, *Jan.* 29, 1909.

BELOVED THOMAS, cher maître et confrère,— Your delightful letter about my Fechner article and about your
having become a professional philosopher yourself came to
hand duly, four days ago, and filled the heart of self and
wife with joy. I always knew you was one, for to be a real
philosopher all that is necessary is to *hate* some one else's
type of thinking, and if that some one else be a representative of the "classic" type of thought, then one is a pragmatist and owns the fulness of the truth. Fechner is indeed a dear, and I am glad to have introduced, so to speak,
his speculations to the English world, although the Revd.
Elwood Worcester has done so in a somewhat more limited
manner in a recent book of his called "The Living Word"
— (Worcester of Emmanuel Church, I mean, whom everyone has now begun to fall foul of for trying to reanimate
the Church's healing virtue). Another case of newspaper
crime! The reporters all got hold of it with their mega-

phones, and made the nation sick of the sound of its name. Whereas in former ages men strove hard for fame, obscurity is now the one thing to be *striven* for. For *fame*, all one need do is to exist; and the reporter will do the rest — especially if you give them the address of your fotographer. I hope you 're a spelling reformer — I send you the last publication from that quarter. I 'm sure that simple spelling will make a page look better, just as a crowd looks better if everyone's clothes fit.

Apropos of pragmatism, a learned Theban named —— has written a circus-performance of which he is the clown, called "Anti-pragmatisme." It has so much verve and good spirit that I feel like patting him on the back, and "sicking him on," but Lord! what a fool! I think I shall leave it unnoticed. I 'm tired of reëxplaining what is already explained to satiety. Let *them* say, now, for it is their turn, what the relation called truth consists in, what it is known as!

I have had you on my mind ever since Jan. 1st, when we had our Friday evening Club-dinner, and I was deputed to cable you a happy New Year. The next day I could n't get to the telegraph office; the day after I said to myself, "I'll save the money, and save him the money, for if he gets a cable, he 'll be sure to cable back; so I'll write"; the following day, I forgot to; the next day I postponed the act; so from postponement to postponement, here I am. Forgive, forgive! Most affectionate remarks were made about you at the dinner, which generally does n't err by wasting words on absentees, even on those gone to eternity. . . .

I have just got off my report on the Hodgson control, which has stuck to my fingers all this time. It is a hedging sort of an affair, and I don't know what the Perry family will think of it. The truth is that the "case" is a particularly poor one for testing Mrs. Piper's claim to bring back spirits. It is *leakier* than any other case, and intrinsically, I think, no stronger than many of her other good cases, certainly weaker than the G. P. case. I am also now engaged in writing a popular article, "the avowals of a psychical researcher," for the "American Magazine," in which I simply state without argument my own convictions, and put myself on record. I think that public opinion is just now taking a step forward in these matters — *vide* the Eusapian boom! and possibly both these *Schriften* of mine will add their influence. Thank you for the Charmes reception and for the earthquake correspondence! I envy you in clean and intelligent Paris, though our winter is treating us very mildly. A lovely sunny day today! Love to all of you! Yours fondly,

W. J.

The "Charmes reception" was a report of the speeches at the French Academy's reception of Francis Charmes. The "Eusapian boom" will have been understood to refer to current discussions of the medium Eusapia Paladino.

The next letter refers to a paper in which both James and Münsterberg had been "attacked" in such a manner that Münsterberg proposed to send a protest to the American Psychological Association.

To Hugo Münsterberg.

CAMBRIDGE, *Mar.* 16, 1909.

DEAR MÜNSTERBERG,— Witmer has sent me the *corpus delicti*, and I find myself curiously unmoved. In fact he takes so much trouble over me, and goes at the job with such zest that I feel like "sicking him on," as they say to dogs. Perhaps the honor of so many pages devoted to one makes up for the dishonor of their content. It is really a great compliment to have anyone take so much trouble about one. Think of copying all Wundt's notes!

But, dear Münsterberg, I hope you'll withdraw a second time your protest. I think it undignified to take such an attack seriously. Its excessive dimensions (in my case at any rate), and the smallness and remoteness of the provocation, stamp it as simply eccentric, and to show sensitiveness only gives it importance in the eyes of readers who otherwise would only smile at its extravagance. Besides, since these temperamental antipathies exist — why is n't it healthy that they should express themselves? For my part, I feel rather glad than otherwise that psychology is so live a subject that psychologists should "go for" each other in this way, and I think it all ought to happen *inside* of our Association. We ought to cultivate tough hides there, so I hope that you will withdraw the protest. I have mentioned it only to Royce, and will mention it to no one else. I don't like the notion of Harvard people seeming "touchy"! Your fellow victim,

W. J.

To John Jay Chapman.

CAMBRIDGE, *Apr. 30*, 1909.

DEAR JACK C., — I 'm not expecting you to *read* my book, but only to "give me a thought" when you look at the cover. A certain witness at a poisoning case was asked how the corpse looked. "Pleasant-like and foaming at the mouth," was the reply. A good description of you, describing philosophy, in your letter. All that you say is true, and yet the conspiracy has to be carried on by us professors. Reality has to be *returned to*, after this long circumbendibus, though *Gavroche* has it already. There *are* concepts, anyhow. I am glad you lost the volume. It makes one less in existence and ought to send up the price of the remainder.

Blessed spring! blessed spring! Love to you both from yours,

WM. JAMES.

The next post-card was written in acknowledgment of Professor Palmer's comments on "A Pluralistic Universe."

To G. H. Palmer.

[Post-card]

CAMBRIDGE, *May* 13, 1909.

"The finest critical mind of our time!" No one can mix the honey and the gall as you do! My conceit appropriates the honey — for the gall it makes indulgent allowance, as the inevitable watering of a pair of aged rationalist eyes at the effulgent sunrise of a new philosophic day! Thanks! thanks! for the honey.

W. J.

To Theodore Flournoy.

CHOCORUA, *June* 18, 1909.

MY DEAR FLOURNOY,— You must have been wondering during all these weeks what has been the explanation of my silence. It has had two simple causes: 1st, laziness; and 2nd, uncertainty, until within a couple of days, about whether or not I was myself going to Geneva for the University Jubilee. I have been strongly tempted, not only by the "doctorate of theology," which you confidentially told me of (and which would have been a fertile subject of triumph over my dear friend Royce on my part, and of sarcasm on his part about academic distinctions, as well as a diverting episode generally among my friends,— I being so essentially profane a character), but by the hope of seeing you, and by the prospect of a few weeks in dear old Switzerland again. But the economical, hygienic and domestic reasons were all against the journey; so a few days ago I ceased coquetting with the idea of it, and have finally given it up. This postpones any possible meeting with you till next summer, when I think it pretty certain that Alice and I and Peggy will go to Europe again, and probably stay there for two years. . . .

What with the Jubilee and the Congress, dear Flournoy, I fear that your own summer will not yield much healing repose. "Go through it like an automaton" is the best advice I can give you. I find that it is possible, on occasions of great strain, to get relief by ceasing all voluntary control. *Do* nothing, and I find that something will do itself! and not so stupidly in the eyes of outsiders as in one's own. Claparède will, I suppose, be the chief executive officer at the Congress. It is a pleasure to see how he is rising to the top among psychologists, how large a field he covers, and with both originality and "humanity" (in the sense of the omission of the superfluous and technical, and preference for the probable). When will the Germans learn that part? I have just been reading Driesch's Gifford lectures, Volume II. Very exact and careful, and the work of a most powerful intellect. But why lug in, as he does, all that Kantian apparatus, when the questions he treats of are real enough and important enough to be handled directly and not smothered in that opaque and artificial veil? I find the book extremely suggestive, and should like to believe in its thesis, but I can't help suspecting that Driesch is unjust to the possibilities of purely mechanical action. Candle-flames, waterfalls, eddies in streams, to say nothing of "vortex atoms," seem to perpetuate themselves and repair their injuries. You ought to receive very soon my report on Mrs. Piper's Hodgson control. Some theoretic remarks I make at the end may interest you. I rejoice in the triumph of Eusapia all along the line — also in Ochorowicz's young Polish medium, whom you have seen. It looks at last as if something definitive and positive were in sight.

I am correcting the proofs of a collection of what I have written on the subject of "truth" — it will appear in September under the title of "The Meaning of Truth, a Sequel to Pragmatism." It is already evident from the letters I am getting about the "Pluralistic Universe" that that book will 1st, be *read*; 2nd, be *rejected* almost unanimously at first, and for very diverse reasons; but, 3rd, will continue to be bought and referred to, and will end by strongly influencing English philosophy. And now, dear Flournoy, good-bye! and believe me with sincerest affection for Mrs. Flournoy and the young people as well as for yourself, yours faithfully,

WM. JAMES.

To Miss Theodora Sedgwick.

CHOCORUA, *July* 12, 1909.

DEAR THEODORA,— We got your letter a week ago, and were very glad to hear of your prosperous installation, and good impressions of the place. I am sorry that Harry could n't go to see you the first Sunday, but hope, if he did n't go for yesterday, that he will do so yet. When your social circle gets established, and routine life set up, I am sure that you will like Newport very much. As for ourselves, the place is only just beginning to smooth out. The instruments of labor had well-nigh all disappeared, and had to come piecemeal, each forty-eight hours after being ordered, so we have been using the cow as a lawn-mower, silver knives to carve with, and finger-nails for technical purposes generally. There is no labor known to man in which Alice has not indulged, and I have sought safety among the mosquitoes in the woods rather than remain to shirk my responsibilities in full view of them. We have hired a little mare, fearless of automobiles, we get our mail daily, we had company to dinner yesterday, relatives of Alice, the children will be here by the middle of the week, the woods are deliciously fragrant, and the weather, so far, cool — in fact we are *launched* and the regular summer equilibrium will soon set in. The place is both pathetic and irresistible; I want to sell it, Alice wants to enlarge it — we shall end by doing neither, but discuss it to the end of our days.

I have just read Shaler's autobiography, and it has fairly haunted me with the overflowing impression of his myriad-minded character. Full of excesses as he was, due to his intense vivacity, impulsiveness, and imaginativeness, his centre of gravity was absolutely steady, and I knew no man whose sense of the larger relation of things was always so true and right. Of all the minds I have known, his leaves the largest impression, and I miss him more than I have missed anyone before. You ought to read the book, especially the autobiographic half. Good-bye, dear Theodora. Alice joins her love to mine, and I am, as ever, yours affectionately,

WM. JAMES.

To F. C. S. Schiller.

CHOCORUA, *Aug.* 14, 1909.

DEAR SCHILLER,— . . . I got the other day a very candid letter from A. S. Pringle-Pattison, about my "Pluralistic Universe," in which he said: "It is supremely difficult to accept the conclusion of an actually growing universe, an actual addition to the sum of being or (if that expression be objectionable) to the intensity and scope of existence, to a growing God, in fact." — This seems to me very significant. On such minute little snags and hooks, do all the "difficulties" of philosophy hang. Call them categories, and sacred laws, principles of reason, etc., and you have the actual state of metaphysics, calling all the analogies of phenomenal life impossibilities.

No more lecturing from W. J., thank you! either at Oxford or elsewhere. Affectionately thine,

W. J.

To Theodore Flournoy.

CHOCORUA, Sept. 28, 1909.

DEAR FLOURNOY, — We had fondly hoped that before now you might both, accepting my half-invitation, half-suggestion, be with us in this uncared-for-nature, so different from Switzerland, and you getting strengthened and refreshed by the change. *Dieu dispose*, indeed! The fact that *is* never entered into our imagination! I give up all hope of you this year, unless it be for Cambridge, where, however, the conditions of repose will be less favorable for you. . . . I am myself going down to Cambridge on the fifth of October for two days of "inauguration" ceremonies of our new president, Lawrence Lowell. . . . There are so many rival universities in our country that advantage has to be taken of such changes to make the newspaper talk, and keep the name of Harvard in the public ear, so the occasion is to be almost as elaborate as a "Jubilee"; but I shall keep as much out of it as is officially possible, and come back to Chocorua on the 8th, to stay as late into October as we can, though probably not later than the 20th, after which the Cambridge winter will begin. It has n't gone well with my health this summer, and beyond a little reading, I have done no work at all. I have, however, succeeded during the past year in preparing a volume on the "Meaning of Truth" — already printed papers for the most part — which you will receive in a few days after getting this letter, and which I think may help you to set the "pragmatic" account of Knowledge in a clearer light. I will also send you a magazine article on the mediums, which has just appeared, and which may divert you.[1] Eusapia Paladino, I understand, has just signed a contract to come to New York to be at the disposition of Hereward Carrington, an expert in medium's tricks, and author of a book on the same, who, together with Fielding and Bagally, also experts, formed the Committee of the London S. P. R., who saw her at Naples. . . . After Courtier's report on Eusapia, I don't think any "investigation" here will be worth much "scientifically" — the only advantage of her coming may possibly be to get some scientific men to believe that there is really a problem. Two other cases have been reported to me lately, which are worth looking up, and I shall hope to do so.

How much your interests and mine keep step with each other, dear Flournoy. "Functional psychology," and the twilight region that surrounds the clearly lighted centre of experience! Speaking of "functional" psychology, Clark University, of which Stanley Hall is president, had a little international congress the other day in honor of the twentieth year of its existence. I went there for one day in order to see what Freud was like, and met also Yung of Zürich, who professed great esteem for you, and made a very pleasant impression. I hope that Freud and his pupils will push their ideas to their utmost limits, so that we may learn what they

---

[1] "The Confidences of a Psychical Researcher," reprinted in *Memories and Studies* under the title "Final Impressions of a Psychical Researcher."

are. They can't fail to throw light on human nature; but I confess that he made on me personally the impression of a man obsessed with fixed ideas. I can make nothing in my own case with his dream theories, and obviously "symbolism" is a most dangerous method. A newspaper report of the congress said that Freud had condemned the American religious therapy (which has such extensive results) as very "dangerous" because so "unscientific." Bah!

Well, it is pouring rain and so dark that I must close. Alice joins me, dear Flournoy, in sending you our united love, in which all your children have a share.   Ever yours,

                                    W. J.

To Shadworth H. Hodgson.

                            CAMBRIDGE, *Jan.* 1, 1910.

A happy New Year to you, dear Hodgson, and may it bring a state of mind more recognizant of truth when you see it! Your jocose salutation of my account of truth is an epigrammatic commentary on the cross-purposes of philosophers, considering that on the very day (yesterday) of its reaching me, I had replied to a Belgian student writing a thesis on pragmatism, who had asked me to name my sources of inspiration, that I could only recognize two, Peirce, as quoted, and "S. H. H." with his method of attacking problems, by asking what their terms are "Known-as." Unhappy world, where grandfathers can't recognize their own grandchildren! Let us love each other all the same, dear Hodgson, though the grandchild be in your eyes a "prodigal." Affectionately yours,

                                    WM. JAMES.

The news of James's election as *Associé étranger* of the Académie des Sciences Morales et Politiques, which had appeared in the Boston "Journal" a day or two before the next letter, had, of course, reached the American newspapers directly from Paris. The unread book by Bergson of which Mr. Chapman was to forward his manuscript-review was obviously "Le Rire," and Mr. Chapman's review may be found, not where the next letter but one might lead one to seek it, but in the files of the "Hibbert Journal."

To John Jay Chapman.

CAMBRIDGE, *Jan.* 30, 1910.

DEAR JACK,— Invincible epistolary laziness and a conscience humbled to the dust have conspired to retard this letter. God sent me straight to you with my story about Bergson's cablegram — the only other person to whom I have told it was Henry Higginson. *One* of you must have put it into the Boston "Journal" of the next day,— *you* of course, to humiliate me still the more,— so now I lie in the dust, spurning all the decorations and honors under which the powers and principalities are trying to bury me, and seeking to manifest the naked truth in my uncomely form. Never again, never again! Naked came I into life, and this world's vanities are not for me! You, dear Jack, are the only reincarnation of Isaiah and Job, and I praise God that he has let me live in your day. *Real* values are known only to *you!*

As for Bergson, I think your change of the word "comic" into the word "tragic" throughout his book is *impayable,* and I have no doubt it is true. I have only read half of him, so don't know how he is coming out. Meanwhile send me your own foolishness on the same subject, commend me to your liege lady, and believe me, shamefully yours,

W. J.

To John Jay Chapman.

CAMBRIDGE, *Feb.* 8, 1910.

DEAR JACK,— Wonderful! wonderful! Shallow, incoherent, obnoxious to its own criticism of Chesterton and Shaw, off its balance, accidental, whimsical, false; but with central fires of truth "blazing fuliginous mid murkiest confusion," telling the reader nothing of the Comic except that it's smaller than the Tragic, but *readable* and splendid, showing that the *man who wrote it* is more than anything he can write!

Pray patch some kind of a finale to it and send it to the "Atlantic"! Yours ever fondly,

W. J.

(Membre de l'Institut!)

The "specimen" which was enclosed with the following note has been lost. It was perhaps a bit of adulatory verse. What is said about "Harris and Shakespeare," as also in a later letter to Mr. T. S. Perry on the same subject, was written apropos of a book entitled "The Man Shakespeare, His Tragic Life-Story." [1]

To John Jay Chapman.

CAMBRIDGE, *Feb.* 15, 1910.

DEAR JACK,— Just a word to say that it pleases me to hear you write this about Harris and Shakespeare. H. is surely false in much that he claims; yet 'tis the only way in which Shakespeare ought to be handled, so his *is* the best book. The trouble with S. was his intolerable fluency. He improvised so easily that it kept down his level. It is hard to see how the man that wrote his best things could possibly have let himself do ranting bombast and compli-

[1] By Frank Harris; New York: 1909.

cation on such a large scale elsewhere. 'T is mighty fun
to read him through in order.

I send you a specimen of the kind of thing that tends to
hang upon me as the ivy on the oak. When will the day
come? Never till, like me, you give yourself out as a
poetry-hater. Thine ever,

James

de l'Institut

(my new signature)

To *Dickinson S. Miller.*

CAMBRIDGE, *Mar.* 26, 1910.

DEAR MILLER,— Your study of me arrives! and I have
pantingly turned the pages to find the eulogistic adjectives,
and find them in such abundance that my head swims.
Glory to God that I have lived to see this day! to have so
much said about me, and to be embalmed in literature like
the great ones of the past! I did n't know I was so much,
was all these things, and yet, as I read, I see that I was
(or am?), and shall boldly assert myself when I go abroad.

To speak in all dull soberness, dear Miller, it touches me
to the quick that you should have hatched out this elaborate description of me with such patient and loving incuba-
tion. I have only spent five minutes over it so far, meaning
to take it on the steamer, but I get the impression that it
is almost unexampled in our literature as a piece of profound analysis of an individual mind. I 'm sorry you stick

so much to my psychological phase, which I care little for, now, and never cared much. This epistemological and metaphysical phase seems to me more original and important, and I have n't lost hopes of converting you entirely yet. Meanwhile, thanks! thanks! [Émile] Boutroux, who is a regular angel, has just left our house. I've written an account of his lectures which the "Nation" will print on the 31st. I should like you to look it over, hasty as it is.

. . . I hope that all these lectures on contemporaries (What a live place Columbia is!) will appear together in a volume. I can't easily believe that any will compare with yours as a thorough piece of interpretative work.

We sail on Tuesday next. My thorax has been going the wrong way badly this winter, and I hope that Nauheim may patch it up.

Strength to your elbow! Affectionately and gratefully yours,

                                        WM. JAMES.

XVII

1910

Final Months — The End

SEVERAL reasons combined to take James to Europe in the early spring of 1910. His heart had been giving him more discomfort. He wished to consult a specialist in Paris from whom an acquaintance of his, similarly afflicted, had received great benefit. He believed that another course of Nauheim baths would be helpful. Last, and not least, he wished to be within reach of his brother Henry, who was ill and concerning whose condition he was much distressed. In reality it was he, not his brother, who already stood in the shadow of Death's door.

Accordingly he sailed for England with Mrs. James, and went first to Lamb House. Thence he crossed alone to Paris, and thence went on to Nauheim, leaving Mrs. James to bring his brother to Nauheim to join him. The Parisian specialist could do nothing but confirm previous diagnoses.

Too much "sitting up and talking" with friends in Paris exhausted him seriously, and, after leaving Paris, he failed for the first time to shake off his fatigue. The immediate effect of the Nauheim baths proved to be very debilitating, and, again, he failed to rally and improve when he had finished them. By July, after trying the air of Lucerne and Geneva, only to find that the altitude caused him unbearable distress, he despaired of any relief beyond what now looked like the incomparable consolations of being at rest in his own home. So he turned his face westward.

The next letters bid good-bye for the summer to two tried friends. Five months later it seemed as if James had been at more pains to make his adieus than he usually put himself to on account of a summer's absence. When Mrs. James returned to the Cambridge house in the autumn, after he had died, and had occasion to open his desk copy of the Harvard Catalogue, she found these words jotted at the head of the Faculty List: "A thousand regrets cover every beloved name." It grieved him that life was too short and too full for him to see many of them as often as he wanted to. One day before he sailed, his eye had been caught by the familiar names and, as a throng of comradely intentions filled his heart, he had had a moment of foreboding, and he had let his hand trace the words that cried this needless "Forgive me!" and recorded an incommunicable Farewell.

To Henry L. Higginson.

CAMBRIDGE, *Mar.* 28, 1910.

BELOVED HENRY,— I had most positive hopes of driving in to see you ere the deep engulfs us, but the press is too great here, and it remains impossible. This is just a word to say that you are not forgotten, or ever to be forgotten, and that (after what Mrs. Higginson said) I am hoping you may sail yourself pretty soon, and have a refreshing time, and cross our path. We go straight to Rye, expecting to be in Paris for the beginning of April for a week, and then to Nauheim, whence Alice, after seeing me safely settled, will probably return to Rye for the heft of the summer. It would pay you to turn up both there and at Nauheim and see the mode of life.

Hoping you 'll have a good [Club] dinner Friday night, and never need any surgery again, I am ever thine,

W. J.

To Miss Frances R. Morse.

CAMBRIDGE, *March* 29, 1910.

DEAREST FANNY,— Your beautiful roses and your card arrived duly — the roses were not deserved, not at least by W. J. I have about given up all visits to Boston this winter, and the racket has been so incessant in the house, owing to foreigners of late, that we have n't had the strength to send for you. I sail on the 29th in the Megantic, first to see Henry, who has been ill, not dangerously, but very miserably. Our Harry is with him now. I shall then go to Paris for a certain medical experiment, and after that report at Nauheim, where they probably will keep me for some weeks. I hope that I may get home again next fall with my organism in better shape, and be able to see more of my friends.

After Thursday, when the good Boutrouxs go, I shall try to arrange a meeting with you, dear Fanny. At present we are "contemporaries," that is all, and the one of us who becomes survivor will have regrets that we were no more!

What a lugubrious ending! With love to your mother, and love from Alice, believe me, dearest Fanny, most affectionately yours,

W. J.

To T. S. Perry.

BAD-NAUHEIM, *May* 22, 1910.

BELOVED THOS.,— I have two letters from you — one about . . . Harris on Shakespeare. *Re* Harris, I did think you were a bit supercilious *a priori*, but I thought of your youth and excused you. Harris himself is horrid, young and crude. Much of his talk seems to me absurd, but nevertheless *that 's the way to write about Shakespeare*, and I am sure that, if Shakespeare were a Piper-control, he would say that he relished Harris far more than the pack of reverent commentators who treat him as a classic moralist. He seems to me to have been a professional *amuser*, in the first instance, with a productivity like that of a Dumas, or a Scribe; but possessing what no other amuser has possessed, a lyric splendor added to his rhetorical fluency, which has made people take him for a more essentially serious human being than he was. Neurotically and erotically, he was hyperæsthetic, with a playful graciousness of character never surpassed. He could be profoundly melancholy; but even then was controlled by the audience's needs. A cork in the rapids, with no ballast of his own, without religious or ethical ideals, accepting uncritically every theatrical and social convention, he was simply an æolian harp passively resounding to the stage's call. Was there ever an author of such emotional importance whose reaction against false conventions of life was such an absolute zero as his? I know nothing of the other Elizabethans, but could they have been as soulless in this respect? — But *halte-là!* or I shall become a Harris myself! . . . With love to you all, believe me ever thine,

W. J.

Read Daniel Halévy's exquisitely discreet "Vie de Nietzsche," if you have n't already done so. Do you know G. Courtelines' "Les Marionettes de la Vie" (Flammarion)? It beats Labiche.

To François Pillon.

BAD-NAUHEIM, *May* 25, 1910.

MY DEAR PILLON,— I have been here a week, taking the baths for my unfortunate cardiac complications, and shall probably stay six weeks longer. I passed through Paris, where I spent a week, partly with my friend the philosopher

Strong, partly at the Fondation Thiers with the Boutrouxs, who had been our guests in America when he lectured a few months ago at Harvard. Every day I said: "I will get to the Pillons this afternoon"; but every day I found it impossible to attempt your four flights of stairs, and finally had to run away from the Boutrouxs' to save my life from the fatigue and pectoral pain which resulted from my seeing so many people. I have a dilatation of the aorta, which causes anginoid pain of a bad kind whenever I make any exertion, muscular, intellectual, or social, and I should not have thought at all of going through Paris were it not that I wished to consult a certain Dr. Moutier there, who is strong on arteries, but who told me that he could do nothing for my case. I hope that these baths may arrest the disagreeable tendency to *pejoration* from which I have suffered in the past year. This is why I didn't come to see the dear Pillons; a loss for which I felt, and shall always feel, deep regret.

The sight of the new "Année Philosophique" at Boutroux's showed me how valiant and solid you still are for literary work. I read a number of the book reviews, but none of the articles, which seemed uncommonly varied and interesting. Your short notice of Schinz's really *bouffon* book showed me to my regret that even you have not yet caught the true inwardness of my notion of Truth. You speak as if I allowed no *valeur de connaissance proprement dite*, which is a quite false accusation. When an idea "works" successfully among *all the other ideas* which relate to the object of which it is our mental substitute, associating and comparing itself with them harmoniously, the workings are wholly inside of the intellectual world, and the idea's value purely intellectual, for the time, at least. This is my doctrine and Schiller's, but it seems very hard to express it so as to get it understood!

I hope that, in spite of the devouring years, dear Madame Pillon's state of health may be less deplorable than it has been so long. In particular I wish that the neuritis may have ceased. I wish! I wish! but what's the use of wishing, against the universal law that "youth's a stuff will not endure," and that we must simply make the best of it? Boutroux gave some beautiful lectures at Harvard, and is the gentlest and most lovable of characters. Believe me, dear Pillon, and dear Madame Pillon, your ever affectionate old friend,

WM. JAMES.

To Theodore Flournoy.

BAD-NAUHEIM, May 29, 1910.

. . . Paris was splendid, but fatiguing. Among other things I was introduced to the Académie des Sciences Morales, of which you may likely have heard that I am now an *associé étranger* (!!). Boutroux says that Renan, when he took his seat after being received at the Académie Française, said: "Qu'on est bien dans çe fauteuil" (it is nothing but a cushioned bench with no back!). "Peut-être n'y a-t-il que cela de vrai!" Delicious Renanesque remark! . . .

W. J.

The arrangement by which Mrs. James and Henry James were to have arrived at Nauheim had been upset. The two, who were to come from England together, were delayed by Henry's condition; and for a while James was at Nauheim alone.

To his Daughter.

BAD-NAUHEIM, May 29, 1910.

BELOVED PÉGUY,— The very *fust* thing I want you to do is to look in the drawer marked "Blood" in my tall filing case in the library closet, and find the *date* of a number of the "Journal of Speculative Philosophy" there that contains an article called "Philosophic Reveries." Send this *date* (not the article) to the Revd. Prof. L. P. Jacks, 28 Holywell, Oxford, if you find it, *immediately*. He will understand what to do with it. If you don't find the article, do nothing! Jacks is notified. I have just corrected the proofs of an article on Blood for the "Hibbert Journal," which, I think, will make people sit up and rub their eyes at the apparition of a new great writer of English. I want Blood himself to get it as a surprise.

I got as a surprise your finely typed copy of the rest of my MS., the other day. I thank you for it; also for your delightful letters. The type-writing seems to set free both your and Aleck's genius more than the pen. (If you need a new ribbon it must be got from the agency in Milk St. just above Devonshire — but you 'll find it hard work to get it into its place.) You seem to be leading a very handsome and domestic life, avoiding social excitements, and hearing of them only from the brethren. It is good sometimes to face the naked ribs of reality as it reveals itself in homes. I face them *here*, with no one but the blackbirds and the trees for my companions, save some rather odd Americans at the *Mittagstisch* and *Abendessen*, and the good smiling *Dienstmädchen* who brings me my breakfast in the morning. . . . I went to my bath at 6 o'clock this morning, and had the Park all to the blackbirds and myself. This was because I am expecting a certain Prof. Goldstein from Darmstadt to come to see me this morning, and I had to get the bath out of the way. He is a powerful young writer, and is translating my "Pluralistic Universe." But the weather has grown so threatening that I hope now that he won't come till next Sunday. It is a shame to converse here and not be in the open air. I would to Heaven *thou* wert *mit* — I think thou wouldst enjoy it very much for a week or more. The German civilization is *good!* Only this place would give a very false impression of our wicked earth to a Mars-*Bewohner* who should descend and leave and see nothing else. Not a dark spot (save what the patients' hearts individually conceal), no poverty, no vice, nothing but prettiness and simplicity of life. I snip out a concert-program (the afternoon one unusually good) which I find lying on my table. The like is given free in the open air every day. The baths weaken one so that I have little brain for reading, and must write letters to all kinds of people every day. A big quarrel is on in Paris between my would-be translators and publishers. I wish translators would let my books alone — they are written for my own people exclusively! You will have received Hewlett's delightful "Halfway House," sent to our steamer by Pauline Goldmark, I think. I have been reading a charmingly discreet life of Nietzsche by D. Halévy, and have invested in a couple more of his (N.'s) books, but have n't yet begun to read them. I am half through "Waffen-nieder!" a *first-rate* anti-war novel by Baroness von Suttner. It has been translated, and I recommend it as in many ways instructive. How are Rebecca and Maggie [the cook and housemaid]? You don't say how you enjoy ordering the bill of fare every day. You can't vary it properly unless you make a *list* and keep it. A good sweet dish is *rothe Grütze*, a form of fine sago consolidated by currant-jelly juice, and sauced with custard, or, I suppose, cream.

Well! no more today! Give no end of love to the good boys, and to your Grandam, and believe me, ever thy affectionate,

W. J.

To Henry P. Bowditch.

BAD-NAUHEIM, *June* 4, 1910.

DEAREST HEINRICH,— The envelope in which this letter goes was addrest in Cambridge, Mass., and expected to go towards you with a letter in it, long before now. But better late than never, so here goes! I came over, as you may remember, for the double purpose of seeing my brother Henry, who had been having a sort of nervous breakdown, and of getting my heart, if possible, tuned up by foreign experts. I stayed upwards of a month with Henry, and then came hither *über* Paris, where I stayed ten days. I have been here two and a half weeks, taking the baths, and enjoying the feeling of the strong, calm, successful, new German civilization all about me. Germany is *great*, and no mistake! But what a contrast, in the well-set-up, well-groomed, smart-looking German man of today, and his rather clumsily drest, dingy, and unworldly-looking father of forty years ago! But something of the old *Gemüthlichkeit* remains, the friendly manners, and the disposition to talk with you and take you seriously and to respect the serious side of whatever comes along. But I can write you more interestingly of physiology than I can of sociology. . . . The baths may or may not arrest for a while the downward tendency which has been so marked in the past year — but at any rate it is a comfort to know that my sufferings have a respectable organic basis, and are not, as so many of my friends tell me, due to pure "nervousness." Dear Henry, you see that you are not the only pebble on the beach, or toad in the puddle, of senile degeneration! I admit that the form of your tragedy beats that of that of most of us; but youth's a stuff that won't endure, in any one, and to have had it, as you and I have had it, is a good deal gained anyhow, while to see the daylight still under *any* conditions is perhaps also better than nothing, and meanwhile the good months are sure to bring the final relief after which, "when you and I behind the veil are passed, Oh, but the long, long time the world shall last!" etc., etc. Rather gloomy moralizing, this, to end an affectionate family letter with; but the circumstances seem to justify it, and I know that you won't take it amiss.

Alice is staying with Henry, but they will both be here in a fortnight or less. I find it pretty lonely all by myself, and the German language does n't run as trippingly off the tongue as it did forty years ago. Passage back is taken for August 12th. . . .

Well, I must stop! Pray give my love to Selma, the faithful one. Also to Fanny, Harold, and Friedel. With Harold's engagement you are more and more of a patriarch. Heaven keep you, dear Henry.

Believe me, ever your affectionately sympathetic old friend,

WM. JAMES.

To François Pillon.

BAD-NAUHEIM, *June* 8, 1910.

MY DEAR PILLON,— I have your good letter of the 4th — which I finally had to take a magnifying-glass to read (!) — and remained full of admiration for the nervous centres which, after 80 years of work, could still guide the fingers to execute, without slipping or trembling, that masterpiece of microscopic calligraphy! Truly your nervous centres are "well preserved" — the optical ones also, in spite of the cataracts and loss of accommodation! How proud I should be if now, at the comparatively youthful age of 68, I could flatter *myself* with the hope of doing what you have done, and living down victoriously twelve more devouring enemies of years! With a fresh volume produced, to mark each year by! I give you leave, as a garland and reward, to misinterpret my doctrine of truth *ad libitum* and to your heart's content, in all your future writings. I will never think the worse of you for it.

What you say of dear Madame Pillon awakens in me very different feelings. She has led, indeed, a life of suffering for many years, and it seems to me a real tragedy that she should now be confined to the house so absolutely. If only you might inhabit the country, where, on fine days, with no stairs to mount or descend, she could sit with flowers and trees around her! The city is not good when one is confined to one's apartment. Pray give Madame Pillon my sincerest love — I never think of her without affection.— I am almost ashamed to accept year after year your "Année Philosophique," and to give you so little in return for it. I am expecting my wife and brother to arrive here from England this afternoon, and we shall *probably* all return together through Paris, by the middle of July. I will then come and see you, with the wife, so please keep the "Année" till then, and put it into my hands. I can read nothing serious here — the baths destroy one's strength so. Whether they will do any good to my circulatory organs remains to be seen — there is no good effect perceptible so far. Believe me, dear old friend, with every message of affection to you both, yours ever faithfully,

WM. JAMES.

The letters which follow concern Henry Adams's "Letter to American Teachers," originally printed for private circulation, but recently published, with a preface by Mr. Brooks Adams, under the title: "The Degradation of Democratic Dogma."

To Henry Adams.

BAD-NAUHEIM, *June* 17, 1910.

DEAR HENRY ADAMS,— I have been so "slim" since seeing you, and the baths here have so weakened my brain,
that I have been unable to do any reading except trash,
and have only just got round to finishing your "letter,"
which I had but half-read when I was with you at Paris.
To tell the truth, it does n't impress me at all, save by its
wit and erudition; and I ask you whether an old man soon
about to meet his Maker can hope to save himself from the
consequences of his life by pointing to the wit and learning
he has shown in treating a tragic subject. No, sir, you
can't do it, can't impress God in that way. So far as our
scientific conceptions go, it may be admitted that your
Creator (and mine) started the universe with a certain
amount of "energy" latent in it, and decreed that everything that should happen thereafter should be a result of
parts of that energy falling to lower levels; raising other
parts higher, to be sure, in so doing, but never in equivalent amount, owing to the constant radiation of unrecov-
erable warmth incidental to the process. It is customary
for gentlemen to pretend to believe one another, and until
some one hits upon a newer revolutionary concept (which
may be tomorrow) all physicists must play the game by
holding religiously to the above doctrine. It involves of
course the ultimate cessation of all perceptible happening,
and the end of human history. With this general conception as *surrounding* everything you say in your "letter,"
no one can find any fault — in the present stage of scientific conventions and fashions. But I protest against your
interpretation of some of the specifications of the great
statistical drift downwards of the original high-level energy.
If, instead of criticizing what you seem to me to say, I

express my own interpretation dogmatically, and leave you to make the comparison, it will doubtless conduce to brevity and economize recrimination.

To begin with, the *amount* of cosmic energy it costs to buy a certain distribution of fact which humanly we regard as precious, seems to me to be an altogether secondary matter as regards the question of history and progress. Certain arrangements of matter *on the same energy-level* are, from the point of view of man's appreciation, superior, while others are inferior. Physically a dinosaur's brain may show as much intensity of energy-exchange as a man's, but it can do infinitely fewer things, because as a force of detent it can only unlock the dinosaur's muscles, while the man's brain, by unlocking far feebler muscles, indirectly can by their means issue proclamations, write books, describe Chartres Cathedral, etc., and guide the energies of the shrinking sun into channels which never would have been entered otherwise — in short, *make* history. Therefore the man's brain and muscles are, from the point of view of the historian, the more important place of energy-exchange, small as this may be when measured in absolute physical units..

The "second law" is wholly irrelevant to "history" — save that it sets a terminus — for history is the course of things before that terminus, and all that the second law says is that, whatever the history, it must invest itself between that initial maximum and that terminal minimum of difference in energy-level. As the great irrigation-reservoir empties itself, the whole question for us is that of the distribution of its effects, of *which* rills to guide it into; and the size of the rills has nothing to do with their significance. Human cerebration is the most important rill we know of, and both the "capacity" and the "intensity" factor thereof may be treated as infinitesimal. Yet the filling of such rills would be cheaply bought by the waste of whole sums spent in getting a little of the down-flowing torrent to enter them. Just so of human institutions — their value has in strict theory nothing whatever to do with their energy-budget — being wholly a question of the form the energy flows through. Though the *ultimate* state of the universe may be its vital and psychical extinction, there is nothing in physics to interfere with the hypothesis that the penultimate state might be the millennium — in other words a state in which a minimum of difference of energy-level might have its exchanges so skillfully *canalisés* that a maximum of happy and virtuous consciousness would be the only result. In short, the last expiring pulsation of the universe's life might be, "I am so happy and perfect that I can stand it no longer." You don't believe this and I don't say I do. But I can find nothing in "Energetik" to conflict with its possibility. You seem to me not to discriminate, but to treat quantity and distribution of energy as if they formed one question.

There! that's pretty good for a brain after 18 Nauheim baths — so I won't write another line, nor ask you to reply to me. In case you can't help doing so, however, I will gratify you now by saying that I probably won't jaw back. — It was pleasant at Paris to hear your identically unchanged and "undegraded" voice after so many years of loss of solar energy. Yours ever truly,

WM. JAMES.

[Post-card]
NAUHEIM, *June* 19, 1910.

P. S. Another illustration of my meaning: The clock of the universe is running down, and by so doing makes the hands move. The energy absorbed by the hands and the

Postkarte

Monsieur Henry Adams
23 Avenue du Bois de Boulogne
Paris

Konstanz, June 26th — Yours of the 20th, just arriving, pleases me by its docility of spirit and passive subjection to philosophic opinion. Never, never pretend to an opinion of your own! that way lies every arrogance and madness! You tempt me to offer you another illustration — that of the hydraulic ram (thrown back twice in an exam? as a 'hydraulic goat' by an insufficiently intelligent student). Let this arrangement of one till, placed in the course of a brook, symbolize the machine of human life. It works, clap, clap, clap, day & night, so long as the brook runs at all, and no matter how full the brook (which symbolizes the descending cosmic energy) may be; and it works to the same effect, of raising so many kilogrammeter of water: what the value of this work as history may be, depends on the

[margin, left side:] The water is put to which the house cd. the ram serve. M. J.

Facsimile of Post-card addressed to Henry Adams.

mechanical work they do is the same day after day, no matter how far the weights have descended from the position they were originally wound up to. The *history* which the hands perpetrate has nothing to do with the *quantity* of this work, but follows the *significance* of the figures which they cover on the dial. If they move from O to XII, there is "progress," if from XII to O, there is "decay," etc. etc.

W. J.

To Henry Adams.

[Post-card]

CONSTANCE, *June* 26, [1910].

Yours of the 20th, just arriving, pleases me by its docility of spirit and passive subjection to philosophic opinion. Never, never pretend to an opinion of your own! that way lies every annoyance and madness! You tempt me to offer you another illustration — that of the *hydraulic ram* (thrown back to me in an exam. as a "hydraulic goat" by an insufficiently intelligent student). Let this arrangement of metal, placed in the course of a brook, symbolize the machine of human life. It works, clap, clap, clap, day and night, so long as the brook runs *at all*, and no matter how full the brook (which symbolizes the descending cosmic energy) may be, it works always to the same effect, of raising so many kilogrammeters of water. What the *value* of this work as history may be, depends on the uses to which the water is put in the house which the ram serves.

W. J.

To Benjamin Paul Blood.

CONSTANCE, *June* 25, 1910.

MY DEAR BLOOD,— About the time you will receive this, you will also be surprised by receiving the "Hibbert Journal" for July, with an article signed by me, but written mainly by yourself.[1] Tired of waiting for your final synthetic pronunciamento, and fearing I might be cut off ere it came, I took time by the forelock, and at the risk of making ducks and drakes of your thoughts, I resolved to save at any rate some of your rhetoric, and the result is what you see. Forgive! forgive! forgive! It will at any rate have made you famous, for the circulation of the H. J. is choice, as well as large (12,000 or more, I 'm told), and the print and paper the best ever yet. I seem to have lost the editor's letter, or I would send it to you. He wrote, in accepting the article in May, "I have already 40 articles accepted, and some of the writers threaten lawsuits for non-publication, yet such was the exquisite refreshment Blood's writing gave me, under the cataract of sawdust in which editorially I live, that I have this day sent the article to the printer. Actions speak louder than words! Blood is simply *great*, and you are to be thanked for having dug him out. L. P. JACKS." Of course I 've used you for my own purposes, and probably misused you; but I 'm sure you will feel more pleasure than pain, and perhaps write again in the "Hibbert" to set yourself right. You 're sure of being printed, whatever you may send. How I wish that I too could write poetry, for pluralism is in its *Sturm und Drang* period, and verse is the only way to express certain things. I 've just been taking the "cure" at Nauheim for my unlucky heart — no results so far!

Sail for home again on August 12th. Address always Cambridge, Mass.; things are forwarded. Warm regards, fellow pluralist. Yours ever,

WM. JAMES.

[1] See the footnote on p. 39 *supra.*

To Theodore Flournoy.

GENEVA, *July* 9, 1910.

DEAREST FLOURNOY,— Your two letters, of yesterday, and of July 4th sent to Nauheim, came this morning. I am sorry that the Nauheim one was not written earlier, since you had the trouble of writing it at all. I thank you for all the considerateness you show — you understand entirely my situation. My dyspnœa gets worse at an accelerated rate, and all I care for now is to get home — doing *nothing* on the way. It is partly a spasmodic phenomenon I am sure, for the aeration of my tissues, judging by the color of my lips, seems to be sufficient. I will leave Geneva now without seeing you again — better not come, unless just to shake hands with my wife! Through all these years I have wished I might live nearer to you and see more of you and exchange more ideas, for we seem two men particularly well *faits pour nous comprendre.* Particularly, now, as my own intellectual house-keeping has seemed on the point of working out some good results, would it have been good to work out the less unworthy parts of it in your company. But that is impossible! — I doubt if I ever do any more writing of a serious sort; and as I am able to look upon my life rather lightly, I can truly say that "I don't care" — don't care in the least pathetically or tragically, at any rate.— I hope that Ragacz will be a success, or at any rate a wholesome way of passing the month, and that little by little you will reach your new equilibrium. Those dear daughters, at any rate, are something to live for — to show them Italy should be rejuvenating. I can write no more, my very dear old friend, but only ask you to think of me as ever lovingly yours,

W. J.

After leaving Geneva James rested at Lamb House for a few days before going to Liverpool to embark. Walking, talking and writing had all become impossible or painful. The short northern route to Quebec was chosen for the home voyage. When he and Mrs. James and his brother Henry landed there, they went straight to Chocorua. The afternoon light was fading from the familiar hills on August 19th, when the motor brought them to the little house, and James sank into a chair beside the fire, and sobbed, "It's so good to get home!"

A change for the worse occurred within forty-eight hours and the true situation became apparent. The effort by which he had kept up a certain interest in what was going on about him during the last weeks of his journey, and a certain semblance of strength, had spent itself. He had been clinging to life only in order to get home.

Death occurred without pain in the early afternoon of August 26th.

His body was taken to Cambridge, where there was a funeral service in the College Chapel. After cremation, his ashes were placed beside the graves of his parents in the Cambridge Cemetery.

THE END

APPENDIXES

APPENDIX I

Three Criticisms for Students

In his smaller classes, made up of advanced students, James found it possible to comment in detail on the work of individuals. Three letters have come into the hands of the editor, from which extracts may be taken to illustrate such comments. They were written for persons with whom he could communicate only by letter, and are extended enough to suggest the *viva voce* comments which many a student recalls, but of which there is no record. The first is from a letter to a former pupil and refers to work of Bertrand Russell and others which the pupil was studying at the time. The second and third comment on manuscripts that had been prepared as "theses" and had been submitted to James for unofficial criticism. They exhibit him, characteristically, as encouraging the student to formulate something more positive.

Jan. 26, 1908.

Those propositions or supposals which [Russell, Moore and Meinong] make the exclusive vehicles of truth are mongrel curs that have no real place between realities on the one hand and beliefs on the other. The negative, disjunctive and hypothetic truths which they so conveniently express can all, perfectly well (so far as I see), be translated into relations between beliefs and positive realities. "Propositions" are expressly devised for quibbling between realities and beliefs. They seem to have the objectivity of the one and the subjectivity of the other, and he who uses them can straddle as he likes, owing to the ambiguity of the word *that*, which is essential to them. "*That* Cæsar existed" is "true," sometimes means the *fact that* he existed is real, sometimes the *belief that* he existed is true. You can get no honest discussion out of such terms. . . .

Aug. 15, 1908.

Dear K——, . . . [I have] read your thesis once through. I only finished it yesterday. It is a big effort, hard to grasp at a single reading, and I'm too lazy to go over it a second time in its present physically inconvenient shape. It is obvious that parts of it have been written rapidly and not boiled down; and my impression is that you have left over in it too much of the complication of form in which our ideas, our critical ideas especially, first come to us, and which has, with much rewriting, to be straightened out. You were dealing with dialecticians and logic-choppers, and you have met them on their own ground with a logic-chopping even more diseased than theirs. So far as I can see, you *have* met them, though your own expressions are often far from lucid (— result of haste?); but in some cases I doubt whether they themselves would think that they were met at all. I fear a little that both Bradley and Royce will think that your *reductiones ad absurdum* are too fine spun and ingenious to have real force. Too complicated, too complicated! is the verdict of my horse-like mind on much of this thesis. Your defense will be, of course, that it is a thesis, and as such, expected to be barbaric. But then I point to the careless, hasty writing of much of it. You *must* simplify yourself, if you hope to have any influence in print.

The writing becomes more careful and the style clearer, the moment you tackle Russell in the 6th part. And when you come to your own dogmatic statement of your vision of things in the last 30 pages or so, I think the thesis splendid, prophetic in tone and *very* felicitous, often, in expression. This is indeed the *philosophie de l'avenir*, and a dogmatic expression of it will be far more effective than critical demolition of its alternatives. It will render that unnecessary if able enough. One will simply *feel* them to be diseased. My total impression is that the critter K —— has a *really magnificent vision* of the lay of the land in philosophy,— of the land of bondage, as well as of that of promise,— but that he has a tremendous lot of work to do yet in the way of getting himself into straight and effective literary shape.' He has *elements* of extraordinary literary power, but they are buried in much sand and shingle. . . .

May. 26, 1900.

Dear Miss S ——, I am a caitiff! I have left your essay on my poor self unanswered. . . . It is a great compliment to me to be taken so philologically and importantly; and I must say that from the technical point of view you may be proud of your production. I like greatly the objective and dispassionate key in which you keep everything, and the number of subdivisions and articulations which you make gives me vertiginous admiration. Nevertheless, the tragic fact remains that I don't feel wounded at all by all that output of ability, and for reasons which I think I can set down briefly enough. It all comes, in my eyes, from too much philological method — as a Ph.D. thesis your essay is supreme, but why don't you go farther? You take utterances of mine written at different dates, for different audiences belonging to different universes of discourse, and string them together as the abstract elements of a total philosophy which you then show to be inwardly incoherent. This is splendid philology, but is it live criticism of anyone's *Weltanschauung?* Your use of the method only strengthens the impression I have got from reading criticisms of my "pragmatic" account of "truth," that the whole Ph.D. industry of building up an author's meaning out of separate texts leads nowhere, unless you have first grasped his centre of vision, by an act of imagination. That, it seems to me, you lack in my case.

For instance: [Seven examples are next dealt with in two and a half pages of type-writing. These pages are omitted.]

. . . I have been unpardonably long; and if you were a man, I should assuredly not expect to influence you a jot by what I write. Being a woman, there may be yet a gleam of hope! — which may serve as the excuse for my prolixity. (It is not for the likes of *you*, however, to hurl accusations of prolixity!) Now if I may presume to give a word of advice to one so much more accomplished than myself in dialectic technique, may I urge, since you have shown what a superb mistress you are in that difficult art of discriminating abstractions and opposing them to each other one by one, since in short there is no university extant that would n't give you its *summa cum laude,* — *I* should certainly so reward your thesis at Harvard, — may I urge, I say, that you should now turn your back upon that academic sort of artificiality altogether, and devote your great talents to the study of reality in its concreteness? In other words, do some *positive* work at the problem of what truth signifies, substitute a definitive alternative for the humanism which I present, as the latter's substitute. Not by proving their inward incoherence does one refute philosophies — every human being is incoherent — but only by superseding them by other philosophies more satisfactory. Your wonderful technical skill ought to serve you in good stead if you would exchange the philological kind of criticism for constructive work. I fear however that you won't — the iron may have bitten too deeply into your soul!!

Have you seen Knox's paper on pragmatism in the "Quarterly Review" for April — perhaps the deepest-cutting thing yet written on the pragmatist side? On the other side read Bertrand Russell's paper in the "Edinburgh Review" just out. A thing after your own heart, but ruined in my eyes by the same kind of vicious abstractionism which your thesis shows. It is amusing to see the critics of the will to believe furnish such exquisite instances of it in their own persons. *E.g.*, Russell's own splendid atheistic-titanic confession of faith in that volume of essays on "Ideals of Science and of Faith" edited by one Hand. X——, whom you quote, has recently worked himself up to the pass of being ordained in the Episcopal church. . . . I justify them both; for only by such experiments on the part of individuals will social man gain the evidence required. They meanwhile seem to think that the only "true" position to hold is that everything not imposed upon a will-less and non-coöperant intellect must count as false — a preposterous principle which no human being follows in real life.

Well! There! that is all! But, dear Madam, I should like to know where you come from, who you are, what your present "situation" is, etc., etc.— It is natural to have some personal curiosity about a lady who has taken such an extraordinary amount of pains for me!

Believe me, dear Miss S ——, with renewed apologies for the extreme tardiness of this acknowledgment, yours with mingled admiration and abhorrence,

WM. JAMES.

APPENDIX II

Books by William James

THE following chronological list includes books only, but it gives the essays and chapters contained in each.

Professor R. B. Perry's "Bibliography" (see below) lists a great number of contributions to periodicals, which have never been reprinted, and includes notes indicative of the matter of each.

(No attempt has been made to compile a list of references to literature about William James, but the following may be mentioned as easily obtainable: *William James*, by ÉMILE BOUTROUX. Paris, 1911. Translation: Longmans, Green & Co., New York and London, 1912. *La Philosophie de William James*, by THEODORE FLOURNOY. St. Blaise, 1911. Translation: *The Philosophy of William James*. Henry Holt & Co., New York, 1917.)

Literary Remains of Henry James, Sr., with an Introduction by
    WILLIAM JAMES. Boston: Houghton, Mifflin & Co., 1884.
The Principles of Psychology. New York: Henry Holt & Co.;
    London: Macmillan & Co., 1890.
    Volume I. Scope of Psychology — Functions of the Brain —
    Conditions of Brain Activity — Habit — The Automaton
    Theory — The Mind-Stuff Theory — Methods and Snares
    of Psychology — Relations of Minds to Other Things —
    The Stream of Thought — The Consciousness of Self —
    Attention — Conception — Discrimination and Comparison — Association — The Perception of Time — Memory.
    Volume II. Sensation — Imagination — Perception of Things
    — The Perception of Space — The Perception of Reality
    — Reasoning — The Production of Movement — Instinct
    — The Emotions — Will — Hypnotism — Necessary Truth
    and the Effects of Experience.
A Text-Book of Psychology. Briefer Course. New York: Henry
    Holt & Co.; London: Macmillan & Co., 1892.

Introductory — Sensation — Sight — Hearing — Touch — Sensations of Motion — Structure of the Brain — Functions of the Brain — Some General Conditions of Neural Activity — Habit — Stream of Consciousness — The Self — Attention — Conception — Discrimination — Association — Sense of Time — Memory — Imagination — Perception — The Perception of Space — Reasoning — Consciousness and Movement — Emotion — Instinct — Will — Psychology and Philosophy.

The Will to Believe, and Other Essays in Popular Philosophy. New York and London: Longmans, Green & Co., 1897.

The Will to Believe — Is Life Worth Living? — The Sentiment of Rationality — Reflex Action and Theism — The Dilemma of Determinism — The Moral Philosopher and the Moral Life — Great Men and their Environment — The Importance of Individuals — On Some Hegelisms — What Psychical Research has Accomplished.

Human Immortality, Two Supposed Objections to the Doctrine. London: Constable & Co., also Dent & Sons; Boston: Houghton, Mifflin & Co., 1898.

The Same. A New Edition with Preface in Reply to His Critics. Boston: Houghton, Mifflin & Co., 1899.

Talks to Teachers on Psychology, and to Students on Some of Life's Ideals. New York: Henry Holt & Co.; London: Longmans, Green & Co., 1899.

Psychology and the Teaching Art — The Stream of Consciousness — The Child as a Behaving Organism — Education and Behavior — The Necessity of Reactions — Native and Acquired Reactions — What the Native Reactions Are — The Laws of Habit — Association of Ideas — Interest — Attention — Memory — Acquisition of Ideas — Apperception — The Will.

Talks to Students: The Gospel of Relaxation — On a Certain Blindness in Human Beings — What Makes Life Significant?

The Varieties of Religious Experience. A Study in Human Nature. The Gifford Lectures on Natural Religion, Edinburgh, 1901–1902. New York and London: Longmans, Green & Co., 1902.

Religion and Neurology — Circumscription of the Topic — The Reality of the Unseen — The Religion of Healthy-Mindedness — The Sick Soul — The Divided Self, and the Process of its Unification — Conversion — Saintliness — The Value of Saintliness — Mysticism — Philosophy — Other Characteristics — Conclusions — Postscript.

Pragmatism. A New Name for Some Old Ways of Thinking. New York and London: Longmans, Green & Co., 1907.

The Present Dilemma in Philosophy — What Pragmatism Means — Some Metaphysical Problems Pragmatically Considered — The One and the Many — Pragmatism and Common Sense — Pragmatism's Conception of Truth — Pragmatism and Humanism — Pragmatism and Religion.

A Pluralistic Universe. Hibbert Lectures at Manchester College. New York and London: Longmans, Green & Co., 1909.

The Types of Philosophic Thinking — Monistic Idealism — Hegel and his Method — Concerning Fechner — Compounding of Consciousness — Bergson and his Critique of Intellectualism — The Continuity of Experience — Conclusions —— Appendixes: *A.* The Thing and its Relations. *B.* The Experience of Activity. *C.* On the Notion of Reality as Changing.

The Meaning of Truth. A Sequel to *Pragmatism.* New York and London: Longmans, Green & Co., 1909.

The Function of Cognition — The Tigers in India — Humanism and Truth — The Relation between Knower and Known — The Essence of Humanism — A Word More about Truth — Professor Pratt on Truth — The Pragmatist Account of Truth and its Misunderstanders — The Meaning of the Word Truth — The Existence of Julius Cæsar — The Absolute and the Strenuous Life — Hébert on Pragmatism — Abstractionism and "Relativismus" — Two English Critics — A Dialogue.

Some Problems of Philosophy. A Beginning of an Introduction to Philosophy. New York and London: Longmans, Green & Co., 1911.

Philosophy and its Critics — The Problems of Metaphysics — The Problem of Being — Percept and Concept — The One and the Many — The Problem of Novelty — Novelty and the Infinite—Novelty and Causation——Appendix: Faith and the Right to Believe.

Memories and Studies. New York and London: Longmans, Green & Co., 1911.

Louis Agassiz — Address at the Emerson Centenary in Concord — Robert Gould Shaw — Francis Boott — Thomas Davidson — Herbert Spencer's Autobiography — Frederick Myers's Services to Psychology — Final Impressions of a Psychical Researcher — On Some Mental Effects of the Earthquake — The Energies of Men — The Moral Equivalent of War — Remarks at the Peace Banquet — The Social Value of the College-bred — The Ph.D. Octopus — The True Harvard — Stanford's Ideal Destiny — A Pluralistic Mystic (B. P. Blood).

Essays in Radical Empiricism. Edited by RALPH BARTON PERRY. New York and London: Longmans, Green & Co., 1912.

Introduction — Does Consciousness Exist? — A World of Pure Experience — The Thing and its Relations — How Two Minds can Know One Thing — The Place of Affectional Facts in a World of Pure Experience — The Experience of Activity — The Essence of Humanism — *La Notion de Conscience* — Is Radical Empiricism Solipsistic? — Mr. Pitkin's Refutation of Radical Empiricism — Humanism and Truth Once More — Absolutism and Empiricism.

Collected Essays and Reviews. Edited by RALPH BARTON PERRY. New York and London: Longmans, Green & Co., 1920.

Review of E. Sargent's *Planchette* (1869) — Review of G. H. Lewes's *Problems of Life and Mind* (1875) — Review entitled "German Pessimism" (1875) — Chauncey Wright (1875) — Review of "Bain and Renouvier" (1876) — Review of Renan's *Dialogues* (1876) — Review of G. H. Lewes's *Physical Basis of Mind* (1877) — Remarks on Spencer's Definition of Mind as Correspondence (1878) — Quelques Considérations sur la Méthode Subjective (1878) — The Sentiment of Rationality (1879) — Review (unsigned) of W. K. Clifford's *Lectures and Essays* (1879) — Review of Herbert Spencer's *Data of Ethics* (1879) — The Feeling of Effort (1880) — The Sense of Dizziness in Deaf Mutes (1882) — What is an Emotion? (1884) — Review of

Royce's *The Religious Aspect of Philosophy* (1885) — The Consciousness of Lost Limbs (1887) — Réponse de W. James aux Remarques de M. Renouvier sur sa théorie de la volonté (1888) — The Psychological Theory of Extension (1889) — A Plea for Psychology as a Natural Science (1892) — The Original Datum of Space Consciousness (1893) — Mr. Bradley on Immediate Resemblance (1893) — Immediate Resemblance — Review of G. T. Ladd's *Psychology* (1894) — The Physical Basis of Emotion (1894) — The Knowing of Things Together (1895) — Review of W. Hirsch's *Genie und Entartung* (1895) — Philosophical Conceptions and Practical Results (1898) — Review of R. Hodgson's *A Further Record of Observations of Certain Phenomena of Trance* (1898) — Review of Sturt's *Personal Idealism* (1903) — The Chicago School (1904) — Review of F. C. S. Schiller's *Humanism* (1904) — Laura Bridgman (1904) — G. Papini and the Pragmatist Movement in Italy (1906) — The Mad Absolute (1906) — Controversy about Truth with John E. Russell (1907) — Report on Mrs. Piper's Hodgson Control; Conclusion (1909) — Bradley or Bergson? (1910) — A Suggestion about Mysticism (1910).

A List of the Published Writings of William James, with notes, and an index; by RALPH BARTON PERRY. New York and London: Longmans, Green & Co., 1920.

INDEX

INDEX

THROUGHOUT the index the initial J. stands for William James. In the list of references to his own writings, arranged alphabetically at the end of the entries under his name, the titles of separate papers are set in roman and quoted, those of volumes in italics.

The words "See Contents" under a name indicate that letters addressed to the person in question are to be sought in the Table of Contents, where all letters are listed.

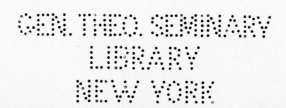

McGrath-Sherrill Press
GRAPHIC ARTS BLDG.
BOSTON